TECHNOLOGY IN *STUDENT AFFAIRS*

Issues, Applications, and Trends

ACPA MEDIA BOARD

Harold E. Cheatham
Editor and Chair
The Pennsylvania State University

Janice Sutera Wolfe
Assistant Editor
George Mason University

Augustine Baron, Jr.
University of Texas

Harry Canon
Aspen Associates

D. Stanley Carpenter
Texas A & M University

H. Jane Fried
Northeastern University

Barbara Jacoby
University of Maryland

Steven Janosik
Virginia Tech

Mike Lopez
Minneapolis State University

Raechele Pope
Teacher's College-Columbia University

Mary L. Roark
State University of New York-Plattsburgh

Melvin C. Terrell
Northeastern Illinois University

Robert Young
Kent State University

TECHNOLOGY IN *STUDENT AFFAIRS*
Issues, Applications, and Trends

Edited by John L. Baier and Thomas S. Strong

Copyright © 1994 by the American College Personnel Association.

Distributed by University Press of America,® Inc.
4720 Boston Way, Lanham, Maryland 20706

All rights reserved
Printed in the United States of America

Library of Congress Cataloging-in-Publication Data

Technology in student affairs : issues, applications, and trends / edited by John L. Baier, Thomas S. Strong.
p. cm.
Includes bibliographical references.
1. Student affairs services—United States—Administration—Data processing. 2. College student development programs—United States—Data processing. 3. College student personnel administrators—United States. 4. Educational technology—United States. I. Baier, John L. II. Strong, Thomas S.
LB2342.9.T43   1994
378.1'94'0420285—dc20   93-23439 CIP

ISBN 1-883485-02-9 (cloth : alk. paper)
ISBN 1-883485-03-7 (pbk. : alk. paper)

∞™ The paper used in this publication meets the minimum requirements of American National Standard for Information Sciences—Permanence of Paper for Printed Library Materials, ANSI Z39.48-1984.

Contents

Preface		vii
Foreword		xi
About the Authors		xiii

Part I:	AN INTRODUCTION TO TECHNOLOGY IN STUDENT AFFAIRS	1
1	The Technology and Information Explosion	3
2	Assessing and Enhancing Technological Competencies of Staff	15
3	A Primer on Information and Computer Technology	27

Part II:	APPLICATIONS OF TECHNOLOGY IN SPECIFIC STUDENT AFFAIRS AREAS	37
4	Academic Advising Programs	39
5	Student Financial Aid	61
6	International Service and Program Offices	71
7	Housing Programs	87
8	Counseling Center Programs	105
9	Teaching-Learning Programs	121
10	Career Planning and Placement Programs	135
11	Student Life, Student Centers, and Student Activities	147
12	Recreational Sports and Wellness Programs	161
13	Student Health Centers	175
14	The Office of the Chief Student Affairs Officer	187

Part III: ADMINISTRATIVE CONSIDERATIONS
          AND IMPLICATIONS FOR THE FUTURE   201
15 Legal Liabilities and Ethical Issues   203
16 Managing Computer Systems and Networks   215
17 Implications for the Future   237

APPENDICES
Appendix A: Listing of Resources by Program Area   243
Appendix B: Glossary   257

Preface

During the past decade, the face of higher education in America has changed dramatically. Despite widespread forecasts of declining enrollment in the 1980s, the last decade saw college enrollments increase from approximately 12,500,000 students in 1980 to over 14,000,000 students today. Many of these new students are non-traditional, high-risk, under-represented minorities, and are likely to be commuting to college and studying part-time. All of these new learners require additional time and support from student affairs professionals in order to help them successfully fulfill their educational objectives and dreams.

Unfortunately, at the same time as the need for expanded and enhanced student affairs services and programs has increased, proportional funding for higher education has either decreased or, at best, remained level at most colleges. And in particular, funding for student affairs programs has been significantly reduced at many colleges.

Therefore, many student affairs divisions have been turning to the use of modern technology wherever possible to help reduce administrative overhead and better meet increasing student needs with the same or reduced numbers of professional staff members.

Despite a literal explosion in the amount of new affordable and user-friendly information and computer technology now available for use in the student affairs area, however, there is no comprehensive reference available which describes and discusses the management issues and the present and future applications of technology to the student affairs.

The purpose of this book is to fill this void. The book begins by discussing the advantages of incorporating information and computer technologies into all student affairs programs, and various methods which can be used for increasing staff competencies in the use of computer and information technology. A brief primer on computer and information technology and terminology is also provided.

The second part of the book addresses the various information and computer systems (hardware and software) that are currently available for each of the functional areas comprising student affairs divisions on most campuses. These include: academic advising; career planning and placement; counseling and testing; financial aid; housing; international student services; learning assistance centers; recreation; student life, student centers and student activities; student health centers; and the office of the chief student affairs officer. The advantages and disadvantages for each software application are provided within each chapter.

Part three of the book presents a discussion of the numerous administrative, legal, and ethical issues which must be considered and addressed in order for a college to successfully computerize its student affairs operations. The book concludes with a chapter on the implications of the technological explosion to the future of student affairs.

Finally, two appendices are presented. The first lists all of the software referenced and provides contact sources for further information. It should be noted that the American College Personnel Association (ACPA) does not endorse any of the products listed. Also the editors and chapter authors are not affiliated with any of the software companies or products listed. The purpose of providing this information is solely to make the reader aware of many of the resources that are currently available for use by student affairs professionals. The second appendix is a glossary of computer terminology found in this book.

We hope this book is useful to student affairs practitioners, student affairs graduate preparation program faculty members and student affairs graduate students. Up to the publication of this book, those practitioners who have been engaged in the computerization of student affairs programs have had to rely mainly on the materials supplied by computer hardware and software vendors, software guides published for specialized areas of practice (i.e. counseling software, placement software), and information obtained at professional conferences or by word of mouth from professional colleagues at other campuses. Most computerization to date, therefore, has been accomplished through trial and error or with the assistance of campus computer center personnel who have a very limited knowledge of the nuances and priorities of student affairs practices. This has resulted in costly errors, both in time and dollars, and an adverse impact on staff member attitudes and confidence in the benefits and utility of using modern information and computer technologies in the delivery of student affairs programs. Hence, we hope a book written by experienced student affairs professionals for student affairs professionals will hasten and assist the proper application of new and emerging technology to administrative practice.

Each chapter author was selected to contribute to this volume based on expertise and experience in personally developing and implementing the broad scale application of the most current information and computer technologies available to his or her area of specialization. We did not ask our authors to define and describe all of the many applications being used throughout the country in their respective areas of specialization. Those are available in the software guides mentioned earlier. Instead we thought that it would be more beneficial to our readers to have them explain in detail how they have applied the use of modern technology on their own and other selected campuses so that our readers could select those applications which might be most pertinent and relevant to their particular needs.

Another use for this book centers on the recently adopted *CAS Standards for Student Affairs' Master's Degree Graduate Preparation Programs* (1986). The standards stipulate that every graduate program (there currently are 87 graduate programs enrolling approximately 1000 students annually) must include a "computer literacy" component, and those programs with an "Administration Emphasis", (which comprise approximately 25% of all programs) must include a specific course, or segment of a course on the administrative uses of computers. We hope that student affairs graduate program faculty and students will find this book useful as a supplemental text to help fulfill the "computer literacy" requirements of the CAS standards.

In closing, we acknowledge many of the special people who made this book possible. In an endeavor of this nature it is often the families of the authors who must give moral support and give up valuable time with their loved ones in order for the authors to complete their work. We are both fortunate to have supportive wives who have provided us with an abundance of encouragement and understanding throughout this project. For Nancy Baier and Pam

Strong we remain forever grateful for your love and support. Our children also saw less of us, but were always in our thoughts. Thank you, Britt and Chris Strong and Karen and John Baier, for making us so very proud of you through the years and for giving us your encouragement to undertake this project.

Completion of this book would also have not been possible without the assistance of our friend and co-worker Ginny Branyon. Her word processing skills were critically important, but her patience and perseverance, draft after draft, transcended far beyond anything for which we could have hoped. Thank you, Ginny, for your hard work and easy smiles.

We are also grateful to Peggy Barr for her review of the prospectus and suggestions for the book. She provided steady encouragement for us to complete this project.

We would also like to acknowledge Colin Marino, a Pre-med student at the University of Alabama, for his technical assistance in the production of the manuscript. His ability to collate information from floppy disks from a wide variety of computers and software programs made the project easier for all of us.

And last, to our friends and colleagues at The University of Alabama and the University of North Texas who gave us encouragement and moral support to undertake and complete this project, we extend our sincere thanks and appreciation. Our hope is that this book will be of value to the student affairs profession, and that in some small way, a student's life will be positively touched because of what we have written.

J. L. Baier
T. S. Strong
December, 1992

REFERENCE

Council For the Advancement of Standards for Student Services/Development Programs (1986). Preparation standards and guidelines at the master's degree level for student services/development professionals in postsecondary education. *CAS standards and guidelines for student services/development programs.* Washington, DC: CAS.

Foreword

The roles and functions of student affairs organizations on college and university campuses are many and varied. Each institution has developed a unique organizational structure, mission, and purpose for student affairs which is responsive to the needs of that college or university. All student affairs units, whether they are part of large or small campuses, two-year or four-year institutions, urban or commuter can profit from increased use of technology in order to better serve both students and our institutions.

This volume, *Technology in Student Affairs: Issues, Applications and Trends*, will be a helpful resource, to individuals who are familiar with the use of technology and those who are novices in the use of technology, to enhance student affairs operations. As Lee Upcraft and I said in *New Futures for Student Affairs*, "we must join the computer and information system revolution" (p.226). To do less does not serve either our institutions or our students well.

Technology, in its' many and varied forms, is a fact of life on most college campuses. Our students have been exposed to technology throughout their educational experiences and our institutions are enhancing technological capabilities each year. For student affairs to be an effective partner in the academic enterprise, we must embrace technology to become more efficient and effective and to gain an understanding of the influence of the technological revolution on the lives of our students.

Student affairs holds a special responsibility to serve our institutions and our students. If we become computer literate and sophisticated in the use of technology, we have the ability to learn more about our students including their backgrounds, their achievements, and their patterns of enrollment that can give us insight into their lives. That insight can assist us in designing programs and services that will more closely meet their needs and in the process increase our effectiveness. Enhanced technological skills also permit us to respond to inquiries, provide answers, and respond to students more quickly. Finally, increased technological sophistication aids us in providing data to our institutions in ways that can be meaningful in setting policy and direction in the years ahead.

Technology is not without problems and part of our obligation as student affairs professionals is to assure that our institutions, our programs, and our services still are responsive to the individual student and that we maintain human contact with them. Student affairs professionals also have a responsibility to assure that institutional processes and procedures remain flexible and responsive to individual life circumstances. Technology should be our tool, not our master.

This volume will assist professionals in gaining knowledge about technology and how to effectively employ it as we meet both our institutional and student obligations. It contains a wealth of information that I found to be useful to me as I pondered questions of the use, expense, and responsibilities associated with the technological revolution. The volume is a practical resource written by professionals for professionals and I am confident that you will find it to be helpful as you develop your plans to become connected with the technological marvels that now are and will be a part of each of our personal and professional lives.

> Margaret J. Barr
> Vice President for Student Affairs
> Northwestern University

REFERENCE

Barr, M.J. & Upcraft, M.L. (Eds). (1991). *New futures for student affairs.* San Francisco: Jossey-Bass.

About the Authors

John L. Baier is Professor of Higher Education and Chairperson of the Department of Higher Education at the University of North Texas. His prior experience includes two years as Professor and Chairperson of Higher Education and six years as Vice President for Student Affairs at The University of Alabama at Tuscaloosa, seven years as Assistant Vice President and Dean of Students at Texas Tech University, two years as Acting Dean and Associate Dean of Student Development at the University of Nebraska and five years as Assistant Dean of Student Life at Southern Illinois University at Carbondale. Baier is the author or co-author of more than a dozen research articles in peer-reviewed journals and three book chapters. He serves on the Editorial Boards of the *Journal of College Student Development*, the *College Student Affairs Journal*, and the *Community/Junior College Journal of Research and Practices*, is a member of the Directorate of ACPA's Commission XII; and is past President of the Texas Association of College and University Student Personnel Administrators. He holds a Ph.D. in Higher Education Administration from Southern Illinois University at Carbondale, an Ed.M. in Counselor Education from SUNY at Buffalo, a Bachelors in Industrial Engineering from GMI Engineering and Management Institute, and is a graduate of Harvard University's Institute for Educational Management.

Thomas S. Strong is Director of Student Services at The University of Alabama at Tuscaloosa. He has over twenty years of experience in student affairs including positions as Director of Recreation, Director of Housing, Assistant Dean of Students, Associate Dean of Students, and Director of Student Services at The University of Alabama. He is an adjunct faculty member for the College of Education and has taught courses in Mexico and Columbia. He has also served as Assistant to the Dean of the College of Education at Virginia Polytechnic Institute and was the Director of Research at The American School Foundation in Mexico City. He has written and received a wide variety of grants. He holds a Ph.D. in Educational Administration and a M.S. in Student Personnel Services from The University of Alabama and a B.S. in Biology from Mobile College.

William Allbritten is Director of the Counseling and Testing Center, Learning Center, and Trio Programs at Murray State University. He has served in his current position for fifteen years. He is also a Professor of Guidance and Counseling at Murray State University. He previously served as a psychometrist at the University of Northern Colorado. Allbritten holds a Ph.D. in College Student Personnel Administration and a M.A. in College Student Personnel Education from the University of Northern Colorado and a B.S. in Mathematics from Northwestern State University of Louisiana. He has published extensively in professional journals and made dozens of presentations at professional meetings.

Ronny Barnes has been serving as Director of Student Financial Aid and Assistant Vice President for Student Affairs at Texas Tech University in Lubbock for the past fifteen years. Prior to his work at Texas Tech he served as Assistant Director of Financial Aid at East Texas State University. He has also been a teacher and a coach. Barnes holds a Ph.D. in Educational Administration and a M.S. in Educational Media and Technology from East Texas State University and a B.S. in Biology and Physical Education from Baylor University. He is an active member of the Texas, Southwestern and the National Association of Student Financial Aid Administrators, and a member of the Advisory Committee of the American College Testing Program, the Texas Higher Education Coordinating Board, and the Panhandle Plains Higher Education Authority.

Sue A. Baum is Division Chairperson of the Department of Computer and Information Science at Enterprise State Junior College in Enterprise, Alabama. Prior to her current position, Baum served for five years as the Director of Academic Computer Services. She is a doctoral candidate in Higher Education at The University of Alabama, holds a M.B.A. from Troy State University, and a B.S.

from Florida State University in Math. She is a member of the Alabama College System Tracking and Placement Committee and has served as an officer of the Alabama Council for Computer Education. She is also a Certified Data Educator.

Emily R. Burgwyn is Associate Director of Housing at Texas Christian University, where she previously served as Assistant Director of Housing for four years and Coordinator of Administrative Services for three years. She is a member of the Southwest Association of College and University Housing Officers Executive Board. She has a B.S. in Therapeutic Recreation from Longwood College, a M.S. in Applied Social Research from Texas Christian University and is a doctoral candidate in Higher Education Administration at the University of North Texas.

Joan M. Comas is Director of the Teaching and Learning Center at The University of Alabama, a position she has held for the past six years. She previously served as Coordinator of the Career Resource Center and Women's Career Services for one and a half years and as a Counselor in the Counseling Center for ten years, all at The University of Alabama. She has been awarded the McKinley Award for outstanding achievement at The University of Alabama and has published extensively in counseling journals. She received her Ph.D. in Counselor Education and M.S. in Counseling and Guidance from The University of Alabama. She received her B.S. in Psychology from the University of Montevallo.

Betty R. Cully currently serves as Assistant Dean of Students for Academic Support at Enterprise State Junior College in Enterprise, Alabama. Prior to her present position, Cully served two years as Director of Student Advancement Services and four years as Director of Student Support Services. She has also held positions in teaching and counseling and has served as the Director of Orientation at other two year colleges. She was named the "Outstanding Freshman Advocate" in 1990 and serves on the Alabama Postsecondary Advisory Committee on Policy Matters. She holds a M.S. in Counseling and Human Development from Troy State University, a B.S. in Secondary Education from West Virginia University, and is a doctoral candidate in Higher Education at The University of Alabama.

David L. Grady serves as the Director of Campus Programs and Student Activities at the University of Iowa. He previously served as the University Ombudsman and Research Associate at the University of Texas at Austin for three years and as an Assistant Director of Student Life at The University of Alabama for four years. He is the co-author of an article published in the *NASPA Journal*, has served as Editor for the National Order of Omega, and received the "Eyes of Texas" Award at The University of Texas-Austin. He holds a Ph.D.in Higher Education from the University of Texas at Austin, an Ed.M. from Harvard University in Educational Administration, and a B.B.A. from Mississippi State University in Finance.

Patricia A. Hollander is the General Counsel of the American Association of University Administrators in New York City. Hollander received her B.S. and J.D. degrees from St. Louis University and serves on the Board of Trustees of Western New England College. Prior to her current position, she was both a faculty member and administrator at State University of New York at Buffalo Faculty of Law and was a visiting Professor at the University of Virginia's Center for the Study of Higher Education. She is the author of *Legal Handbook for Educators* (1978); *Computers in Education: Legal Liabilities and Ethical Issues Concerning Their Use and Abuse* (1986); former principal editor of *The Computer Law Monitor* (1983-1990); and co-author of *A guide for Successful Searches for College Personnel: Policies, Procedures, and Legal Issues* (1987).

Molly M. Lawrence is Director of Student Financial Services at The University of Alabama, a position she has held for two years. She also serves concurrently as the Assistant to the Vice President of Student Affairs for Financial Management and she has an additional twenty years of administrative experience in other areas of Student Affairs. She is a member of the National Association of Financial Aid Administrators and has been a regional officer in the National Association of Student Personnel Administrators. She has been a member of the Regional Council for American College Testing and is a member of numerous honorary societies. She received her M.S. in Accounting and her B.S. in Business from The University of Alabama.

Joseph Gregory Leonard has been serving as the Director of International Student Affairs at The University of Alabama for the past fourteen years. He previously served as a Special Assistant to the Vice President and as Director of the Counseling Department at the Institute of International Education in Houston, Texas. He also has worked at the Greenbriar Counseling Center and the Texas Outward Bound School and served in the Peace Corps. He holds a M.A. in Education and a B.A. in Sociology from The University of North Carolina at Chapel Hill. He is currently a member of the Microcomputer Special Interest Group, the Council of Advisors to Foreign Students and Scholars, and the Government Regulations Advisory Committee of the National Association of Foreign Student Advisors: Association of International Educators, and a frequent contributor to NAFSA publications.

Gary D. Melaney is Director of Student Affairs Research, Information and Systems (SARIS) and Assistant Professor in the Center for the Study of Adult and Higher Education at the University of Massachusetts at Amherst. Melaney also has more than ten years experience as a research administrator at Ohio State University, having served as the Assistant Director of the School of Public Administration and as the Research Administrator of the Polimetrics Laboratory. He holds a Ph.D. in Higher Education, a M.A. in Political Socialization and a B.A. in Political Science, all from Ohio State University. Melaney is the author or co-author of over thirty articles in peer-reviewed journals and five book chapters. He also has served as a reviewer of research proposals for the Association for the Study of Higher Education.

Judith G. Miller is Director of Institutional Research at Enterprise State Junior College in Enterprise, Alabama. Miller has been in her current position for five years and previously served as Director of Guidance Services for one year and Director of Student Support Services for six years. She has also served as Director of Financial Aid for two years at Hopkinsville Community College. She holds an Ed.D. from Vanderbilt University in Higher Education Administration, an Ed.S. in Student Personnel Work in Higher Education and a M.S. in Guidance and Counseling from Troy State University, and a B.S. from Radford College in English and History Education. She has served as an officer in the Alabama Association for Women Deans, Administrators and Counselors and the Alabama Association for Institutional Research, and as the Chairperson of the Chancellor's Committee for Statewide Student Tracking and Placement of the Alabama State Junior College System.

Steve J. Miller is the manager of Computer and Information Services for the College Placement Council, Inc., a position he has held for the last six years. He previously served as a systems analyst for Century Systems Design. He is the author of *CPC Computerization Sourcebook*, has authored chapters in other books, and is currently writing a column for "Spotlight", College Placement Council's biweekly newsletter, on technology products, issues, and trends impacting career planning, placement and recruitment. He received his B.S. in Computer Science from Rutgers University in 1984.

Donald B. Mills is Acting Vice Chancellor for Student Affairs at Texas Christian University. Mills has over twenty years of administrative experience at Texas Christian University. Prior to his present position he served as Associate Vice Chancellor for Student Affairs, Associate Dean of Students and Director of Housing, and Director of University Programs. He holds an Ed.D. from the University of North Texas in Higher Education, a M.Div. from Texas Christian University in Christian Ethics, and an A.B. from Harvard University in Government. He has been awarded the "Distinguished Service Award" from the Texas Association of College and University Student Personnel Administrators and has served as president of the organization. He has also served as a State President of NASPA as well as a member of the ACE/NASPA Richard Stevens Institute staff. He is the author or co-author of four book chapters on a variety of student affairs issues.

Craig M. Ross is Associate Director of Recreational Sports at Indiana University in Bloomington. Ross has wide and varied experience in the field of Recreation. He has served five years as Assistant Director and three years as Coordinator of Recreational Sports at Indiana University, one year as Assistant Professor of Recreation at the University of Southern Mississippi, and three years as a community center director for the Memphis Park Commission. He has also been a teacher and a coach. He has served as Chairman of the Professional Development Curriculum Committee, Chairman of the Computer Utilization Committee, Chairman of the Career Placement Center, and as a State Director of the National

Intramural-Recreational Sports Association. He has co-authored a textbook on Recreation and written extensively in recreational sports journals. He holds a Doctorate in Recreation from Indiana University, and a M.S. in Recreation and a B.S. in Physical Education from Memphis State University.

Edward G. Whipple is Vice President for Student Affairs at Eastern Montana College in Billings, a position he has held for the past three years. His prior experience includes five years as Director of Student Life at The University of Alabama, three years as Associate Dean of Students at Texas Tech University, and one year as Greek Affairs Coordinator at Iowa State University. He holds a Ph.D. in College Student Services Administration from Oregon State University, a M.A.T. from Northwestern University in English Education, and a B.A. from Willamette University in English. He is the current NASPA State Director for Montana and has co-authored several articles for the *NASPA Journal* and *Journal of College Student Development*.

William Mark Whitson currently serves as Managing Director of Pine Valley Retirement Community in Tuscaloosa, Alabama. Prior to assuming his current position in 1991, Whitson served as the Assistant Director of the Student Health Center at the University of Alabama for six years. He also previously worked for eight years in nursing home administration where he designed and implemented management information systems. He holds a B.S. in Business Administration from The University of Alabama and is a member of the Executive Board of the Southern College Health Association of the American College Health Association. He is also an adjunct Professor in Health Care Management at The University of Alabama and is a licensed nursing home administrator.

Part I

An Introduction to Technology in Student Affairs

This introduction begins with a summary of the rapid rise in the use of information and computer technology in student affairs and a discussion of how this use enhances the delivery of services to students and increases the effectiveness and efficiency of routine administrative functions.

Chapter Two examines the need for staff training from the introductory phase of the technology transfer process to the continuing education of staff as new systems and programs are brought on line and technology advances.

Last, because there are large numbers of student affairs professionals and graduate students who are not as technologically literate or comfortable with using computers as they should be, Part I concludes with a brief user-friendly primer on information and computer technology and terminology so that all readers might benefit from the special applications and issues described in Parts II and III. A glossary of computer terminology used throughout the book is also provided in Appendix B.

Chapter 1

The Technology and Information Explosion

Thomas S. Strong

History will no doubt show that the emergence of the microcomputer in the 1980s played a very important role in permanently changing the ways student affairs organizations administer their programs and student services. However, until the introduction of the low cost personal computer, the only path available for computerizing routine management systems on most college campuses was through the mainframe computer via dumb (non-interactive) terminals or punch cards and required using very expensive and problem-prone customized software programs. Therefore, only functions requiring the management of large data bases, such as admissions, financial aid, registration, and student billing could efficiently utilize computer technology in the 1970s and early 1980s.

The introduction of the IBM personal computer (PC) in 1981 spawned the sale of millions of PCs and a staggering variety of excellent new software packages. This caused much of higher education, and particularly student affairs, to embrace the widespread use of computer technology for routine administrative functions. Complete PC hardware packages that once sold for four to five thousand dollars in the mid-eighties now sell for one to two thousand dollars. At the same time, advancing technology has caused the power of these machines to increase dramatically in speed, memory, and the ability to run complex software programs. Today's $2,000 PC system is now as powerful as the million dollar mainframe computer of twenty years ago. The quality of the software available has also improved dramatically. As a result, the emphasis in teaching computer science in high schools and technical colleges has shifted from teaching programming skills to teaching students how to use "off the shelf" software and how to modify that software to meet specific customer/employee needs.

"User-friendly" is the mandate that guides the design of hardware and software in today's competitive, rapidly changing, and advancing technological market. Marketing strategies for both new computers and software programs now emphasize ease of use, in addition to computing power and low price.

The purpose in this chapter is to provide an introductory perspective on the current status of computer and information technology in student affairs. The chapter first examines the rise of technology in higher education and in student affairs; second, it briefly discusses how student affairs can benefit from these technological advances; and it concludes with an examination of a few of the central issues that must be addressed in order to successfully utilize modern technology in student affairs operations.

A HISTORICAL PERSPECTIVE ON THE ADVANCEMENT OF TECHNOLOGY IN HIGHER EDUCATION AND STUDENT AFFAIRS

Although many people may argue whether the technological revolution in higher education began with the advent of the mainframe computer in the late 1950s or with the introduction of the personal computer in the late 1970s, most scholars agree that the technological revolution in education actually began in the mid 1960s with the establishment of the Public Broadcasting System and the widespread use of television and video technology for teaching preschool age children both at home (i.e. Sesame Street, Captain Kangaroo, and Mister Rogers) and in the schools. For the first time in history, a generation of Americans not only became comfortable learning from an impersonal two-dimensional video screen, but became convinced that learning via images and sounds produced on an electronic instrument was not only possible, but convenient, entertaining, and effective.

Following 20 years of numerous advances in television technology, in the late 1970s the home video cassette recorder (VCR) was developed. Because of the VCR's relatively low cost, portability, easy use, quality images, and wide variety of applications, the VCR became an instant success not only in the home, but also in schools and colleges throughout the country. As the technology of video cameras, production capabilities, and VCRs were further improved, so too did public and educator confidence increase that technology could effectively be used to improve education. The widespread use of the VCR and video technology both at home and at school reinforced the notion that human beings could effectively learn from a two dimensional video screen and that modern technology was something to be embraced rather than feared.

Thus, through television and video technology, a generation of college students, faculty and administrators learned to depend on, trust, and appreciate the positive value of technology in education. This served as the foundation for the general acceptance and use of computer and information technologies that we find in higher education today.

The first large mainframe computers had thousands of vacuum tubes, were the size of a room, and had strict environmental standards for their location. As technology progressed (i.e., the computer chip), the computers shrank in size and became much more powerful.

The minicomputer evolved from the mainframe. It was not nearly as powerful as the mainframe but was smaller in size and far less expensive to purchase and maintain. This made it the ideal machine for business applications and other uses that did not require the massive computing power of a mainframe computer.

Computers continued to shrink in size and price, and by 1980 several commentators were predicting that computers would be as common as television in American households before the end of the century. The introduction of the personal computer (PC) by Apple Computer in the late 1970s and by IBM in 1981 put low priced microcomputers within the reach of small businesses, college faculty and staff, and other professionals for the first time. Although PCs are not yet as common as television sets in American homes, they are found extensively in every segment of society.

Ironically, institutions of higher education are often the last to exploit the advances and new technologies that they help to create. This is primarily due to institutional inertia, as well as a lack of adequate resources to procure the equipment and facilities required to apply new technologies on the college campus. Therefore, the broad scale use of the computer for the traditional administrative, teaching and research missions of higher education was slow to develop.

Computers were first used in higher education in the teaching and research mission of the institution. It is generally easier to justify requests for funding new technology that is going to be used for teaching and research than it is for administrative purposes. However, after central computer centers (housing large mainframe computers) became established on college campuses, administrative applications soon followed. Most early administrative applications involved business functions such as accounting, purchasing, payroll and personnel. But these were soon followed by numerous student affairs applications.

Admissions and records offices used the mainframe computer for everything from recruiting and registering students to storing and retrieving academic records. Housing offices used the mainframe computer for making assignments, billing and tracking students, and financial aid offices managed their aid-packaging and loan programs and produced financial aid award letters on the mainframe. Although the minicomputer would find itself being used in a few student affairs offices in the 1970s (i.e. student centers and student health centers), it took the introduction of the microcomputer in the 1980s to enable more widespread computer utilization in most student affairs divisions.

Many of the early PC applications centered around word processing and data management. Indeed, many PCs are still used primarily as word processors. But, as the machines and programs became more user friendly and as a new generation of computer literate personnel became available to use them, other applications soon emerged that enabled student affairs administrators to administer additional programs more efficiently and effectively with the use of computers.

For example, in a survey conducted by Morris Welch of Louisiana State University for the Association of College and University Housing Officers (1986), it was found that housing offices were using computers for all of the eighty-one different applications listed on his survey, ranging from data manipulation to the control of heating and cooling systems. This extensive use of the computer clearly illustrates how pervasive the use of technology has become across a broad range of administrative functions. And in many cases, function begets function. When a computer or some other form of technology is introduced into an administrative process, it spurs usages not conceived of prior to the introduction of the first use of technology.

Evidence of the growth of computer usage in student affairs' operations and programs can also be found beyond the campus. Each year more and more professional conferences and seminars are being offered on high tech applications for student affairs. Bleuer and Walz (1990) recently pointed out that sessions exploring the broad role of computer use in counseling began at the 1984 annual conference of the American Association for Counseling and Development, and by 1987, sessions devoted exclusively to overviews of various types of computer software were common place. This trend continues today as most professional associations in student affairs devote more and more conference time to the use and management of information and computer technology.

There is also an expectation from students that the computer will be used in more student services programs. Reports from the United States Census Bureau (1991) show that forty-four percent of college students used computers in 1989 compared to only thirty-one percent just five years earlier. The traditional college age group held the highest proportion of computer usage of any age group (about half). The report also showed that 46 percent of males and 41 percent of females now use computers in their academic classes. This trend should continue as students embrace technology more and more as an integral part of their educational experience. Therefore, the student affairs practitioner should not be surprised to find the use of computer and information technology in almost every aspect of his/her job during the next decade.

BENEFITS OF USING TECHNOLOGY IN STUDENT AFFAIRS

There are many benefits to be derived from employing technology in student affairs programs and services. First, it allows for the management of large amounts of data in ways that were not possible a generation ago. Most of the major systems that fall under the student affairs umbrella must use large data bases in order to effectively deliver their services to students. From the study of these data bases we are able to introduce facts into the decision making process that allow us to make administrative judgements and decisions in a more timely and informed manner. This results in better overall services for the students.

Computers and other related high tech devices also allow student affairs professionals to offer their services with increased speed and accuracy. Turn around time in some cases is almost instant. For example, students no longer have to wait days or weeks for course selection approval or financial aid notification.

Reduced administrative cost is yet another benefit to be derived from the use of modern computer and information technology. Production of documents that might have taken weeks previously can now be produced in hours. With computer automation it is also possible to reduce clerical and administrative time devoted to certain routine administrative tasks. For example, using computers, housing assignments can be handled by one person rather than several, and entrance to recreational facilities can be fully automated so that no personnel are required to staff entry points.

The proper use of technology also can encourage more effective communication. Mail merge programs allow for personalized responses to large numbers of parents and students. Computer linkages through the use of modems allow remote locations to also access numerous campus programs and services. Desk-top publishing has also given student affairs professionals the opportunity to produce quality printed documents that just a few years ago were possible only if one employed the services of an expensive printing shop. This allows for less expensive and more timely student publications. If we can more effectively communicate with students, then we can expect students to take greater advantage of the services and programs we provide for their benefit.

There are also some current student affairs programs and services that would not be possible without the use of modern technology. For example, complex databases that show similarities of interests with successful people in particular careers and can present possibilities for students who use these databases for career exploration, require the use of sophisticated inter-active computer programs. Inter-active tutorial programs that allow students to supplement their in class time with high quality out of class learning opportunities and automated registration through the use of touch tone telephones that eliminate long lines and allow for instantaneous course selections and changes are other examples.

The quality of word processing can also be dramatically improved with the use of computer technology. Electronic dedicated word processors and word processing programs for microcomputers allow for continuous revision of documents with a minimum of turn around time. Administrators who might have been reluctant to make changes in typed documents because the retyping would have taken hours, now can make changes that range from one word or two, to massive revisions that change entire sections, all in just a few minutes time. Word processing enhancement probably represents the single biggest impact that technology has had on the day-to-day routine of most student affairs staff members.

All of the advantages listed thus far are very important and, individually, each could stand alone and represent sufficient justification for employing the use of modern computer and information technology in student affairs. However, the single most significant reason for the use of modern technology in student affairs is that its use enables the expansion of "high touch" activities without the addition of more professional staff members. High touch activities are those opportunities that allow staff to interact on a one-to-one basis with students, parents, and others. They are important because they provide the highest level of satisfaction for both parties. By freeing our professionally trained staff members from mundane clerical tasks, they will have more time to create programs, talk with parents and work with students in a more personal and effective manner; thus, they are able to more efficiently use their time for people centered activities.

In summary, by properly using modern computer and information technology, student affairs organizations can enhance the delivery of student services, activities, and programs and increase the overall effectiveness and efficiency with which they perform related administrative functions. These benefits include, but are not limited to: (1) reduced administrative overhead costs related to maintaining files, generating reports, keeping statistics, etc.; (2) reduced number of human errors resulting in improved record accuracy; (3) improved intra-and-inter departmental communications; (4) improved collection and use of administrative data (i.e. fiscal, usage, personnel, and facility) needed for planning, policy analyses and decision making; (5) reduced publication costs for handbooks, brochures, course schedules, directories, calendars, forms, letters, flyers, etc., while simultaneously improving their timeliness and appearance; (6) increased speed and simplification of data collection, analyses, and report production; (7) possible reductions in clerical and support staff needs; and (8) increased time professional staff members may spend engaged in "high touch" activities with prospective students, students' parents, faculty, alumni, and other staff members. Therefore, every student affairs organization should attempt to properly integrate and apply modern computer and information technology to its routine administrative functions whenever possible.

ISSUES IN TECHNOLOGY IN STUDENT AFFAIRS

Administrators considering the computerization of their programs or the introduction of other technologies must confront a myriad of issues that can delay or confound progress toward this worthwhile goal. Included among them are cost, selection of hardware and software, legal and ethical questions, security of files, records and equipment, staff development, and general resistance toward change. All of these issues are addressed in considerable detail in Parts II and III of this book.

There are three issues, though, which encompass all of the above and are of paramount importance when giving consideration to the expanded use of technology in student affairs. They are: (1) the need for strategic planning of technological resources; (2) avoiding the danger of becoming routinized and impersonal in the use of technology; and (3) ensuring equitable access to technological resources for both students and staff.

Strategic Planning

The first issue to be considered when planning to introduce or expand the use of technology in student affairs is the need for strategic planning. Don Mills (1990), writing about the technological transformation of student affairs, suggests that the first step is to establish strategic planning which uses environmental scanning in the planning model. By using environmental scanning as a technique, all staff become involved in a continuous planning process and new information can routinely be introduced into discussions regarding possible technologies to be adopted.

Mills also emphasizes that four other conditions should exist in order to successfully plan for applying technology to student affairs administration. First, there should be a central authority appointed to plan and coordinate the implementation of technology for daily administrative practice. This person must be granted the authority to oversee the process from the Chief Student Affairs Officer (CSAO) and should work to avoid a duplication of resources and assure that plans are consistent with divisional and institutional goals.

Second, other members of the institutional community should be involved in decisions regarding the use of technology in student affairs. Shared use of computer hardware and software by other campus departments or agencies may be possible, thus reducing the cost for all users. This will also allow student affairs to call upon the expertise of others to avoid mistakes and allow for the most judicious expenditure of funds.

Third, consideration should be given to societal developments external to the campus. These developments range in scope from increased dependence on the advancement of electronic technology in our daily lives, to increases in crime and drug use. Student affairs professionals must constantly be aware of societal trends that affect the way high school students think and create expectations of what college will be like. If expectations and reality are significantly different, students may be dissatisfied with their educational experience. In some cases it may be necessary to accommodate the expectations of students; in other cases students may need some assistance in helping them to change their expectations to a more realistic appraisal of the institution and its programs. In either case, the use of technology in the delivery and administration of student programs and services will be impacted. For example, in the past ten years we have seen the widespread introduction of computer registration, electronic admittance to facilities, complex programs that match roommates and computerized job searches for graduating students.

Finally, a strategic application of technology will likely require a considerable expenditure of funds. Student affairs administrators should therefore, seek assurance at the beginning of the planning process that the institution is committed to the initial cost of acquiring the system and to the continuing costs of operating and maintaining the system from year to year. Because sophisticated technologies are not inexpensive, there should be a firm institutional commitment to embracing technology before a student affairs component attempts to employ these new technologies in its daily activities.

Maintaining Human Priorities

The second issue that must be considered before a student affairs organization considers expanding its use of computer technology is the danger of becoming impersonal, routinized or standardized in the approach to work. The computer makes it very easy to personalize written responses to individuals. But it also may cause some administrators to approach student problems and solutions impersonally if they are not careful. The danger is that they may become complacent and allow a computerized response to suffice when such is really not appropriate to a particular situation.

For example, a prospective student may write the admissions office requesting general information and also may ask a specific question about a personal problem or concern. Too often the solution may be to send "letter b" that answers most of the questions, but fails to provide all the specific information requested. Not only does the prospective student not receive what he/she requested but he/she may be left with the impression the university is too bureaucratic and insensitive to student needs. This is just the opposite of the "high touch" service most student affairs offices try to provide. Therefore, although computers can save time and money, student affairs professionals must be very careful that they do not let them blur our historic focus on helping, educating and serving students as individuals.

Ensuring Equal Access

Access for students and staff to the use of technological resources is another issue that needs to be addressed when considering using technology in student affairs. Some colleges and universities now require that all entering students have a personal computer to use in conjunction with classroom assignments. This requirement portends the possibility that some students may be denied admission if they cannot afford the added expense. The use of a computer in the classroom is one that must be encouraged, but should not be done in such a way that access is limited for a certain group of students, such as those who are less affluent, disabled, or otherwise disadvantaged. There are many ways to avoid this problem, such as installing computer labs in residence halls, classroom buildings, the student center, the library, and other such facilities. But whatever the solution, equitable student access must be provided.

Equal access to computers must also be provided to student affairs staff members who need them to do their jobs. For example, if it is a requirement of a person's position description that he/she know how to utilize a computer for word processing, data collection, fiscal management, maintaining records, and performing routine office functions, the college has an obligation to provide that person with access to and training for the needed hardware and software to do the job. Unfortunately, some colleges and universities are requiring staff members to be computer literate and competent, but then are not providing them with appropriate access to and/or training for the technology necessary to get their job done efficiently. This may result in some applicants for employment being unfairly denied employment because they do not presently have the "skills" needed to perform the job, and/or an employee being unfairly penalized during evaluation periods for not meeting productivity standards. It is, therefore, important to ensure appropriate computer access for all staff members whose position descriptions require the use of computer technology.

By addressing each of these issues before embarking upon any significant computerization in student affairs, there is an increased chance that the effort will not only meet with success but also avoid wasting valuable time and resources.

It is the intent of this book to provide a practical guide for student affairs administrators who are considering the introduction or expansion of technology into their program and service areas. This book, therefore, suggests strategies for enhancing staff competencies in computer applications, provides a primer on computer technology and terminology for those professionals who are not yet technologically literate, presents a series of chapters that describe the many different uses of technology in component areas of student affairs, examines the legal and ethical issues surrounding the use of technology in higher education, and offers a number of recommendations on what needs to be done to ensure that the continued use of technology in student affairs is successful and proper.

The opportunity to touch the lives of students in a significant and meaningful way almost always results from one-on-one contact between students and staff. By properly employing technology, student affairs professionals can have more time for interaction with students that might make a significant difference in a student's academic success and/or personal development. It is, therefore, incumbent upon all student affairs professionals to learn how to properly apply and manage modern computer and information technology in the performance of their daily activities.

REFERENCES

Bleuer, J. C. & Walz, G. R. (1990). Outlook on computers in counseling. In J. C. Bleuer, M. Maze & G. R. Walz (Eds.), *Counseling software guide* (pp. 239-252). Alexandria, VA.: American Association for Counseling and Development.

Mills, D. B. (1990). The technological transformation of student services. In M. J. Barr & M. L. Upcraft (Eds.), *New Futures for Student Affairs: Building a Vision for Professional Leadership and Practice* (pp. 138-159). San Francisco: Jossey-Bass Publishers.

Welch, M. (1986). Housing and food service functions performed on computers. *Data from a survey distributed to the Association of College and University Housing Officers - International.*

U.S. Bureau of the Census, Current Population Reports, Series P-23, No. 171, *Computer use in the United States: 1989.* U.S. Government Printing Office, Washington, D.C., 1991.

Chapter 2

Assessing and Enhancing Technological Competencies of Staff

John L. Baier

Don Mills (1990) recently wrote, "Student affairs is typically viewed as a professional area that focuses on the person. . . . There is little mention of technology in the student affairs literature. . . . Indeed, student affairs is considered by many to be the 'high-touch' counterpart to the 'high-tech' aspects of campus life (p. 138)". However, as indicated in the previous chapter, by properly using modern computer and information technology, student affairs organizations can enhance the delivery of student services, activities, and programs and increase the overall effectiveness and efficiency with which they perform many of their related administrative functions.

All student affairs professionals should, therefore, know how to properly use modern computer and information technology in their daily activities. As Barr and Upcraft (1990) urged in *New Futures for Student Affairs*, the student affairs profession should join the computer and information system revolution and do the following:

1. Develop computer-assisted ways of managing information about students, services, programs, and facilities and institutions in general.

2. Make better use of computer technology for planning, facilities management, resource allocation, record keeping, and other management functions.

3. Ensure that student affairs staff are computer literate and update professional staff development to include technological advances.

4. Serve as guardian against the dehumanization of students and staff that can occur with the increased use of computer technology.

5. Assist in the development of policies regarding both academic freedom and academic dishonesty when using computers.

Thus, for the remainder of the twentieth century it will be necessary for all student affairs organizations that have not already done so, to actively engage themselves in the broad scale computerization of their programs, services, and administrative functions. Also, those organizations that have already begun the process, will need to upgrade their hardware and software, and integrate the newer technologies (such as CD-ROM and interactive multimedia) into their operations. To accomplish this, most student affairs professionals will need to acquire and/or increase their technological literacy level as well as their comfort level with using advanced technologies in their daily activities. In short, they must learn how to properly use "high-tech" to enhance "high-touch", rather than fear it, and they must do it in a way that "ensure[s] that [the] student affairs administrator is managing the system—rather than the system managing the administrator" (Mills, 1990, p. 151).

The purpose of this chapter is to discuss various approaches to assessing and enhancing the technological competencies of both incumbent and future student affairs staff members. The chapter is organized into three sections. The first section assesses the current status of computer literacy and competence within the student affairs profession, or stated differently, the technological readiness of the profession. The second section describes various methods through which the technological competencies of current staff members can be enhanced. The chapter concludes with a discussion on how the student affairs profession can increase the technological literacy and competence of future staff members.

ASSESSING THE TECHNOLOGICAL LITERACY AND READINESS OF THE PROFESSION

The slowness of many student affairs divisions in the early 1980s to embrace and engage the expanded use of computer and information technology in their day to day activities was due to a number of factors. Among them were the lack of the funding needed to procure and maintain new computer hardware and the lack of suitable software and/or the programming support to meet the particular needs of student affairs programs. However, two of the biggest obstacles were the technological illiteracy of many student affairs staff members (especially Chief Student Affairs Officers), and the general discomfort and apprehension of large numbers of professional staff members to trust and embrace the use of technology in their daily activities.

Much of the early computerization of student affairs programs and services in the late 1970s and early 1980s was accomplished through "trial and error" by campus computer center personnel and computer equipment vendors. These computer experts possessed considerable technical computer knowledge but had a very limited knowledge of the nuances and human priorities of the student affairs profession. They, therefore, unwittingly developed software applications which were convenient to computer center personnel but not very personal or convenient for student affairs staff and students. Thus, many costly errors were made, both in time and resources, and the computer tended to foster and symbolize a growing sense of distrust and impersonalization on many college campuses. This adversely impacted the attitudes of many student affairs staff members toward, and confidence in, the potential benefits to be derived from incorporating additional computer applications in the delivery of student affairs programs, services, and administrative functions.

The past five years, however, have evidenced dozens of new computer applications in many student affairs divisions. There were several factors that caused this dramatic shift in the span of only a few years. First, there has been a literal explosion in the amount of new affordable and "user friendly" computer equipment and software programs that could readily be utilized in the management and delivery of student affairs programs and services.

Second, the expectations of the students changed. Most of today's students were raised on television images (i.e. Sesame Street, CNN, and MTV), and many now bring to college their own TVs, VCRs, CD stereo systems, telephone answering machines, FAX machines, personal pagers, cordless or cellular telephones, and personal computers and ink-jet or laser printers. They are also familiar with and competent at using word processing, spreadsheet, and desktop publishing software. Therefore, because most of today's college students have been exposed to computers and information technology since nursery school, they not only appreciate and use technology themselves on a daily basis, but expect that their colleges also utilize technology wherever possible. Hence, student affairs professionals have had to become more technologically literate and competent in order to keep up with their students.

Third, as university and student affairs budgets began shrinking nationwide in the late 1980s, college administrators and faculty members alike began exploring new ways to use technology more effectively as a means of reducing administrative overhead expenses and instructional costs. Through this process, student affairs administrators discovered that many of their traditional "high-touch" functions and activities could be enhanced, rather than diminished, through the use of modern information and computer technology.

All of these factors contributed to the broader acceptance of computer and information technology by student affairs professionals. Hence, the willingness to use technology in student affairs is now present on most campuses. Unfortunately, however, willingness does not equal readiness. To be ready to fully embrace modern technology in their daily activities, many student affairs administrators must first increase their technological literacy level and then learn how to actually use and depend on computers themselves. The following section addresses ways in which staff technological literacy and competency levels can be enhanced.

Enhancing Staff Technological Literacy and Competencies

Having access to modern computer and information technology is of little value if one does not have staff members who know how to use it properly. Because so many current student affairs practitioners entered the profession before much of the computer and information technology available today was even invented, and because most people who are attracted to the profession are more "people" rather than "thing" oriented, it is vital the profession embarks upon a major technological literacy and competency training effort within the framework of existing staff and personal development training programs. There are numerous ways in which this can be accomplished. They include computer usage short courses and workshops, reading and publication of technology related newsletters and magazines, employee suggestion programs and contests, tutoring programs, self-paced video learning modules, and computer equipment loan programs. A brief description of each follows.

Computer Usage Short Courses and Workshops

On most large college campuses, continuing education departments, staff training offices, and central computer centers offer short courses and workshops on how to use basic word processing, spreadsheet, database, and desktop publishing software programs. Short courses usually consist of two to ten one-hour sessions spread over a two or three week time frame. Workshops usually run one or two days from 9 am to 4 pm. Selected workshops and courses are typically offered several times each semester and are offered free of charge to university personnel or a small fee is charged to cover the costs of instructional manuals, use of the computer lab, and instructional personnel. Introductory courses, encompassing several hours of group instruction followed by several hours of independent lab homework assignments, and more advanced courses which include several hours of individual tutorial sessions or small group classes followed by several hours of homework assignments, are usually offered.

Other short courses and workshops are also offered by community colleges, local computer retail outlets, and by commercial computer instruction centers such as Mac Academys and IBM Customer Service Centers. Short courses taught by for-profit agencies usually cost $25 - $100 per hour of instruction. Although expensive compared to non-profit campus based programs, they have been reported to receive high satisfaction ratings from people who have taken the courses and should be considered by staff members who work at a campus that does not offer lower cost "in-house" instruction. For about $500 of instructional costs and by spending approximately 20-40 hours of time practicing on a personal computer, most individuals can become fairly proficient in word processing, spreadsheet, database, and desktop software. In addition, dozens of individuals who have taken short courses or attended workshops (from either computer center personnel, continuing education departments, community colleges, and/or commercial centers) have reported to this author that the courses/workshops have not only increased their computer usage skills and competency level, but have also stimulated their desire to increase their computer literacy further through additional instruction or some of the independent self-help techniques and programs discussed below.

Newsletters and Magazines

An excellent way to keep abreast of practical computer applications and technological advances is to regularly read computer related newsletters and magazines. There are dozens of general monthly computer magazines (i.e., *PC World, Computing, MacUser, PC Magazine*), as well as several excellent program specific computer newsletters (i.e., *Computers in Recreation*) from which student affairs professionals can choose. Each magazine and newsletter regularly has articles on what new hardware and software has just been released, as well as critiques of their value and usefulness for various applications and users. Therefore, by reading at least one such publication each month, a computer literate staff member should be able to stay current with very little effort and a technological novice should be able to develop a reasonable level of technological literacy within a short period of time.

Because reading about technology and technological applications is so central to both becoming and remaining technologically literate and competent, student affairs divisions should consider publishing a short in-house "Computer Applications in Student Affairs" newsletter of their own or add a "computer/technological advances" section to an existing student affairs division staff newsletter. This special newsletter or section of an existing newsletter should highlight both current and potential applications as well as list courses, workshops, and other instructional resources that staff members could avail themselves of to learn both present and future applications. *The Chronicle of Higher Education* includes a regular "Information Technology" section which provides similar information on a macro scale. A locally produced in-house publication should address these issues on the micro level.

The publication of an in-house computer newsletter or computer section of an existing newsletter would also symbolically communicate to the staff that becoming and remaining technologically literate and competent is an expectation of the job and a personal responsibility of each staff member.

Suggestion Programs and Contests

Another way to symbolically communicate to a student affairs staff that technological literacy and competency is an important job requirement is to sponsor division-wide contests and suggestion programs which increase customer satisfaction, student service, administrative effectiveness, speed of processing information, accuracy of records, timeliness of reports, and reduce administrative inefficiencies and operating expenses. By rewarding staff members and departments with small fiscal rewards and other incentives (i.e., new computer equipment or assignment of a portion of the annual savings to the division to extra operating funds for the department which developed the improvement) it is not only possible to save thousands of dollars in annual operating costs, but also helps motivate staff members to embrace the use of technology to enhance the delivery of improved student services and programs as well as increase administrative efficiency and effectiveness.

Tutoring Programs

Several universities have computer-based honors programs which enroll dozens of very bright and talented computer literate students who can receive academic credit for tutoring faculty and staff members on how to properly utilize computers in their teaching and/or administrative responsibilities. A "learning contract" for tutoring instruction is usually developed between the honors program student (tutor) and the staff member (student) describing the number of tutoring sessions that will be provided during the course of the semester and the learning objectives to be achieved by the staff member. This contract is then approved by the honors program supervisor (faculty member) and at the completion of the semester the tutor is graded on his/her ability to help the staff member achieve the specified learning objectives. This arrangement, therefore, places a certain amount of pressure on both the honors program tutor and the staff member to work hard at accomplishing the learning contract objectives.

The University of Alabama in Tuscaloosa has such a program in place. Through this program, over the past five years, student tutors have taught numerous senior administrators and faculty members in the proper use of PCs for routine word processing, spreadsheet analysis, desktop publishing, and database management.

Colleges and universities that do not have such a tutoring program can accomplish similar results by using work study students who are either majoring in computer science or have developed computer expertise in some other way. Computer literate work study students can be assigned to tutor individual staff members in the financial aid office, placement center, student center, housing office, student health service, etc. Tutoring sessions can be directed at specific software applications for particular departments (i.e., career counseling software such as SIGI Plus) or can be general in nature (i.e., word processing or desktop publishing software).

Self-Paced Video Learning Modules

Using self-paced video learning tapes is yet another way for staff members to learn inexpensively how to use PCs and the extensive library of software programs available for them. Many distributors of computer self-instruction videos are available throughout the country. For example, one of the larger distributors of self-instruction video tapes for Macintosh computer users is Florida Marketing International in Orlando, Florida. They market the MacAcademy Video Training Series consisting of numerous individual tapes (about one hour in length each) that teach the user how to use Macintosh computers (i.e., Basics 1 & 2 and Advanced Mac), and Macintosh software (i.e., Microsoft Word, Microsoft Works, Aldus Pagemaker Volume 1 & 2, Excel (1, 2 & 3), and Hyper Card). Each tape is designed to "walk" the learners through each program step by step so that they can master the program at their own pace and in the privacy of their own home or office. Proven self-instruction teaching techniques make learning fast and easy. The showing of the monitor and keyboard simultaneously also allows one to better see the effects of each keystroke or click on the mouse. Also, since each tape can be purchased with a site license for instructional use within an individual office for approximately $40 each and can be played over and over and used by several individuals within an office, the per-person cost is very small for such an excellent training aid.

Similar video tapes can also be purchased for IBM compatible computers. One of the more popular series for IBM compatibles is marketed by Video Projects of Salt Lake City, Utah. Their tapes cost approximately $70 each and provide instruction for the use of Windows, DOS Intermediate, Lotus 1,2,3 Intermediate, and

WordPerfect (Introduction and Intermediate). They are also of very high quality.

Computer Equipment Loan Programs

One of the major obstacles to staff members becoming computer literate is not having convenient access to a PC for practice and experimentation after office hours. Office computers are not generally made accessible to staff members after working hours for personal use because of security and copyright concerns. Thus, unless a staff member has purchased a fairly powerful PC for home use, along with a full complement of software (i.e. word processing, database management, spreadsheet), or is given evening/weekend access to a similarly configured office computer system, it is unlikely that the staff member will experiment with new program applications or think of using a computer for routine word processing and data management functions "after hours". This inhibits the staff member's potential interest in developing new computer skills and applications.

One technique that can be used to overcome this problem is to establish a computer equipment loan program within the division or college. Staff members should be permitted to "check out" a PC (with appropriate software) and a printer for limited periods of home use. Such loan programs will not only encourage staff members to become more computer literate and competent, but will also whet their appetite for the purchase of their own computer system in the future. Once people have discovered the vast potential of the computer to assist in the production and maintenance of routine correspondence, reports, papers, mailing lists, resume' and financial records, and the relative ease with which they can be used, the more likely they will be to embrace their use in all of their daily activities and look for new applications to simplify their work and personal affairs. Thus, having a modest computer equipment loan program in place can have a dramatic positive impact on expediting the competency levels of professional staff members who otherwise may resist becoming computer literate.

Ensuring Future Staff Technological Competencies

To ensure that new people who enter the profession are technologically literate and competent, in addition to providing all of the above staff development programs and incentives, the profession also needs to encourage each of the student affairs graduate preparation programs to follow the Council for the Advancement of Standards (CAS) for Student Services/Development Programs **Preparation Standards and Guidelines at the Master's Degree Level for Student Services/Development Professionals in Postsecondary Education** which were adopted in 1986. These standards and guidelines call for the inclusion of a computer literacy and computer applications component in all student affairs graduate preparation programs, regardless of the programs' emphases (student development, administration, or counseling).

Although the **CAS Standards** were adopted by the profession six years ago, because no existing higher education accreditation body uses the **CAS Standards** to review or approve student affairs graduate programs, they have yet to be followed by most of the 87 graduate programs from which approximately 500 new professionals are employed each year. Unless graduate preparation programs are required to follow the CAS computer literacy standard, the profession will find itself in an endless cycle of having to train most student affairs staff members through "on-the-job" training programs. Because there are so many other things that must be continually taught to staff members through limited and minimally funded staff development programs (e.g. changes in the law, changes in federal/state financial aid regulations, new medical information, new institutional policies and procedures, strategic planning techniques, leadership skills, multicultural issues, substance abuse issues, etc.) the profession should seriously consider requiring all future staff members to be technologically literate and competent as a condition of employment. If this were done, it would only take a few years to significantly raise and maintain the technological competency level of the entire student affairs profession.

CONCLUSION

In conclusion, even if millions of dollars are spent on sophisticated computer hardware, unless there are technologically literate staff who are knowledgeable about how to efficiently and properly utilize it, the profession will not be able to obtain the enormous potential benefits to be derived from modern technological advances. The profession must, therefore, invest in the most complex piece of technology, the education of the student affairs staff member.

The first step is to become technologically literate. Staff members can accomplish this by investing a little time doing such things as: attending in-service training programs, computer short courses and computer usage workshops; periodically reading computer magazines and newsletters; watching self-paced learning video tapes; purchasing a PC for home use; observing others who are more skilled at using technology than they are; experimenting with new computer systems and software programs; and, attending computer related conferences.

Student affairs professionals must not just learn how computers work, however. They must learn when it is appropriate to use them for specific purposes. Because student affairs is a "people oriented" profession that values human interaction and the individuality of college students, it is not always appropriate to utilize every new technological advancement. The benefits of efficiency may be more than offset by the dehumanization of the campus's teaching and learning environment. It is, therefore, important that professionals learn when not to use computers, as well as, when to use them. That means they also have to learn how to be good technology consumers. That can be accomplished by attending student affairs conference sessions on technological applications, reading professional journal articles and books, talking with colleagues on other campuses, and using cost-benefit analysis to evaluate the value of possible new applications before any equipment or software is purchased.

What must be avoided at all costs, though, is to fear using technology at any time, because, as discussed in the previous chapter, the potential benefits to be derived from the proper use of modern technology are too great. It is, therefore, imperative that all student affairs professionals become and remain technologically literate and competent if the student affairs profession is to be able to fulfill its historical mission during the twenty-first century.

REFERENCES

Barr, M.J., & Upcraft, M.L. (Eds.) (1990). *New futures for student affairs.* San Francisco: Jossey-Bass.

Council for the Advancement of Standards for Student Services/Development Programs. (1986). Preparation standards and guidelines at the master's degree level for student services/development professionals in postsecondary education. *CAS standards and guidelines for student services/development programs.* Washington, DC: Council for the Advancement of Standards.

Ferrante, R., Hayman, J., Carlston, M.S., & Philips, H. (1988) *Planning for microcomputers in high education: Strategies for the next generation*, ASHE-ERIC higher education report no. 7, Washington, DC: Association for Study of Higher Education. Mills, D.B. (1990). The technological transformation of student services. In M. J. Barr, & M. L. Upcraft (Eds.), *New futures for student affairs.* (pp. 138-159). San Francisco: Jossey-Bass.

Chapter 3

A Primer on Information and Computer Technology

John L. Baier

The remaining chapters of this book were written with the assumption that readers would have at least a basic knowledge and understanding of modern information and computer technology and terminology, thus this section is provided as a courtesy to those readers who may not currently be as technologically literate as they would like. Although the following user-friendly summary of current information and computer technology and terminology is brief, coupled with the glossary in the appendix, it should be adequate to allow the newcomer to technology to be able to understand and benefit from the rest of this book. Those readers who are already technologically literate may wish to skip this chapter and proceed directly to Parts II and III.

COMPUTER HARDWARE

Computers come in four general types: mainframe, mini, micro and portable.

Mainframe Computers

Mainframe computers were originally developed in the late 1950s. As indicated previously, they were large and cumbersome and often required an entire room (which had to be dust free and temperature controlled), generated a great deal of heat, needed to be serviced regularly, and had very limited memory and computing power by today's standards. For example, the same computing power of a 1950s analog computer (16 K) costing upwards of $1 million can be purchased today as a hand held calculator with a solar powered battery for less than $100.

With the invention of the computer microchip in the 1970s, computer power, memory, flexibility, and dependability increased rapidly while cost, size, and programming complexity dramatically decreased. Today, almost every college campus maintains at least one mainframe computer system for academic and administrative computing (requiring the storage, retrieval and manipulation of large databases) and the production of complex reports or simulations. On large campuses mainframes are generally used to maintain registration files, store and retrieve student data, maintain personnel records, process payroll, schedule classes, maintain accounting records, handle purchasing functions, maintain student financial aid data, and handle student billing systems. Because of their power and the large institutional bureaucracies that have been created to procure, maintain, and upgrade them (i.e. Computer Centers and Management Information Systems Offices), it is likely that mainframe computer systems will continue to be utilized on most college campuses well into the 21st century.

Minicomputers

Minicomputers have been available since the early 1970s. They are significantly less powerful but also less expensive than mainframe systems. They are usually purchased and programmed to perform specific functions, such as managing alumni office records, managing student health service medical and pharmacy records, managing housing reservations and assignments, and managing food service programs (i.e. Vali-Dine Systems). More widespread use in higher education beyond these types of specialized applications, however, will probably never materialize. The introduction of relatively inexpensive, but very powerful microcomputers in the early 1980s, coupled with the technology to inexpensively network microcomputers via LANs (Local Area Networks) or WANs (Wide Area Networks) has resulted in the minicomputer becoming almost obsolete on many campuses. In fact, many desktop microcomputers are now more powerful than minicomputers were just a few years ago, and they are less expensive to purchase, easier to program and use, more flexible, and require less space and maintenance. As microcomputers become even more powerful, as their hard disk storage capacity increases, and as campuses install more LANs and WANs between offices and buildings, the microcomputer may some day make the mainframe computer obsolete for everything but sophisticated academic research and the sharing of data and transactions among numerous databases.

Microcomputers

Microcomputers were first introduced by the Apple Computer Company in 1976. Although other companies like Tandy and Commodore introduced their own versions a couple of years later, it was not until IBM introduced the PC (personal computer) in 1981 that the widespread use of microcomputers in higher education began. Since that time, microcomputers have pervaded every aspect of the educational environment. A typical microcomputer configuration (costing $2000-$4000 in 1992) includes two to eight thousand megabytes (2-8 MB) of random access memory (RAM), eighty to two hundred and fifty megabytes (80-250 MB) of hard disk memory, a high resolution color monitor, a 386 or 486 microprocessor chip, an 1.4 MB 3 1/2" disk drive, and an ink jet or laser printer. This microcomputer hardware package offers the same computing power and printing capabilities as yesterday's small mainframe or large minicomputer system which cost upwards of $100,000 and required a computer programmer to run it. So the dramatic advances in computing technology have placed the equivalent of a small "computer center" on each individual's desk for his/her personal use.

Portable Computers

Portable computers became available in the late 1980s and have since been rapidly gaining acceptance in both education and business. As the name implies, portable computers can operate on either battery (usually three to six hours before needing to be recharged) or regular electrical power, are small in size, and very light weight. They are about the size of a small brief case or large notebook and usually weigh less than ten pounds. Yet, they have the same computing power, speed, sharp liquid crystal display (LCD) screens, memory and software and graphics capabilities as desktop PCs.

Portable or mobile computing has become a way of life for people whose business takes them away from their office. Until recently, however, most portable computers lacked the ability to easily network with other computers. But in 1992, NCR introduced the NSX/20 Notebook Computer, which with a Local Area Network (LAN) adapter or an integrated telephone modem, can take advantage of AT&T's worldwide connectivity to let their new portable computers network from anywhere in the world to anywhere else in the world. Easily networked portable computers are now also available from NEC, IBM, Apple and other computer manufacturers. They generally cost about twice as much as a similarly powered and equipped desktop personal computer, but their smaller size and portability are fast making them the computer of choice for most business people and college professors and administrators.

COMPUTER OPERATING SYSTEMS

Computers utilize one of several different types of disk operating systems. The most common are CP/M developed by Apple in the late 1970s for its Apple line, Macintosh Systems 5-7 developed in the 1980s by Apple for its Macintosh line, MS-DOS developed by Microsoft Corporation in the early 1980s for IBM and compatible PCs, and IBM's own OS/2 developed in the late 1980s for its current line of microcomputers. By the mid-1990s, Apple and IBM will produce jointly a new disk operating system, called Taligent, for use on their new compatible IBM and Macintosh computer systems.

IBM currently dominates the microcomputer market in higher education, but other manufacturers such as Apple, AT&T, Compac, and Zenith have significant market shares. With the exception of Macintosh, all other manufacturers produce computer equipment that is compatible with IBM's, but following the release of the new operating disk system being jointly developed by IBM and Apple, all microcomputers produced in the late 1990s should be compatible with each other. This will eliminate the last major obstacle to the further integration of microcomputers in education.

COMPUTER SOFTWARE

Regardless of the disk operating system utilized to operate a microcomputer there are four general types of software programs commercially available for computers: word processing software, spreadsheet software, database software, and desktop publishing software. Each serves a unique function, is relatively easy to learn and inexpensive to purchase. In addition to these general purposes, there is a proliferation of software for specific other purposes.

Word Processing Software

Word Processing Software (i.e., WordPerfect, Microsoft Word, Wordstar, MacWrite) allows the computer user to not only utilize the computer for routine typing tasks but also permits numerous variations of formats and type styles within a single document, the movement of blocks of copy within a document and between documents, spelling checks, properly positioned footnotes, headers and footers, insertion of graphs and tables produced by other programs, document and file saving, mail merging (automated addressing and mailing features), and other operations. Coupled with the wide variety of letter and typesetting quality printers available, the output of these word processing programs is first class.

Spreadsheet Software

Spreadsheet software programs (i.e., Lotus 1-2-3, Excel, Quattro, Visicalc, Multiplan) create a numerical table, or spreadsheet, in which any cell may contain either original data, a permanent label, or a formula to calculate new data from data entered in one or more of the other cells. Each time any cell is altered, all the dependent formula cells are automatically recalculated. Sections of the spreadsheet may also be moved or copied at will without inhibiting the recalculation of the dependent data. This type of software is very useful for determining the financial impact of changing housing occupancy rates, bond interest rates, enrollments, and other such applications involving "what if" type questions. By using spreadsheet software it is possible to ask and answer literally dozens of hypothetical "what if" financial and enrollment questions within the span of a single work day. Before the advent of computers, determining the impacts of the same number of scenarios would have been impossible, impractical or both. Hence, spreadsheet software is one of the most useful types of software for the decision maker to have on his/her computer.

Database Software

Database software programs (i.e., dBase, Condor, Pfs:File, Powerbase, PCFile) are designed to manage a series of information items for a group of individual entities. Each piece of data is a field, each group of fields about a single entity is called a record, and each set of records is called a file. The logic behind database software programs is similar to the manner in which office filing systems have been historically maintained, but it is all done electronically and eliminates the need for file folders and filing cabinets. For example, instead of keeping thousands of separate pieces of paper to record student transcripts, grades, residence hall assignments, home addresses, etc. for each student in a series of file folders stored in a bank of filing cabinets, with database software, one can store and retrieve any or all of this information electronically (in any order desired such as alphabetically, zip code, GPA, residence hall, state, gender, race, etc.) in a matter of minutes.

Desktop Publishing Software

Desktop publishing software (i.e., PageMaker) was created in the mid 1980s. It has rapidly become one of the most popular and useful software programs on the educational market. It can be used to produce newsletters, announcements, flyers, brochures, and a host of other short documents. Desktop software displays on the computer screen how the printed page will look and allows the user to incorporate graphs, drawings, pictures, and other graphics into a document that has the appearance of having been professionally typeset. It has an enormous number of applications in student affairs, many of which are described in the following chapters of this book.

COMPUTER NETWORKS

The full benefits of using computer technology cannot be obtained if most campus computers are not networked to each other and to the central campus mainframe computer. Networks allow for on-line interactive communication with any other connected computer. The proper development of Local Area Networks (LANs) which link computers within a single building or portion of a building and Wide Area Networks (WANs) which link computers between buildings and/or between campuses is very important to the effective and efficient use of computer databases, software programs, and electronic communications. Therefore, it is imperative that student affairs organizations carefully develop appropriate networking systems to meet the particular needs of their campus. As with other computer related matters, a whole new lexicon has evolved to define and describe the various components of computer networks. Because of the complexity of this aspect of "computer speak" this book contains a whole chapter devoted to networking (see Chapter Sixteen, "Managing Computer Systems and Networks"). Included in that chapter is a brief description of the relevant terms and technology pertaining to networks. The glossary in the appendix also defines network related terms.

CD-ROM TECHNOLOGY

CD-ROM (compact disc-read only memory) is a data publication and retrieval system for use with computer systems. It works much like a compact disc for a home stereo system. Data is stored as three dimensional pits on a disc and then sealed with a protective coating. A CD-ROM drive is connected to the computer and reads data from the CD-ROM. CD-ROM discs differ from floppy disks and hard disk drives (normally used in microcomputers) in that they use a laser beam rather than a magnetic head to retrieve stored data. This eliminates wear of the disc surface and prolongs the useful life of the CD-ROM almost indefinitely.

The primary advantage of the CD-ROM technology over the floppy or hard disk drive technology, however, is in the tremendous amount of information which can be stored on a CD-ROM. A single CD-ROM has the same storage capacity as 1520 floppy disks. At the present time, the information on most commercially available CD-ROM discs is written for MS-DOS computers, but Apple Computer is rapidly developing its own capability for reading CD-ROM discs and several disc publishers have started producing discs for Apple computers as well.

Because CD-ROM is currently a "read-only" technology, it is not possible for the user to add to or modify the data on a CD-ROM disc. Although this is an advantage for many educational applications and eliminates the chance of inadvertently erasing data, it is presently considered a medium for publication rather than for storage of large data bases which need to be periodically updated.

THOR-CD TECHNOLOGY

To correct for this deficiency in CD-ROM technology, several companies are now working on the development of CD-compatible discs capable of being erased and re-recorded. One such disc is called THOR-CD (developed by Tandy Corp in 1990). It can repeatedly record, play back, store and erase sound, data or video on a disc that can be used with all existing CD audio and CD-ROM players. The advancement of THOR-CD technology may further diminish the need for mainframe computers with large hard disk memory capacities. For example, with a THOR-CD, a financial aid office could easily store all of its student files for several years on a single THOR-CD and make corrections and updates to it from a computer located on a financial aid officer's desk. Other student files could similarly be stored and updated almost instantaneously. The savings in time, equipment and staff can be enormous.

INTERACTIVE MULTIMEDIA TECHNOLOGY

The potential for interactive multimedia is limitless. Although the term "multimedia" has been used for decades, recently it has become the buzzword in educational technology to describe the fusion or interactivity, of video technology with the enormous power of the computer and CD-ROM/THOR-CD technology. Interactive multimedia technology combines speech, enhanced music, video images, animation, and computer capabilities into a unified system. It lends itself to instruction based on the very different ways students learn because it can access and produce information using a variety of media in a coordinated nonsequential way. The technologies that are driving the use of interactive multimedia include the advancement in the way video images can be stored and accessed through CD-ROM/THOR-CD technology and new computer technology which allows for the fusion of video images and computer graphics on the same screen instead of two separate screens. The emergence of faster, more powerful computers has also been significant. At the beginning of this decade, all of the major computer companies began racing to assemble hardware that will allow the delivery of multimedia programs. It is, therefore, likely that interactive multimedia hardware and software will become the new standard in computer and information technology by the beginning of the twenty-first century.

SUMMARY

This brief primer on current computer and information terminology and technology is not presented with the intent of covering all of the vast array of technologies which exist today. Rather the intent, consistent with the mission of this book, is to provide student affairs practitioners and graduate students who are unfamiliar with general computer and information terminology and technologies with enough background information to understand the powerful tools computers can be and the enormous potential they have for enhancing student affairs administrative practice and program effectiveness on a daily basis.

It is suggested that the reader refer back to this chapter or the glossary when encountering unfamiliar terminology in Parts II and III. This practice will not only assist the novice to become more technologically literate, but will also increase the value he or she will be able to obtain from each of the following chapters.

Part II

Application of Technology in Specific Student Affairs Areas

The chapters contained within Part II cover most of those services found in a typical student affairs organization. They are arranged sequentially in the order that a student might use the services over the span of his/her academic career.

Chapters 4 through 10 cover those services that most students depend on during the general matriculation process. In order of presentation they are: Academic Advising Programs (Chapter 4), Student Financial Aid (Chapter 5), International Service and Program Offices (Chapter 6), Housing Programs (Chapter 7), Counseling Center Programs (Chapter 8), Teaching-Learning Programs (Chapter 9), and Career Planning and Placement Programs (Chapter 10).

Chapters 11 through 13 address co-curricular and wellness programs. They include Student Life, Student Centers and Student Activities (Chapter 11), Recreation Sports and Wellness Programs (Chapter 12) and Student Health Centers (Chapter 13).

Part II concludes with a chapter on how the Office of the Chief Student Affairs Officer (CSAO) can utilize technology to more effectively coordinate and administer the diverse staff, programs, and budgets common to most comprehensive student affairs divisions (Chapter 14).

Chapter 4

Academic Advising Programs

Betty Cully
Sue Baum
Judith Miller

In today's high tech world, the automation of student advisement in education has not been neglected. Several institutions and organizations sponsor national conferences which address computer-assisted advising: Brigham Young University, the League for Innovation in the Community College, the National Academic Advising Association (NACADA), and the American College Testing service (ACT) are a few.

Even so, the definition of computer aided student advisement is elusive because institutions define it differently. According to the literature, computer aided advisement may range from simply providing on-line catalogue information for students to integrating state-wide advisement where the system audits student records and gives transfer and graduation information based on the student's major, courses taken, and intended transfer institution.

Computer aided advisement has been defined as "a computer program that stores and matches degree requirements and student academic records" (Spencer, Peterson, and Kramer, 1983). An important criterion in designing a computer aided advisement system is the emphasis on the word "aid" and the acceptance of less than 100% accuracy. It should also be noted that as Bays (1984) pointed out, in the interest of cost savings and timeliness, a system that is 98% accurate should be considered acceptable. A 2% machine entry error factor is far superior to the much greater human error factor common to traditional paper and folder advisor systems. Spencer, Peterson and Kramer (1983) further recommend that, in general, a comprehensive student advisement system should provide the following information:

1. Detailed individual evaluation of all graduation requirements for each student.
2. Immediate access to information for students, faculty and administrators.
3. Immediate assessment of progress toward graduation for students.
4. All requirements for graduation stated and tracked.
5. Requirements within the major categorized.
6. Approved degree program individually tailored, inserted, and tracked.
7. Number of classes, number of semester hours, and combinations of each tracked.
8. Prerequisites for required courses listed.
9. Narrative information provided.
10. All credit, substitutions, and waivers included.
11. Instant update capability provided.
12. Each student allowed to "shop" for a major and immediately review change of major consequences.
13. Requirements tracked as frequently as every semester, but each student tracked by date of entry into major.
14. Two or more majors capable of being tracked. As with all automation efforts, the advantages must be weighed against the disadvantages, especially since student counseling and advisement are such personal, "high touch" areas of the educational process.

Bellenger and Bellenger (1987) list several benefits of computerization in dealing with people problems. First, is time efficient. Academic counselors using a computerized system are saved the time consuming effort of collecting facts about curriculum, majors, and prerequisites, and thus are able to spend more time actually counseling students face to face. Another major benefit is cost savings since the price of hardware has declined dramatically in recent years. Job descriptions may change as a result of computer introduction, but these changes extend the provision of personal services to students. Finally, computerized advisement systems provide more accurate information than manually compiled systems. This fact diminishes information disappearance, information delay, and information distortion.

In implementing a computer aided student advisement system, it seems that the main disadvantages are people- oriented problems. The new users of a system—counselors, faculty and even students—may exhibit unfavorable reactions to the system. In many cases when a new system is introduced, work divisions and responsibilities change and informal relationships are disrupted. Also, the personalities and backgrounds of new users affect their reaction to the new system. Bellenger and Bellenger (1987) suggest several steps to help avoid these behavioral problems.

1. Ensure strong endorsement of the project from the top.
2. Appoint future users to work with computer specialists in the design of the system.
3. Schedule regular meetings with the design team and future users for input and feedback.
4. Make certain new users understand exactly what the new system is intended to do and agree that it will be useful.
5. Do several trial runs with the new system to be sure it is error free.
6. Provide adequate training for new users.
7. Evaluate the system by the users after it is in operation and make modifications.

Several colleges and organizations have shared information concerning their respective systems and, where indicated, their future plans for expansion. The following information includes both commercially available and "in-house" computer-assisted advisement systems currently in use and in various stages of development.

COMMERCIALLY AVAILABLE SYSTEMS
People Oriented Information Systems for Education (POISE)

Campus America-Administrative and Instructional Systems for Education has served the higher education market since 1977 with administrative software for admissions, financial aid, registration, academic history, degree audit/academic advisement, fiscal management, student billing/receivables, payroll, personnel, development/alumni, and campus automation (word processing, electronic mail, microcomputer software). Each POISE module is built on DMS-Plus, a relational database management system (RDDMS) and fourth-generation language (4GL). The system offers a powerful report-writer, information-retrieval system using multiple keys, screen generation, an English-like query language, and interfacing to MS-DOS and PC-DOS microcomputers. DMS-Plus has multiple user levels which include the operator, intermediate user, advanced user, and application developers.

The POISE Degree Audit/Academic Advisement System (DA/AA) tracks students' progress toward degree choices and includes majors and minors. An excerpt from the company's sales brochure describes the CAI component:

> The Degree Audit/Academic Advisement System uses data from several sources (including current student schedules and historical course information) to evaluate a student's progress toward a degree. Using a "computerized" course catalog, the system produces a degree audit transcript reflecting the current status of each of the degree requirements. An advisor, with the student present, may use the system to interactively evaluate possible degree plans and to plan a schedule of classes to fulfill the requirements. Multiple catalog years may be defined using DAReL (the Degree Audit Requirements Language). DAReL is a nonprocedural English-like language based on 'Expert Systems' technology. The system will accommodate CLEP, transfer credit, and 'life experience' provisions, as well as individualized programs of study (Campus America, 1991).

An interesting feature of this system is that it allows for interactive "degree shopping" which would be a valuable asset for advisors. The principal output of the DA/AA is the degree audit transcript which is similar to an academic transcript and includes data reflecting unfulfilled requirements as *incomplete*, current requirements as *in progress*, and fulfilled requirements as *complete*.

Two other modules, the POISE Registration and Academic History System must be installed prior to use of the DA/AA component. The cost of this module is based on the model of VAX computer used.

POISE was designed to operate on Digital Equipment Corporation VAX/VMS, and PDP/RSTS Systems. DMS-Micro is available on MS-DOS and PC-DOS. Also DMS-MicroNET is available on PC-NET allowing institutions to use the same RDBMS on its personal computers.

If colleges are interested in POISE, Campus America will provide a listing of the POISE User's Group who may be called upon as references for the system. Both public and private two-year and four-year institutions are represented. If a college becomes a subscriber, Campus America provides training, support and documentation for the users of POISE.

Contacts at two colleges spoke favorably about the POISE Degree/Audit/Academic Advisement module (See Appendix). Personnel at Washington and Jefferson, a private four-year college in Pennsylvania, commented that the system was flexible and accommodating to even their most unusual core requirements for graduation. They have entered one catalog in the system and are considering adding another catalog soon. At this time, the college is using the program for degree audit only, but has plans for the future to link the main network to microcomputers for professors' use in advising. Twenty to thirty employees may access and use the program at a time. Programming for the system is simple and becomes more meaningful with continued use. Comments regarding technical support were favorable.

At Gwynedd-Mercy College, a two-year private college with an enrollment of 2000 in Pennsylvania, personnel who programmed the system have given ownership of POISE to the registrar's office where personnel have learned to operate the system without needing continued support from the administrative computing division. College personnel remarked that it was somewhat difficult to streamline each and every program change; therefore, changes in the system are made annually. At Gwynedd-Mercy College, advisors are given a hard copy of the degree audit generated in the registrar's office to share with students and aid in the personalization and accuracy of the advisement process.

TEAMS 2000

Teams 2000 software, developed by Computer Management & Development Services (CMDS), is a dynamic and comprehensive set of modules designed for the higher education environment. Teams 2000 application modules include Admissions/Recruitment,

Financial Aid/Need Analysis, General Ledger, Accounts Receivable, Accounts Payable, Purchasing, Registration, Development/Alumni, Payroll, Fixed Assets, and Advising/Degree Audit. Each module is capable of standing alone, but the integration of the modules lends this commercial package its power. Since information entered in one module is shared by all to prevent redundancy, assure consistency, and improve efficiency, using all modules needed by the institution helps eliminate program customizing difficulties.

Teams 2000 makes use of IBM hardware, provides growth potential with the AS/400 series of computers, takes advantage of the AS/400 technology and relational database, and provides special features such as windows, office integration, and executive menus for decision support. Although Teams 2000 seems the answer to many problems regarding information collection and retrieval, particularly in the area of academic advising using computers, this software is expensive. Pricing as of September 1991 quoted the least expensive module, Fixed Assets, at $3,675, while the module for advising costs approximately $23,000. This commercial system would, therefore, appeal more to larger colleges, or two-year college systems, rather than to individual small schools with comparatively smaller budgets. For example, the University of Kentucky and the University of Kentucky Community College System is presently converting its 14 community colleges to IBM AS400 hardware and Teams 2000 software packages. According to the coordinator of Business and Information Services at Hopkinsville Community College in Kentucky, after overcoming initial problems with start-up and working through tailoring the system to meet several colleges' needs, this program should work well. He also indicated that problems seem to occur when purchasing only some of the modules and then expecting the system to work as smoothly as when all program components are used.

ACTIONTRACK

ActionTrack, developed and marketed by Noel/Levitz Centers, Inc., is a software package designed to boost retention success through assistance with monitoring and tracking students and to customize college services to meet individual student needs. ActionTrack consists of four major components: Early Alert, Academic Monitoring, Individualized Retention Plan Development, and Comprehensive Retention Reporting. Upon request, Noel/Levitz will send an institution a demonstration disk which is easy to review. The Academic Monitoring module is designed to enable an institution to follow systematically the progress of a specific population of students. For example, ActionTrack would allow an institution to follow the academic performance of honors students, adult learners, athletes, and students with specific majors, such as engineering or nursing. Other uses include monitoring special interest groups, underprepared students, dropout-prone students, and others. ActionTrack allows for downloading student information routinely gathered by an institution, such as ACT or SAT scores and other demographic and academic information. This information can then be accessed by a counselor or advisor. A Retention Management System provides to the advisor a range of individual and/or institutional actions based on the individual student's data that could encourage the student's success. Several colleges and universities use this commercially developed software. According to the director of Student Support Services at Pueblo Community College, Colorado, the system demonstrates great flexibility in developing special plans for students. Students can set objectives and these objectives can be monitored. ActionTrack is networked at Pueblo Community College, which allows several offices to use the software. The Pueblo Community College director of Student Support Services highly recommends that institutions involve their users and computer personnel in all initial and final communications with the software vendor prior to purchasing software.

The coordinator of the Retention Management System at California State, Northridge, relies on ActionTrack in the advisement and counseling process, particularly with special student populations and with undeclared students. He states that ActionTrack combines information about both the cognitive and the affective areas of student development. Many commercially developed software programs deal with only the academic areas and do not allow for inclusion of other student development factors. The coordinator of the Retention Management System at California State, Northridge, particularly likes the versatility of the program. It allows an institution to build, change, and add as needs arise. California State, Northridge, uses the College Student Inventory portion of the program for entering first year students; this inventory is sent to Noel/Levitz to be scored. The results are returned by computer disk which is then entered into the ActionTrack system. There is a fee for the scoring.

ActionTrack is relatively inexpensive, thus within the range of most college budgets. As of October 1990, the company advertised a price for the four modules installed on one PC site and a two day on-campus consultation by a Noel/Levitz ActionTrack specialist for $8,900. The cost for the program installed on 2 PC sites totaled $9,400 and the cost for 3 sites was $9,700.

IN-HOUSE DEVELOPED SYSTEMS

Enterprise State Junior College

Enterprise State Junior College (ESJC) in Alabama, uses an IBM System 38 for which computer personnel and college counselors have designed and implemented a student advising sheet. This advising sheet lists students' personal biographic data, ASSET placement scores, cumulative grade point averages, total hours completed, developmental courses required, grades for completed courses and a list of current courses, and transfer requirements for specific majors at most institutions in Alabama and many out of state. Tailored information is based on the student's educational intentions. Each quarter, new student advising sheets are run and issued to academic advisors who share the information with their advisees. Four offices within ESJC's Student Affairs Department may run the student advising sheets anytime during the quarter; this facilitates students making future academic plans at other than peak advisement periods.

In addition, to aid advisement, the college has implemented an Early Warning System for developmental students and a Course Progress Program which interrelates with a Waiver Program. Students are required to enroll according to their ASSET scores in the proper developmental course level for math, English, reading, or to enroll for the proper prerequisite courses. Waivers may be issued to students, however, and entered into the system's Waiver Program. The course progress program recognizes these waivers and ignores waived students on initial class rolls. Those students who have improperly enrolled in courses are marked with an asterisk on the class rolls at the beginning of the quarter and are not permitted to stay in class.

In addition, each quarter at midterm a letter is generated through the system and mailed to developmental students who are in academic jeopardy. The advantage to this program is that students needing academic help are warned to get assistance early enough in the term to make a difference in their end-of-quarter grades.

The major advantage of this system is that the programs are custom-designed to ESJC's unique needs. The system was relatively inexpensive because the software was written by the college's administrative computer services personnel and the System 38 is also used for other administrative purposes. Since ESJC is a commuter school, the system has resulted in saving valuable academic advisement time. Also, the student has immediate and accurate information needed for making personal advisement decisions. These features have resulted in a high satisfaction rate for the program from both students and advisors.

The major disadvantage of this system is that the IBM System 38 is becoming obsolete and needs replacing at a time when the institution and the state are suffering a shortage of funds. Also, the System 38 currently does not have the ability to link with state-wide or national advisement networks. In addition, more computer clerical support is needed in the counseling office because updates from four-year transfer institutions often arrive weekly. Changes in the system which require re-programming are also slow. For the Early Warning System, enabling faculty to enter their own mid-quarter data would ease the burden of extensive data entry placed on the academic support office. At times, retrieving needed information is slow and hinges on mainframe use by other offices. Access to information needs to be enhanced.

Future plans are to make the advising sheets more reader-friendly, implement a new marking system for courses students have fulfilled, and design a graduation audit which may be used by both counselors and admissions staff for all degrees offered at the institution More terminals or emulated microcomputers are needed for students and advisors to personally access transfer, advisement, and graduation information.

Massachusetts Bay Community College

At Massachusetts Bay Community College (MBCC), the ACADEMIC ADVISING INFORMATION SYSTEM (AVIS) is an on-line advising sub-system of the Student Information System (SIS). The Director of Administrative Software Development at MBCC describes the system as an application developed using the INGRES

Database Management System (DBMS). Administrators, registrar's staff, and admissions staff may access AVIS information. The five major areas of information are Assessment and Placement, Prerequisite and Transfer, Academic Record, Degree Audit, and Graduation.

The ASELF sub-system module provides information for advisors and students themselves. Advisors can access the data of their advisees only. Students can access their own advising information to assess their progress in terms of degree requirements based on courses they have taken. A unique feature of ASELF is the "journal conference" which allows both advisors and students to make comments during advising sessions. Also, administrators can perform degree audits on-line. The ASELF modules are: Assessment and Placement Check; Prerequisite Check; Course Schedule and Catalog Information; Degree Audit Report, Advisors/Advisees Journal Notes and Students Biographic Information; Graduation Checkout and Curriculum Information; and Graduation Approval.

The college lists the following advantages to AVIS: increased productivity, high performance, availability, integration, flexibility, security control, portability, maintainability, functionality, user-friendly, and customized. The only disadvantage to the system is that it must run on INGRES DBMS. The software needed is INGRES DBMS and the hardware is any VAX/VMS family (mini, micro, or VAX station).

The college reports that the system is cost effective because it eliminates paper work, increases productivity, reduces time, is user independent, is decentralized, and requires minimal training time for users.

Key features of the system are the security control on the database and application, increased efficiency in decision making and user-independence, and portability of the application to other institutions.

Future enhancement currently being implemented is the transfer into MBCC module which allows the data entry clerk to enter all transfer courses into a student's record via student ID. The dean/division chair will evaluate these transfer credits for a particular major indicating which courses will apply to the student's program. The degree audit application will provide the on-line transfer courses' evaluation. The degree audit system will keep the audit trail of transfer credit for each major for which a student is evaluated. A second enhancement will allow transfer from MBCC to other institution modules. This application translates MBCC course credit to receiving institutional equivalent credit.

Valencia Community College

Leonard Burry, assistant vice president for computer services at Valencia Community College, shared information regarding the degree audit/counseling component which is one of the most complex applications the college had to develop and which is still evolving. The system has both on-line and batch versions of this function. Students at VCC have five years to graduate under the catalog in effect when they select a degree program. After that they must fulfill the requirements of the catalog in use when they apply for graduation.

The advantages to this in-house developed module are that it is very efficient and fast. The system is designed to expand to deliver a long-range educational plan that will interface with Valencia's registration and assessment processes. The output produces very "readable" reports. Advisement has become more effective and accomplished in a much shorter timeframe than previously required.

The start-up costs included salaries for three programmers. Maintenance costs are negligible as the system is driven by user-entered parameters. The software programs needed are IBM DOS, CICS, and COBOL language; the hardware needed is an IBM mainframe and terminals.

The system is quite cost-effective because the design imposes relatively little overhead/processing workload on the mainframe. "Batch-mode" reports can carry more descriptive text (for self-advisement) than on-line graduation checks which are assumed to be counseling tools. The system feeds from registration and assessment. Work continues to interface with registration (mandated remediation). Registration already supports automated prerequisite checks.

The recommendation for the future is to develop a comprehensive computer-based educational planning function. Objectives for this individualized educational plan representing completed, required, and recommended courses would be comprised of the following:

1. To facilitate the construction of an appropriate educational plan for each student in a medium and format that can be

quickly "understood" by the persons involved with registration so that, as an example, the student can be informed at registration that the math course selected is inappropriate or appropriate for his/her educational goals.
2. To reduce the number and duration of counseling sessions necessary for each student. The hope is that the student and counselor will develop an appropriate and lasting plan that will require little change during the first session and the integrated computer system will then inform and guide the student throughout his or her career at the College.
3. To improve accuracy and completeness of the educational plan. Since the plans are stored on and/or generated by the computer, there is less margin for human error.
4. To offer the student more specific guidance on the degree audit/counseling report, specifically course requirements for various majors at transfer institutions.

Burry suggests implementing these functions in four different ways or a combination of these ways.
1. Florida operates the "SOLAR" facility though its educational computing network. Valencia Community College would like to download files from all state community colleges and universities, abstract the list for specific lower division course recommendations for every degree program in every state university, and build disk records on their mainframe that translate those specific lower division course recommendations into educational plans. Then, when a student indicates his/her long-term educational goals to a counselor, the counselor and student can select the most appropriate of those plans and the mainframe will build an educational plan for that student from the record derived from SOLAR information.
2. Counselors and representatives of the various academic departments can build their own educational plans for students who are uncertain about their goals beyond the Associate's Degree or are intending to earn a particular two-year vocational degree. These Valencia-specific records will conform with the coding structures and formats of the educational plan generated from SOLAR files.

3. The system should be designed to examine placement test scores recorded for the student and to add any remedial coursework mandated by those test scores to the student's educational plan record.
4. Design of the system should allow counselors to make adjustments in any of the student's educational plans by adding electives to support individual student goals.

Burry has researched and described the Student Services System, and he is currently working to bring this research up to date in case the Valencia system is marketed.

University of Wisconsin System

When students are preparing to transfer, obtaining information about course equivalencies is often confusing. A recent article describes a pilot-project begun in 1988 and developed by the University of Wisconsin System and the System schools that is improving articulation problems in this state (Staff, 1990). The Transfer Information System (TIS), a microcomputer-based information program for the UW System and Vocational, Technical, and Adult Education (VTAE), is funded by the legislature to enable students desiring to transfer to institutions of higher education within the state to have easy access to up-to-date transfer information. Also, the system will provide a vehicle for admissions staffs throughout Wisconsin to facilitate communication regarding course and program changes.

When completed, TIS will equate a course taken at any UW System or VTAE institution with courses at other UW colleges, and will reflect completed courses' application toward degree requirements. No computer knowledge is required to use the system which is designed for students, staff, and faculty to operate.

Montgomery College, Maryland

Price and Miller (1988) describe this multi-campus community college's successful effort in initiating a pilot project in 1981 which was designed to accomplish the following objectives:
1. To provide students with a list of Montgomery College courses that would transfer into specific majors at local colleges and universities;

2. To provide critical advising information relevant to each program at each four-year transfer institution, such as competitive admission and GPA requirements and names of contact people;
3. To dispel the persistent rumor that Montgomery College courses do not transfer;
4. To provide samples of articulation information to high school counselors so that they could also respond to this rumor;
5. To update the information continuously, thereby benefiting from the contacts between the transfer counselors and the transfer institution.

Price and Miller suggest the initial draft of the program of courses should be developed by the community college's central articulation office and forwarded to the four-year institutions for review. Once the four-year transfer institutions have revised and returned the information to the two-year college, the corrections or changes are entered into the microcomputer and the draft status is removed.

For the system to operate appropriately, all campuses must have identical computer hardware and software. At least once a term, disks should be updated, and all programs should be reviewed by the articulation office and transfer institution at least annually. The date of last review should be included on the information sheet distributed to all users.

The costs for a computer and printer are around $3,000. The annual cost for the disk information and the 80 bound copies for the college is approximately $3,500. The personnel costs require about 480 hours per year for a professional to develop and review the program articulation and about 960 hours of clerical support initially, then being reduced with the growth of the program.

Price and Miller report many advantages to this program. Students now have a hard copy of current transfer information. Also, the various transfer institutions' requirements are translated to the community college equivalencies, so students can compare various transfer institutions' requirements. Advisors can provide more accurate data more quickly. Questions regarding course transferability are answered for college and high school personnel. Transferring students are assured of the fit of their first two years into the curriculum of the transfer institution. The need to update computer-based transfer information opens channels of communication between two-year and four-year institutions. Since students are confident of which courses transfer, they are more likely to stay at the community college for two years. A final benefit is that the program format enhances community college curriculum development and the review process of transfer programs.

Future plans include extension of this college-wide computerized student information system making student tracking possible from the freshman through the senior year.

Response at Montgomery College has been extremely positive and this "process gives credibility to academic advising at the community college as well as at the receiving institution" (Price & Miller, 1988, p. 44).

Robert Morris College

Robert Morris College in Illinois, has designed an award winning dynamic computerized advisement system which calculates, defines, and displays a student's academic progress within the context of the student's major field of study. This student records management information system integrates student advising and academic audits with the admissions, registration, and automated transcripts process (Staff, 1991).

According to the college's description, the system has three major parts: (1) a statistical page, (2) the checksheet, and (3) course restrictions. The statistical page identifies courses completed, quality point average, transfer credits, CLEP, advanced standing, credits-in-progress, and pre-registered credits. After fulfillment of respective categories, the statistical page also displays additional credits needed for graduation.

The checksheet is a printout of the academic major checksheet prepared by the academic department updated from the computer records for courses completed and in-progress. Course requirements met and unmet and course restrictions are listed. The checksheet system is used as a stand-alone for student advisement, as an integral part of the registration process, and as a degree audit tool.

Advantages to the system for improved academic advisement are improved accuracy, immediate recognition of courses needed for students who are changing majors, a decrease in the amount of paper work needed, and an increase in quality advisement time for students. In addition, the system has reduced clerical time and eliminated the need for an expensive micrographics system to produce transcripts.

The system was developed on a Prime computer system and the programs were written in COBOL language. The system is accessible through terminals for 130 faculty advisors and professional staff. This innovative system has saved the college an annual $78,000 for which they received a $10,000 award from the National Association of College and University Business Officers and USX Foundation's annual Cost Reduction Incentive Awards Program.

Pennsylvania State University

As described in *The Freshman Year Experience Newsletter*, Penn State's student electronic portfolio provides another look at future use of technology to enhance advisement. New students are asked to complete an Educational Planning Survey which is added to the university's student data base. Once these data elements are keyed and matched with the student's high school GPA, placement test scores, and SAT scores, each student then has an advising screen which forms the core of the electronic portfolio.

When students meet with advisors, the date, advisor conducting the session, college of enrollment, content of advising session, referrals, and majors of interest are recorded on the screen. The individual advising portfolios begin prior to pre-college advisement and follow the student until graduation.

Another positive value of the electronic portfolios is the enhancement of institutional research. Large scale reports of interest to the college which can be generated from this data can give a comprehensive profile of the freshmen class. Student affairs professionals can use the data to learn the number of advising contacts, types of contacts, referrals, choices of majors, individual advisor workloads, and patterns of contacts which aids in planning and management of the advisement process.

Northwest Mississippi Community College

At Northwest Mississippi Community College, a computer based advising program was developed to address the problem of providing accurate and timely information for student advising to academic advisors. Funded in part through a Title III grant, STARS

(Student Tracking Advising and Retention System) became a significant answer to improving this college's advising and retention procedures. STARS programming was done in-house using dBase III+ and compiled using Clipper. According to the STARS programmer and director, the information is downloaded from the System/36 using a program called dBase Direct/36 directly into a dBase III+ file. The STARS program accesses this database and does not directly access the data on the System/36. This procedure was established to ensure security, but it does sacrifice immediate on-line information. The data is accurate only as of the time downloaded, but the downloading is done frequently. The STARS program prints on the screen or printer read-only information. The STARS printout takes a major program of study and shows the student's progress toward graduation. The program allows flexibility for changing majors to see what additional requirements will have to be met. Students and advisors can play "what if?"

The advantages of the STARS program include ease of access to the mainframe data, linkage to advisement information for faculty advisors and students, and ability to download files from the mainframe into dBaseIII+ format. Using dBase III+ format allows easy transfer of data for institutional research purposes into such software packages as SPSS PC+ for statistical analysis.

Disadvantages of this program primarily involve lack of on-line access to the mainframe. The direct on-line method can be used, however, once issues concerning confidentiality and data integrity have been addressed.

Equipment and costs for this program include a mainframe computer, dBase Direct 36, 38 or 400 (approximately $2,600-$3,000), dbase III+ (@$400), PC hardware (recommended 120 meg hard drive, 2 to 4 meg RAM @$2,800), printer (@$600-$2,000), and PC's for faculty advising offices or advisement lab. Other software programs necessary are Clipper, PC Support, and STARS (in-house developed program).

The program is cost effective in that it uses less programming time than other similar programs. People familiar with dBase III+ may access information in ways they need it, rather than requesting programming from the computer center. Information can also be placed on a single diskette and manually transported to branches or offices not connected to the main computer. The results are better information for students, and as a consequence, higher student retention. A degree audit is also included in STARS, which involves the student course history and progress toward graduation.

Florida Community College at Jacksonville

The Dean of Student Affairs-South Campus of Florida Community College at Jacksonville (FCC), describes their computerized academic advising system as excellent. This system relies heavily on the SOLAR (Student On Line Advisement and Articulation) system. FCC provides each student with a Graduation Status Sheet (GSS) mailed each term to all students who have six or more credits earned. This GSS informs the student of progress toward graduation and additional courses needed.

The SOLAR project was started in the late 1980s by the Division of Community Colleges, Florida Department of Education, and has now developed to include all majors for all nine state universities in the state of Florida. This data is on-line available via a state network called FIRN (Florida Information Regional Network). The concept behind SOLAR is simple. A student would select the community college they are attending, the university they plan to attend and their intended major. The system then provides the student with an inventory of community college core requirements as well as a listing of the specific prerequisite courses to be taken at the community college which are required or suggested by the university for the program in which the student is interested. The student also receives information regarding admission to the university program they selected and a listing of course requirements for the junior/senior years at the university. In addition to the course and admissions information, SOLAR also provides step-by-step information about the transfer process as well as general admission requirements for freshmen entering a public community college or a state university.

SOLAR is housed on an IBM 3090 mainframe computer at Northwest Regional Data Center (NWDRC) in Tallahassee, FL. The system is networked to all 28 community colleges, state universities, and many other educational sites via the Florida Information Resource Network (FIRN).

Most academic advisors and counselors in community colleges have access to a terminal either at their desks or in a centralized advising location. The accessibility to current information in an on-line advising situation greatly assists the student. Changes and updates to the system occur almost daily. The system also allows community colleges and universities to inform students early about upcoming changes in program requirements or new requirements and their effective dates. SOLAR is menu driven, contains on-line help sessions, and free access and service for educational entities. Plans for the future include a micro computer version to provide additional access.

THE FUTURE

As technology changes, improves, and becomes less expensive, it will be incorporated into student advisement systems. The use of CD-ROM (Compact Disc-Read Only Memory) should fill a niche in comprehensive systems because of its tremendous storage capacity. Many volumes of catalog information can be stored on a single compact disc. Long distance access and networking will also be used more effectively in the future with the great strides that are being made in communications links, both long and short distance, and in optic fiber transfer and storage. These advancements will enable entire school systems and even whole states to share and coordinate course, transfer, and student information. Interactive capabilities through touch screen devices will enhance the access of advisement databases for students, faculty, and administration, thus improving the service and productivity of advisors.

As computing power becomes more available in price to student affairs offices, it will be necessary for advising personnel to be involved in all aspects of designing a college student information system. This observation was advanced by Johnson (1990):

> As management information systems become more important in student affairs, the responsibility falls on the student affairs professionals to take a proactive stance and be involved in the design and implementation of these systems. If the strong, proactive stance is not taken, these systems will still be implemented by individuals from outside the student affairs profession and the students' best interest will not be a high priority. This increase in efficiency and effectiveness will provide a greater service to the student population as a whole. Service to the student is the mission of student affairs. If steps can be taken to better assist the students, student affairs professionals are responsible to take these challenges (p. 138).

Colleges attempting to begin systems of computerized advisement should be encouraged that many other institutions have succeeded in developing outstanding systems. These institutions have attacked and, in most instances, overcome the problems they faced: lack of computer knowledge, budget difficulties, software selection and/or development, and data confidentiality. It should be exciting to colleges which are beginning systems during times when the technology has never been so advanced and the costs so reasonable. A personal computer in an individual's office now has the capability and power once found only in large, expensive, mainframes. Service to students with accurate, timely advisement, information for accountability, and information for research and development are all available.

For colleges which have years of experience in advising students using computerized processes, now is the time to assess current methods and systems and revise equipment and procedures by exploring what others are doing, using what will work in one's own environment, and filing the rest. State educational systems should also take note. Often state-wide networks and state developed systems are much more cost effective than institutionally developed systems and have the added advantage of providing comparable standardized information. Technology changes daily, and dedicated educators who are committed to serving students with the best information available will find ways to do so, even in times of limited funds. The future will bring many as yet unknown technological advancements and it will be exciting to see how they may be implemented in the effective advising of students to enhance "high touch" activities through the use of high technology.

REFERENCES

Bays, C. (1984). Computer-aided advisement language at the University of South Carolina. *College and University*, 60, 32-36.

Bellenger, J.E. & Bellenger, D.N. (1987). Guidelines for computerizing your information system for academic program counseling: Dealing with people problems. *NASPA Journal*, 14, 53-60.

Johnson, De. E., & Yen, D. (1990). Management information systems and student affairs. *Journal of Research on Computing in Education*, 23, 127-139.

Kelly, J. (1991). Electronic portfolios: Advising toward the year 2000. *The Freshmen Year Experience Newsletter*, 3,(3), p. 5.

Kramer, G.L., Peterson, E.D. & Spencer, R.W. (1983). Designing and implementing a computer assisted academic advisement program. *Journal of College Student Personnel*, 24, 513-518.

Price, T.S. & Miller, R.J. (1988). Putting technology to work for transfer students. *AACJC Journal*, 51(2), 44.

Chapter 5

Student Financial Aid

Ronny Barnes

Financial aid offices have historically been one of the primary users of information and computer technology in student affairs. Financial aid offices utilize computers to manipulate large amounts of data, make awards, keep records, and access student information data files to mail award notifications and to credit financial aid to student tuition and fee bills.

Computer automation has also become quite valuable in the process of record verification. This process entails the comparison of data secured from the financial aid application with other documents such as Internal Revenue forms. With the side variety of programs, living arrangements, and external costs.

Another major use of computers in financial aid offices is the determination of the student's specific cost of attendance; this is the cost figure on which most financial aid awards are based. It is not unusual today for an institution to have as many as a dozen different costs of attendance for their students.

Application tracking is yet another important financial aid procedure which can be enhanced through the use of computer technology. This is the process by which each student's application is monitored for completeness and correctness and then notified via letter if any additional information or forms are required. Before computer automation, this was one of the most time-consuming processes in the management of student financial aid. Computer technology has not only reduced the time necessary to track applications, but also increased record accuracy and reduced the number of clerical staff required to perform these functions.

Financial aid offices are now also finding it cost effective and advantageous to use computer technology to electronically transfer funds within the university and from outside the institution, such as loan proceeds transferred from a bank to the institution's account. They are also finding it beneficial to participate in the federal government's Pell Grant Electronic Data Exchange Program and similar state financial aid program electronic data exchanges and computer networks. These electronic networks and tape exchange programs save weeks of application processing time, reduce human errors, and significantly reduce the number of fee deferments which otherwise would have to be granted to a large number of Pell Grant and state grant applicants waiting to receive official notification of their awards at the beginning of each new semester, quarter or term.

Although most early financial aid software was developed for use on campus mainframe computers, during the past five years, a wide variety of excellent financial aid specific computer software has also been developed for use on the more powerful personal microcomputers that are now available. The purposes of this chapter are first to provide an overview of the available software in the financial aid field today and then to discuss the questions that a financial aid officer should ask of the vendor and him/herself when reviewing prospective software and hardware systems for his/her particular campus.

COMMERCIALLY AVAILABLE STUDENT FINANCIAL AID SOFTWARE

The following is a summary of the various software programs which are commercially available for use in the typical student financial aid office. Each short review is meant to provide the reader with some technical information along with a brief description of each system's design and application by installation size.

Student Aid Reporting and Analysis System (SARA)

The American College Testing Program offers three systems acceptable for various size schools. These systems range from a small PC driven stand alone system to a fully integrated mainframe system. The smallest of these is called SARA. SARA is ACT's comprehensive microcomputer-based system for student financial aid administration. This menu-driven system was developed for small to medium sized institutions that do not need an integrated multi-station system.

For the small institution, SARA is a good system which performs most functions expected of a financial aid system. The only major weakness is that since it is microcomputer driven, data from other systems must be downloaded, manually entered, or otherwise transferred from a fileserver or central computer data file.

To operate SARA, ACT recommends an IBM or IBM compatible personal computer, such as an IBM PS/2 Model 50 or higher, with at least 640K of RAM, a 20 megabyte or larger hard disk and IBM or MS-DOS version 3.3 or later. Also a quality printer is recommended to print student letters and award notifications.

Network Student Aid Reporting and Analysis System (Network SARA)

ACT also offers an enhanced version of SARA for larger institutions which need multiple workstations. Network SARA, as ACT calls it, is an enhanced version of SARA with greater capacities and networking capabilities.

In this system the workstations must be IBM PC's or 100% IBM compatible. The fileserver and PC that controls the work stations must be "Novell Certified" IBM compatible. Each workstation must have 1024K or addressable RAM and 565K free RAM. At least one workstation must have a floppy disk drive and if DOS 4.1 is used, memory-manager software is required to free up 565K of RAM. The operating system is Novell Netware 286 or 386.

SAFE

ACT recently acquired Information & Communications, Inc. (ICI) of La Jolla, California. This merger provided ACT with a mainframe system for larger user institutions called SAFE. SAFE is an integrated multi-level, multi-year system that performs all the major financial aid functions including: application processing, document tracking, need analysis, budgets, awarding, report and letter writing, and fund management.

SAFE runs in the IBM mainframe environment - OS or DOS. It is a modular system written in ANSI COBOL with VSAM KSDS file structure and standard VSAM access routines. This is a well designed and well maintained system which will accept electronic application from any of the national processors.

Student Aid Management System (SAM)

SAM, from Sigma Systems Inc. is another veteran system for mainframe operations. This integrative system also supports all functions required to properly manage the financial aid functions for even the largest of programs. SAM operates in a variety of computer systems, primarily IBM: VM, MVS, VSE and DEC: VMS. The environments it can function in are IBM: MVS/CICS/VSAM, VSE/CICS/VAAM, IMS/DC, and DEC: RMS. Data base configurations compatible for SAM are IBM: IMS, ADABAS, SUPRA, IOMS/S, VM/ORACLE, SQL/DX and DEC: ORACLE. The SAM system is programmed in COBOL and VS-COBOL-II.

Financial Aid Management System (FAMS)

FAMS is a component of Information Associates Student Information System family of software products for institutions of higher education. This system performs all necessary functions for the effective management of the student financial aid process, is fully integratable, and allows the user maximum flexibility in institutional design options.

FAMS is programmed in COBOL and COLOL II and runs on either IBM: MVS/XA, MVS/ESA or DEC: RMS. The primary design of this system is to operate best in an IBM: MVS/CICS/VSAM, DOS/VSE, DOS/ESA environment although it is operable in DEC: RMA. In IBM systems, FAMS uses VSAM/DB2 database.

Financial Aid Module (AID)

AID is produced by Software Research Northwest, Inc. to work in an interactive mode with its other student information systems. Based on information available at this writing, AID is designed to run on Hewlett-Packard equipment and can be designed to fit the needs of any size institution. This system supports all the necessary functions for the operation of the financial aid office.

SELECTING THE RIGHT SOFTWARE SYSTEM

With so many different software systems now available, how does the financial aid officer decide which system is right for his/her particular needs and campus? Based on over fifteen years experience as a director of a financial aid office at a large state university, this author suggests that the following questions be asked and answered before any institution, large or small, proceeds with purchasing and installing a computer assisted financial aid management system.

Determining Institutional Needs

To start the process, the financial aid administrator, in conjunction with the computer support staff, should first identify all the data elements needed in the financial aid management system. This is particularly true when thinking of institutionally specific financial aid programs such as scholarships and short term loans. It is frustrating to set up a new system and find that there is no way to identify a large group of students for a major scholarship program.

After this list is compiled, the next step is to establish a list of all functions the system is to be able to perform. From this list will come the questions the vendor must be able to answer in the affirmative in order to supply the system needed.

The following is a sampling of questions which can be used to evaluate the vendor responses to your institution's request for a quotation or bid.

1. Does the system have the capability to monitor and track the various elements of the financial aid applications and produce letters notifying the applicants of the elements received and of those that are needed?
2. Can a process be initiated to perform a "needs analysis" which includes calculations of expected parental and student contributions toward educational costs in accordance with the approved methods of needs analysis as accepted by the Department of Education and computation of the Pell grant index?
3. Does the system provide the capability to construct student expense budgets from one to eight standard budgets

or numerous individualized budgets, subtract from the budget any known resources available to the student, including parent and student contributions, resulting in the student's net financial need, and print notification of ineligibility or eligibility to the student?

4. Can a process be initiated to "package" the student's financial aid request based on the net financial need and packaging parameters supplied by the institution that meet federal, state, and institutional restrictions and priorities for both type and amount of award?

5. Does the system provide the funds management capability that includes a three-level encumbrance and expenditure control process described as follows:

    a. Encumbrance at the time of the award and deduction from the funds available.

    b. Release of encumbrance when the award is declined or conversion of the encumbrance to a permanent encumbrance when the award is accepted.

    c. Authorization of payment and release of encumbrance?

6. Can a process be initiated to format and print a notification to advise applicants of the financial aid award being offered and the basis upon which the award is being made?

7. Can a process be initiated to select in-process awards, display or print out the amount of the award payment, and list details of the total disbursements?

8. Can a process be initiated to format and print the federal "Fiscal-Operations Report"?

9. Can a process be initiated that checks all applicants' records to see that eligibility criteria are maintained throughout the year?

Visiting Other Schools

After requesting that each vendor complete a questionnaire answering such questions as above, the next step is to review the results and start visiting other campuses which have installed their systems. As a part of the bid request, each vendor should be requested to supply a list of current installations using their system. From this list one can select comparable schools to visit. Visiting is probably the most important aspect in the entire search. Talk to users. Talk to their computer support people. Here one will find the true picture of what each system can do.

One of the biggest surprises to many institutions when installing a fully automated online financial aid system is the enormous amount of computer capacity such a system requires. Normally while selecting a system, those faced with the task of reviewing other installations tend to look at how the system functions in the aid office. Does it meet the day to day operational needs? This is good for the daily user to know; however, one should also look behind the scene. How much storage does the system require for start-up? After five years? Do the batch programs run in an efficient manner or do some schools experience problems with the batch programs eating up "wall clock" time? How quick is response time in peak use times such as registration when everyone is trying to access the computer's central processing unit at the same time? These behind the scene considerations can become the most critical areas to the effective and efficient operation of the financial aid system.

Maintaining the System

Another critical area to consider after identifying prospective systems is maintenance. Many schools are surprised when they discover that their maintenance agreement only covers updating their system with the new federal regulations each year. It is dismaying to find a major flaw in your design and realize that it will cost extra to have the vendor help make needed modifications. A good understanding with the vendor about what maintenance covers and in what manner the maintenance will be delivered is necessary. In the cases of federal regulations, will these come in the form of new programs on tape that can be installed and recompiled, or are change lists sent which institutional programmers must install? Is the maintenance provided institution-specific or is it market-wide? In most cases, federal regulation changes are done once for customers for each vendor. As a result, the specific institution must be careful to track any changes made to the system purchased so that when updates and modifications come from the vendor, the institution knows how to adapt this maintenance to its "modified system".

The last and perhaps most important area of maintenance is its cost. The longer term maintenance contract one can negotiate the better. It is not unusual to see maintenance costs increase each year when in fact they should decrease. If a vendor is only providing federal regulation updates in its maintenance and if it has a growing number of clients, one would think that as the cost is spread over more users it should go down. Experience has shown that this, however, is not always the case.

Installing the System

Once the system is selected, an institution schedule must be determined. Since financial aid runs on an annual cycle the most logical time to bring a new system on-line is early in the application/award cycle. This would probably be January for most institutions.

Most institutions will wonder whether they need to run a parallel system in their old mode as a backup in case there is a failure in the installation of the new system. The answer to that question rests with the implementation schedule that is established for the new system. It is very important to allow adequate time in the schedule for adequate testing. The amount of time allowed for testing will determine the need for a backup system. If adequate testing has taken place, the need for a backup system is lessened. Testing should be done in volume using real data. In many cases, preliminary tests are run on "test or demonstration" data. This is far from a true test. These tests should be conducted using "live" data interfaced or loaded in the same manner as it would be in production. The time required for testing can vary. However, the best way to estimate this is based on the length of each cycle. A cycle is the process from the loading of application data through all of the functions of tracing, budget construction, verification, awarding, notification, and funds transfer. If this cycle is one week, then allow three cycles for testing. Therefore, one is given two cycles (weeks in this case) to test, and an additional cycle to make adjustments. The more extensive the amount of testing at the time is installed, the less likely the institution is to experience problems or delays once the system is made operational.

If the new system selected is replacing an existing computer system there will also be a need to write transactions which will load aggregate data from the old system to the new system. One should consider this in the installation process as early as possible. In many cases these data can provide volume data for some testing. It may also be desirable to include this in the purchase or installation contract.

SUMMARY

Until recently, financial aid processing, packaging, awarding, and record keeping on many small campuses that did not have the support of a large mainframe computer center, had to be done manually because of the lack of affordable and suitable computer hardware and software. There are now excellent and relatively inexpensive financial aid software programs for microcomputers to perform these functions. In addition, there are microcomputer software programs for managing student part-time employment records and veterans benefits. Within the past couple of years, several excellent PC software programs have also become available for managing student loan programs and counseling students about their loan obligations (i.e., *Perkins Loans by Software* and *Student Loan Counselor-Plus* from ETS). Therefore, it is the rare student financial aid office that does not now utilize modern computer and information technology in the administration and delivery of its services.

The need for financial aid offices to not only be computer literate but also sophisticated in the evaluation and use of complex computer assisted financial aid management systems is now paramount in the profession. Students, as well as other college administrators, expect and require computer competency from the modern financial aid office.

As should be apparent from this brief description of financial aid software programs and the technical questions which need to be resolved before purchasing any new financial aid management system, without proper planning and technical sophistication, a tremendous amount of waste may occur from purchasing the wrong type of system for a particular campus's needs. It is, therefore, imperative to make sure that one selects the right hardware and software for a particular campus, not just a good system someone else uses, someplace else. If the wrong system is selected, one will be plagued with problems, complaints, errors, and will waste thousands of dollars. However, by properly selecting, installing, maintaining and upgrading the right system, the quality of services can be enhanced and an institution can save thousands of dollars in annual operating expenses.

Chapter 6

International Service and Program Offices

J. Greg Leonard

This chapter should be of particular interest to professionals in the field of international education. It has been composed with a rather broad spectrum of administrators in mind, including foreign student and scholar advisers, international admissions specialists, administrators responsible for encouraging United States students to study abroad, and administrators of intensive English language programs for foreign students.

The information in this chapter is to be viewed in light of two propositions. The first is that technology should serve as a tool to decrease the amount of time devoted to work which does not involve "high touch" activities. More time can be created for staff/student interaction if technology can increase our efficiency and productivity. The second proposition is that technology can be used to enhance interaction and communication with our clients. This use of technology presents new and challenging opportunities for improvement in those communication relationships.

CULTURAL DIFFERENCES AND TECHNOLOGY

Most college and university administrators, research scholars and professors who work with international students contend that there is no more challenging nor rewarding work on campus. In many respects, the same may be said of the use of technology in attempting effectively and efficiently serve this client population.

At the core of this technological challenge is the concept of cultural values. While the dominant values of American culture emphasize individuality and a preoccupation with external "things", the dominant values of many other cultures (including many subcultures within American society) emphasize the "group" and place great importance upon personal relationships. That raises a very important issue. How does one use technology with a client who considers many forms of its use to be barriers to personal relationships?

Most cultures value technological development. Indeed, many innovations in technology have resulted from the work of individuals who are not members of the dominant culture. Listening to the evening news reports on the latest advances in technology will be amaze one with the percentage of researchers interviewed who speak with foreign accents.

Many cultures eschew the use of technology when it is perceived as an interference to the development and maintenance of personal relationships. For example, using a financial spreadsheet can accomplish amazing projections but when it comes to closing a business deal, the personal relationship is an absolutely essential ingredient without which nothing will be accomplished.

One might suggest that technological advances are causing substantive change within most cultures and that these changes are subtly moving humankind toward more compatible values which may eventually transcend many cultural differences in communication. Regardless of movement in this area, significant cultural differences exist in communication and these differences represent a special challenge to international educators.

The topic of "culturally appropriate technology" in relation to curriculum content is one which is familiar to many academicians. Now international administrators must also ask if in the light of technological advances in information management and communication they are being sensitive to cultural differences in their non-academic communication and work with international students?

GETTING STARTED: DETERMINING NEEDS

Hardware

Many international service and program offices have clearly arrived at the long-predicted milepost called "information overload". The quantity of information received daily from the postal service, FAX machine, electronic mail and the telephone is truly overwhelming. The variety of information international educators and administrators are expected to have at their fingertips is equally awesome. The field is changing so rapidly, that the wisest choice is to utilize new computer technology to help improve the management of all of these information demands.

Every staff member, whether professional or clerical, should have access to a computer terminal. Because desktop models usually have more storage capability and may be easily connected to computer networks, it is recommended that they be used as basic equipment in international programs offices, all office computers should be connected via a local area network (LAN) and, if possible, to at least one other network which connects them to computer users outside their own campus (a global network). A detailed discussion of local area networks is presented in chapter sixteen of this book and should be referenced if one is considering designing a network for his or her office.

Many different student databases can be accessed through the use of LANs. Those who work with foreign students and scholars have an unambiguous need to have continuous access to information on students, and frequently will also need access to different records within this database simultaneously. Computer networking is the only effective and efficient way of obtaining this capability.

SOFTWARE

Integrated Software

Virtually all software used by international services offices should be "integrated". This means that, from the user's perspective, it works together as one package. The user should be able to move from word processing to a database program to a spreadsheet program with few keystrokes. Further, it should be able to quickly copy material from a database program or a spreadsheet program into the word processing software so that the material can be easily used in a report or other document being prepared.

Microsoft Windows is an example of a popular program which integrates other applications for IBM and IBM-compatible computers. It integrates software applications such as Microsoft Word for Windows, databases such as dBase, and spreadsheets like Excel. Macintosh computers from Apple have integrated software capability already built-in as part of their microprocessor design.

Word Processing Software

The backbone of all international services work is word processing and, therefore, each computer should have word processing software installed. In addition to the routine types of word processing required by most student affairs offices, foreign student/scholar service offices are also responsible for high-volume production of certain federal government forms and for issuing documents which certify different types of information on individual students and scholars.

Database Management Systems (DBMS)

A good database management system is fundamental to the proper functioning of any international services office. Foreign student offices are required by federal regulations to gather, maintain and report certain information about their students. In addition, data is needed for internal planning purposes, for institutional planning, and by external organizations.

Perhaps the most important external organization requesting data on international student enrollment is the International Education Data Collection Committee (IEDC), composed of the American Association of Collegiate Registrars and Admissions Officers (AACRAO), NAFSA: Association of International Educators, and the Institute of International Education (IIE).

An internal DBMS should be multifaceted and designed to meet the needs of the office without unnecessarily duplicating information contained in the student information system maintained by the college. Some duplicate information may be essential and can help to assist the college in keeping its mainframe information accurate for student records since it will probably be necessary to add certain fields of information to the main student data file in order to produce reports and complete federal forms. General application databases may be tailored to meet an office's particular needs by the college's systems information office, or excellent software programs designed specifically for international student offices can be purchased commercially. Some current available packages follow:

PC Automated International Student Records System

This database is available for both Macintosh and IBM-compatible computers from the Career Services Office at Brooklyn College. It sells for approximately $200 and a demonstration disk is available upon request.

IVYSOFT Foreign Student Database Management System

Ivysoft International produces this customized software. It was originally developed for Memphis State University and may be purchased for approximately $300.

International Student and Scholars Management System

Education Catalysts, Inc., has this database available for purchase. It operates on Macintosh computers. Originally developed for the Massachusetts Institute of Technology as a foreign scholars database, it has now been expanded to include students. Purchase prices begin at $300 and vary according to school size.

Data Perfect

This package, produced by the Word Perfect Corporation, was prepared for the NAFSA national conference and demonstrated at that meeting. It is available as a demonstration disk for about $10. They also have available a free video entitled "Are You Cut Out for Data Perfect?".

Q & A

Available from Symantec Corporation, this database was also demonstrated at a recent NAFSA conference, it was designed for general international student office requirements.

Many colleges have created customized database programs independently and some of these packages are also available for others to use. For example, the University of Michigan's International

Center has a student/scholar database developed on dBase IV software. A FoxPro version may soon be available. It is one of the most complete databases for foreign student and scholar offices that is available today. It is be available in IBM, Mac and UNIX formats.

Most database programs will need to be modified to meet foreign student and scholar information needs as federal regulations change. For example, some databases currently available do not allow close monitoring of lawful status. The expiration date of INS Form I-20 has become very important and some databases do not contain this field. Some do not provide for fields to facilitate programming, such as codes for officers of student organizations. Others do not allow for clear distinction among records of students who have been admitted but are yet to arrive, students who are currently enrolled, students on curricular or post-completion practical training, and inactive student records.

Any use of a database program should facilitate efforts at reducing paperwork. If adequate fields are established for notes recording the content of guidance and advising sessions with students, there should be no need to keep physical copies of such information in student files. If all staff members have access to the database, ideally through a LAN, all would know what has occurred during staff contacts with a student.

For more information on foreign student and scholar database design or modification, three documents are available from NAFSA. Those publications are: (1) "Computer Systems for International Education", (2) "NAFSA Working Paper #3: Foreign Student Data-Base Development for NAFSA and NAFSA Members", and (3) "NAFSA Working Paper #11: Data Collection for Foreign Scholars". Some of the information contained in these publications is very helpful; some is helpful only as a general guideline. Recent changes in federal regulations and further changes anticipated in the future will require that NAFSA provide updates and revisions for its membership.

Desktop Publishing

Desktop publishing software has become very sophisticated and it represents one of the more complex packages to master. However, documents produced with desktop publishing packages such as Ventura and PageMaker are virtually indistinguishable from those coming from commercial printers.

Written communication is very important in international services offices. Oral communication should be reinforced by newsletters, handouts, and other printed documents since most international students are functioning in a second language. Therefore, by using desktop publishing software, international services offices can readily facilitate the timely production of newsletters, handouts, and other such documents.

ASSOCIATION SUPPORT AND RESOURCES

NAFSA: Association of International Educators

NAFSA, its subdivisions and its services represent absolutely essential resources in the area of technology use by international educators. Formerly the National Association for Foreign Student Affairs, the organization changed its name to more accurately reflect its membership, which includes much more in the field of international education than foreign student advising. The membership components of NAFSA are called sections and include:

1. ADSEC: Admissions Section
2. ATESL: Association of Teachers of English as a Second Language
3. CAFSS: Council of Advisers to Foreign Students and Scholars
4. COMSEC: Community Section
5. SECUSSA: Section on U. S. Students Abroad

Most members of the association have a primary affiliation with one of these sections. Some members have dual or multiple responsibilities on their campuses, and may be actively involved with more than one section. Besides the five major sections, NAFSA's organizational structure includes smaller groups of people which have a more focused interest on particular topics. These subgroups are called Special Interest Groups (SIGs) and Professional Educator Groups (PEGs).

All of the principal NAFSA sections and many of the special subgroups are interested in the use of technology and how it might further their work. NAFSA will make available to interested individuals information to facilitate contact with members of the national sectional teams and sectional representatives in each region of the United States, and provide information on all its SIGs and PEGs.

NAFSA will also provide information on the appropriate use of technology in the cross-cultural setting, and facilitate contact with professionals in the field who are experts on computer technology and its application. Additionally it offers informational and training sessions on the use of technology at each of its national conferences and during many of its regional and local meetings.

MICROSIG: NAFSA Microcomputer Special Interest Group

MicroSIG is the Special Interest Group which focuses its attention upon computer technology as it relates to NAFSA and the organization's five principal sections.

The goal of MicroSIG is to assist NAFSA and its members to fully utilize modern technology as it applies to international educational exchange. Conceived in 1984 and birthed the following year, MicroSIG's first directory of members' E-Mail addresses contained only twelve listings. It currently contains hundreds of listings. MicroSIG established the INTER-L electronic mail distribution system through which many NAFSAnet (NAFSA network) communications pass and has recently supported the creation of another distribution system which specifically serves professionals responsible for study abroad programs (the SECUSSA section of NAFSA).

MicroSIG publishes a periodic newsletter which is highly recommended for international educators interested in technological advancement. Past issues have contained articles on the MicroSIG organization, E-Mail and networking for the membership; using a word processor to compose E-Mail messages; software which will print INS Forms I-20; special prices on computer books and software for non-profit organizations; and electronic communication and the future of educational advising.

OSEAS: NAFSA Overseas Exchange Advisers Professional Interest Group

One of NAFSA's Professional Interest Groups (PEGs), OSEAS includes exchange advisers and program administrators in university, government, private, United States Information Service (USIS) and Fulbright advising centers in over 130 countries. This group is of particular interest to international admissions and study abroad professionals, but also can be effectively utilized by other international educators when appropriate.

Two OSEAS directories are available from archives maintained by the INTER-L electronic mail distribution system and these directories include telephone, FAX and E-Mail information on over 600 advisers. Information is indexed by country, city, and institution. Mailing addresses are not provided since these directories are not intended to facilitate bulk recruitment mailings. This OSEAS database constitutes the largest known collection of information on exchange advisers in other countries.

Admissions personnel may be especially interested in this information since it allows the possibility of E-Mail correspondence directly with officials of foreign institutions for clarification of foreign transcript information and assistance with evaluations. Study abroad professionals may also be interested in this information because it allows direct contact with administrators in foreign institutions who are responsible for coordinating international programs and services, and with personnel in OSEAS advising centers. These contacts are valuable for establishing new study abroad programs and enhancing currently existing programs.

Many OSEAS advising centers do not have E-Mail capability at the present time but some do. This situation should improve considerably in the next few years.

NAFSAnet

Many individuals representing all sections and groups within NAFSA are linked together through a computer communication network known as NAFSAnet (the NAFSA network). This network is not really a unique physical communication network but is just a term which has been given to the rapidly increasing communication which has been taking place among NAFSA members who have access to computer networks.

The NAFSAnet communication network is made possible by technical support from MicroSIG and is facilitated by an electronic mail distribution system known as INTER-L, which is managed by MicroSIG. Since NAFSAnet has much in common with global computer communication networks and since INTER-L distributes mail worldwide, both of these topics are discussed in more detail later in this chapter.

The Answer Project - An International Education Knowledgebase

The ANSWER project is a database that allows access through a computer to an information management tool which contains extensive data on international and cross-cultural programming, federal regulations affecting foreign students and scholars, the administration of study abroad programs for United States students, international admissions and foreign credential evaluation, English as a Second Language (ESL) program administration and curricula, plus other information of interest to international educators. This database is capable of multiple searches, an electronic locator for cross-referenced information, and the data is constantly updated.

NAFSA recently received a grant from the Fund for the Improvement of Postsecondary Education (FIPSE), to initiate the ANSWER project. This effort will result in the most comprehensive information management tool available to professionals in the field of international education. While the concept is still evolving and will likely not reach culmination for a few more years, the types of data to be collected, stored, managed and retrieved have already been identified by task forces and focus groups representing each of the five NAFSA sections. Technical specifications are being developed and prototype demonstrations for the membership are now available.

This "knowledgebase", once operational, will be accessed via an E-Mail type of computer communication network. Start-up, operational and maintenance costs, along with NAFSA's ability to recover those expenditures, will determine the pace at which the various database components can be developed.

MicroSIG is developing a training program in preparation for the advent of this knowledgebase. This training will initially focus upon expanding the technological and computing knowledge of participants, and will be offered at conferences and meetings.

GLOBAL COMPUTER COMMUNICATION NETWORKS AND LIST SERVICES

Global Networks

Local area networks connect computer users in an office, a building or a particular administrative division, usually through hardware called fileservers. Wide area networks (WANs) may encompass an entire campus and these networks usually function through the school's mainframe computer center. Global networks are networks of mainframe computers. Anyone who has access to a mainframe computer which is on a global network has the ability to electronically communicate with anyone else on the network.

Most college mainframe computers are tied into computer communication networks which, through connections with other networks called "gateways", stretch throughout the world. Familiar examples are Bitnet or Internet, two academic computer networks, and Compuserve or MCI Mail, two commercial E-Mail networks. Most institutions facilitate easy and free access to communication networks for all faculty, staff, and students with mainframe computer accounts.

If access is available to a dedicated terminal connected to the mainframe computer, then it is possible to access outside computer networks. If access is through a microcomputer which can access the school's mainframe, then it would also be possible to access global computer networks. Access can also be achieved through a modem to the school's mainframe computer.

If the school is not connected to an external computer network, which is more likely to be true for relatively small schools, it may be necessary to encourage the administration to establish such a link. Until the connection is made, one may have to explore the possibility of linking his/her computer to a modem and subscribing to a commercial computer network such as those mentioned earlier. Care should be taken to examine not only start-up costs but also the cost of actually using the system once access is gained.

Electronic Mail (E-MAIL)

Electronic mail may now be the single most important communication and information management link the international service office has with the outside world. To communicate with someone through E-Mail, the E-Mail address must be known. Such addresses have a standardized format which consists of a user ID, the word "at" or the symbol "@", and the user's mainframe computer "node".

All people linked to the same mainframe computer use the same node for their E-Mail addresses. For example, all staff at the NAFSA office in Washington, D. C., have "NAFSA.ORG" as their node. NAFSA's Microcomputer Special Interest Group maintains a directory of all NAFSA members who have registered their E- Mail addresses with the organization.

If there is a choice of more than one network on your campus, you should always use the same network which the intended recipient of your message uses. The reason for this is that communication within the same network does not require the message to pass through a "gateway" connecting one network to a different network. "Interbit" is the name of the gateway between Internet and Bitnet. E-Mail which must pass through a gateway sometimes requires "protocol conversion", a process which modifies the message so that it can be properly formatted and transmitted through a different operating system. Protocol conversion occurs automatically but the address one uses to pass through a gateway is different from same-network E-Mail addresses and the conversion process can delay transmission. Fortunately for most users in United States higher education, the gateway between Bitnet and Internet is "invisible" from the user's perspective. Gateways with some other networks are not as easily traversed and require special addresses.

Subscribing to bulletin boards, distribution lists and other E-Mail services on different networks is also different. LISTSERV is the name used for distribution systems on Bitnet; NEWSGROUPS is the name of these systems on Internet, for example.

When access is available to E-Mail one should subscribe to INTER-L, an electronic mail list which is described in detail in a later section. By subscribing to INTER- L, an E-Mail address can be added to the NAFSAnet Directory.

NAFSAnet

As mentioned previously, many international educators are linked together through a computer communication network known as NAFSAnet. Communications among NAFSAnet users take place in two ways: (1) directly from one user to another or (2) through an

E-Mail distribution service, INTER-L, which sends communications to all subscribers of the service.

NAFSAnet communications from one user to another move from mainframe computer to mainframe computer much as a physical letter moves through the postal service. This is accomplished by one user sending the communication to another user by employing personal E-Mail addresses. Using a personal E-Mail address means only the person who has that address receives the communication.

While INTER-L facilitates NAFSAnet electronic mail communication among those with both general and specific interests in international education, a list service called SECUSS-L (SECUSSA - List) is available to those with a particular interest in study abroad (NAFSA's SECUSSA section). Two other list services, TESL-L (Teachers of English as a Second Language - List) and SLART-L (Second Language Acquisition, Research and Teaching - List), exist for those with an interest in English as a second language and second language acquisition.

It should be noted that just as rapid advances in medicine are presenting challenges to the fields of law and ethics, swift technological advances are presenting challenges to professional associations in our field. NAFSAnet is "officially" recognized by NAFSA, and both INTER-L and SECUSS-L have a very close relationship with the association. The associational affiliations of TESL-L and SLART-L are more tenuous in nature. TESOL, an association of Teachers of English to Speakers of Other Languages, does not "officially" recognize TESL-L although it promotes the list service in some of its literature. Many members of NAFSA's ATESL section are subscribers to TESL-L but an "official" relationship does not exist with the association.

Inter-L

INTER-L is a network that saves all messages until it's convenient to view them. Conversely, communication is sent to each and every "listener" on the network for them to access at their convenience. It's restricted in the sense that only international educators or those with a particular interest in international education have access to the party line.

The power of this communication tool is awesome and it's absolutely free. For example, suppose a subscriber sends out a question over the network about an immigration question or requests help.

By typing out an E-Mail message to INTER-L which asks other subscribers for assistance, the message is automatically sent to all INTER-L subscribers. Not all will respond, of course, but many of those who share this interest and have information or ideas to offer will respond.

INTER-L subscribers will automatically receive all numbered "Updates" from NAFSA's Government Relations staff in Washington. These are communications of particular interest to international educational exchange professionals and they summarize the latest information on proposed legislation, anticipated and current federal regulations, and regulatory interpretation. In addition, INTER-L may be used to advertise position openings in the field, to publicize the availability of grants which seek to promote exchange, to notify users of professional meetings, and so forth.

INTER-L also provides a reference library to its subscribers. This library includes files or notebooks such as NAFSANET ETIQUETT, NAFSANET GUIDE, NAFSAFAX DIRECTRY and NAFSANET DIRECTRY. It also contains a directory, compiled by the Overseas Exchange Advisers (OSEAS) Database Project, of overseas contacts; articles of interest to international educators; the U. S. Department of State travel advisories; and a log or notebook of all messages handled by INTER-L, listed by week, for the preceding three months.

NAFSA is considering offering an E-Mail service separate from INTER-L, which, probably for a subscription fee, will provide users with the "Government Affairs Bulletin", the updates from their Government Relations staff and a host of other "official" information encompassing the full range of NAFSA's professional interests. However, INTER-L will continue to perform an invaluable service for its users.

CONCLUSION

Advances in technology can be utilized in a variety of ways by international educators and can be employed in a sensitive manner when used for communication across cultural boundaries. Within all international services offices staff must take full advantage of current technological capabilities to maximize time for "high-touch" activities which are, the critical activities from the clients' perspective. This means networking office computers (a local area network or LAN) and automating word processing, record keeping and reporting work. In addition, international educators should work toward establishing a computer network encompassing all international service and program offices on campus (an expanded LAN or a wide area network, WAN), and efficiently utilize the enhanced communication and coordination capabilities such networking facilitates.

Moving beyond the campus boundaries, international educators must also be constantly aware of new capabilities being developed by institutions in the forefront of technology use, and must be networked with other professionals in the field. Electronic communication via global communication networks and electronic mail distribution systems which operate on those networks are revolutionizing communication and access to information just as much as satellite technology has revolutionized the reporting of news.

Utilization of advances in technology can be needlessly confining if we remain captive to thought and behavior patterns established during the days of manual typewriters and rotary telephones, however. Technological advances open up new and creative ways of approaching the fulfillment of professional responsibilities, and all international educators need to think in new and creative ways to make full and appropriate use of these capabilities.

Chapter 7

Housing Programs

Donald B. Mills
Emily Burgwyn

Housing is another department in student affairs that lends itself easily to computerization and the use of technology. The basic function of housing requires the collection of information and the manipulation of data. Technology enables the housing professional to conduct tasks in a manner that is more efficient than manual collection and manipulation of data but does not change the essential role of the practitioner. Technology should be viewed only as an asset to provide service; it should never be considered an end in itself. Careful consideration of desired results must precede any consideration of the use of technology.

The implications of adding technology to the management functions of a housing office are critical. Before decisions are made to use computers and before software is selected, policy questions must be decided. If technology is to be a management tool it must support policies, not determine them. For example, the relative importance of various criteria for assigning roommates is appropriately a management decision; therefore, technology must be selected which allows the flexibility to weigh the criteria by policy. There must also be the flexibility to make changes in the criteria as necessary by environmental imperatives such as changing demographics.

While technology does not change the purpose of housing, it does change the delivery of housing functions. Reports may be tailored for specific needs. Information for decision-making can be readily accessible. The maintenance of files becomes more space efficient and the use of historical data becomes easier. The subtle inducements of using machine generated data must be carefully monitored, however. Because the sheer volume of data can be so easily accessed, the housing professional may choose to have more information rather than only pertinent information. There exists always the temptation to interact more with machinery than with people. The housing professional must continue to collect information about attitudes, preferences, and satisfaction directly from students and staff in a variety of forms. While data collection that can be processed by machine is more "clean," the messy process of data collection by focus groups, surveys with open-ended questions, and face to face conversations may provide the affective information necessary to make those decisions that enhance the residential and educational experience of the primary constituency, students.

This chapter examines a variety of typical housing functions and discusses ways that the housing professional can best utilize technology to perform them. It should be noted, however, that the discussion will be conducted from the point of view of housing practitioners, not from a perspective of technical expertise.

BRIEF HISTORY

Student affairs persons are fond of declaring that they represent the "high touch" aspects of higher education in an environment that is increasingly "high tech." While those who focus on residential life programs might continue to maintain this position, those engaged in the operational aspects of a housing program have recognized the value of technology for many years. The sheer volume of financial and individual student information led to use of computers to organize information and to ease the record keeping pressures on staff. Many of those who turned earliest to technology did so in an effort to avoid increasing personnel costs. Automating financial information for housing programs became common, if not the norm, over twenty years ago. For example, Texas Christian University offered a nascent computerized room assignment program in 1975 (although today it would be seen as awkward and totally inadequate). In the earliest usages, most of the computing was conducted on a mainframe computer that housing officers shared with other university departments. The primary benefit was the speed available in crunching volumes of numbers and pieces of information. Very few persons recognized the range of opportunities that would become available by the 1990s.

While many institutions began to understand the benefits of computerizing financial and statistical information, cost was a continuing problem. While businesses could purchase computing equipment and use tax depreciation rules to help finance the purchase, institutions of higher education were funding purchases from current funds. In an era when funds were tight, the purchase and use of large computing equipment was difficult. The introduction of the microcomputer, the forerunner of today's personal computer changed the environment dramatically.

The personal computer provides technology inexpensively and provides very powerful management tools for practitioners. The last decade witnessed not only an expansion of available hardware, but also of software so the housing professional began to recognize the myriad of possibilities from technology. The housing office could now respond more quickly to changes and to analyze important information more completely. Services for students could be more immediate and tailored to individual needs and requests. The personal computer has become almost an indispensable management tool.

THE MANAGEMENT PERSPECTIVE

Developing a housing program that is responsive to the needs of students and the needs of the institution is the overall goal of any housing management official. The adoption of technology as one of management's tools requires that the manager apply the same perspective to the adoption of technology as to the adoption of any other management tool.

Any technology must be evaluated on the basis of its effectiveness and efficiency. Will this technology enable the housing staff to complete needed tasks more quickly and accurately? Will this technology enable them to complete necessary tasks better? These two questions are the essence of effectiveness and efficiency. In an environment where student needs and expectations change rapidly, technology must be flexible, affordable, and ultimately supportive of housing programs. Failure to assure these characteristics can easily result in technology efficiently performing unnecessary or ineffective tasks.

The management perspective of technology must also consider the cost/benefit ratio for new technologies. While this might sound simple enough, ultimately understanding the true nature of costs and benefits strikes to the core of the manager's responsibilities. And the costs can be very subtle when the use of time-saving technology might result in additional projects and the need for more staff. The benefits might not be readily perceived in strictly financial terms. Nor should they be judged solely on the basis of quantity of production. Losses in contact with students or the tendency to view students as data rather than customers are costs as well.

Nevertheless, the manager's primary function in evaluating technology is the determination that technology will assist in meeting both short-term and long-term goals, and that these goals are met in an efficient, effective manner. Further, technology must enable the housing professional to better understand the environment of the institution and to develop programs that best provide support to the student's residential and educational needs and goals.

APPLICATIONS

The operation of a housing office includes the recruitment of students, the assignment of students to rooms, the maintenance of residence halls, and the collection of charges. Techniques of marketing and record-keeping are essential. The use of technology is designed to provide the customer with immediate and high quality service. Information must be made available in a manner that improves responsiveness and enhances satisfaction. The following discussion of applications of technology is organized by the various functional areas where a housing office interacts with a student customer.

Marketing

The first contact made with students is recruiting them to live in the residence halls. How are they recruited? Where is the population pool created? The housing professional must also ask what technology can be used to make their residence halls competitive and attractive with the competition? These questions deal with marketing, publications, contracts and assignments, correspondence, and customer service. Generally, the applicant pool is established from two sources, students who resided in residence halls the previous year and students new to an institution. To recruit these students, campus housing programs are competing with other housing opportunities for students, e.g. off-campus apartments, Greek housing, or at home with family. For those with high demand for facilities, they might neglect the "Madison Avenue" approach and assume the attitude that if you don't take what we offer, move over because there is someone behind you who will! Those who are "begging" students to stay in their facilities have learned that slick, easy to follow publications (and re-evaluation of policies) are the necessary state of the art. Housing professionals have therefore, become sophisticated users of desk-top-publishing software, laser printers, graphics and pictures, and advanced data collection devices. Some have moved to electronic data collection.

Many housing departments have gradually moved from hand drawings and "clip art" to Arts & Letters software; from a Xerox "Zelda" mainframe to PostScript printing on an IBM mainframe with a high speed laser printer. Both approaches offer efficient means for mass communication and office productivity. On the Texas Christian University (TCU) campus the housing office has evolved to Harvard Graphics from PF Write, from mainframe Script to Waterloo Script, and from daisy wheels and dot matrix printers to laser technology. It is amazing how much quicker and more efficiently it is now possible to produce far more appealing and professional looking publications. And this professional look is necessary to keep the attention of a visually sophisticated student body.

Marketing, of course, involves much more than word processing and desktop publishing. The relationship with other offices or units in the institution become paramount to an effective system. The ability to retrieve information about prospective residents requires not only a working, communicative relationship with the admissions office, but also the ability to capture the data from another office in a timely and efficient manner.

Establishing a Database

For the manager, the ability to transfer the data about prospective residents from a machine in one office to a machine in another reduces the cost of personnel. In essence this can be accomplished through shared "databases" or "interface technology". This raises the issue of network systems or shared mainframe files.

There are benefits and drawbacks to a shared mainframe environment. It reduces the need to spend resources to duplicate common information shared by many offices or units such as mailing address, billing address, major, and other basic demographic information. The mainframe can serve as a "fileserver" and export data to personal computers (PCs) where modifications and adjustments can be made without competing with other units for mainframe time and resources. PC software can be utilized to speed up modifications and configure the data to formats more suitable for housing personnel. In the past, TCU has relied on mainframe resources to handle file management, primarily because PC capacity was not yet sufficient to store and manipulate large databases. With the arrival of megabyte hard drives and megabyte RAM, a PC environment is becoming more practical, even for larger institutions.

There are drawbacks to relying on a mainframe environment. Many users are competing for resources concurrently. As a result, priorities must be established between competing departments to drive access, storage capacity, and processing capabilities. Often these priorities result in slower response time and scheduling delays in receiving reports. Additionally, when a high number of users have access to the mainframe for any variety of computing applications, security becomes a major issue with the need for varying levels of access and controls.

What should a typical housing database include? What data are important to store? Obviously, this will vary from school to school, but included on most campuses are the following: student name; some sort of identification number; a permanent address; a billing address; a next of kin address and phone numbers; hours enrolled for the term; classification; a number of "report flags" used to identify various correspondence and contacts made; housing reservation status; specific residence hall and roommate assignment preferences (i.e., choice of hall; personal characteristics used in making assignments such as smoking, drinking, study habits, neatness, interests, musical interests, etc.); actual hall and room assignment; room phone number; rental rate for the student room; dates of file activity (reservation receipt, assignment, assignment changes); and meal plan if required as a part of housing package.

Correspondence

Correspondence with potential residents begins after the database is established. In a PC environment, a combination of Word Perfect 5.0 and Arts & Letters on a Post Script laser printer will reduce production time, avoid the cost of typesetting, and improve recruiting publications significantly. Additionally, by merging name and address files, extracted from the database, with word processing, it is not difficult to personalize all correspondence.

Data Collection and Use

Through the use of electronic technology, data can be collected from students for use in successfully providing appropriate housing. Information collected from students on housing applications may be used to determine assignment preferences, establish contract terms, and to credit deposits. At TCU, manual data entry was considered too time consuming, carried a high degree of errors, and was just not a fun way to work. Thus, a move was made to a scannable form (aka "bubble sheets")housing application . The forms were designed by TCU personnel and produced by National Computer Systems in Owatonna, Minnesota. Customized software, developed by the TCU Information Services Department, was necessary to read the application and create transactions to feed the database. Personnel responsibilities shifted from clerical data entry to evaluation of data integrity. Information collected in this manner was more accurate with a significant decrease in errors. Further, this process provided more opportunities for students to make changes in their housing requests, to make the changes more easily, and to have information available in the database much earlier in the process.

After data is collected, it must be put into usable formats for data manipulation. Report generator software and editing functions are usually used to configure the data into appropriate form. A variety of software exists for this function. Most database packages (DataPerfect, MicroSoft Works) come with report and query options. This process extracts information in the database to satisfy various needs. For example, one can create files of names and addresses of only specific types of students, such as those who have submitted a housing reservation, to merge with a word processing program (WordPerfect, Waterloo Script) to create a letter thanking them for their reservation and what they should expect next. Or, one could create a list of potential residents and their home phone numbers, sorted by geographic location, to be used for a phone-a-thon to prospective students. Or, one could use the report generating or query function to answer ad hoc questions such as how many new freshmen students who have been admitted to the institution have sent a housing reservation. The possibilities are limited only by the data contained in the database.

Room Assignments

After the pool of residents for housing has been established, the difficult tasks of assigning students with other students to specific rooms begins. This is an area of computer assistance that is still evolving. Each institution has its own unique set of policies, procedures, traditions, and priorities that make pre-packaged assignment software difficult to develop and market. There have been a number of software companies who have tried to provide quality assigning software. However, because of each institution's unique processes, the cost of modifications and enhancements to software often exceed the cost of software developed in-house.

In making the decision about assignment software, decisions must be made on both cost and quality of service dimensions. Is the purchase or development of assigning software cost effective? That is, will the product produce what is necessary without additional work or data manipulation by the housing staff? When evaluating automation, efficient use of resources (machine as well as personnel) is an issue that cannot be overlooked. Another component of the decision to have a computer do room assignments is the impact on the personal touch; do students lose individual attention when roommate matches are made by machine?

Applied Collegiate Systems, a division of Griffin Technology, Inc., currently is marketing a Housing Information System designed for single user PC-DOS or MS-DOS, PC local area network (LAN) use, VAX/VMS (mainframe) use, or Novell networks. This is a comprehensive system that includes a module for facilities and for residents, an automated assignments module, an accounts receivable module, an automated billing module, a maintenance/inventory module, and a conference services module.

Another commercially available software package is called SSH (The System for Student Housing) and marketed through SofTech Associates, Inc., in Piscataway, New Jersey. This PC based system includes automated assignments, automated resident student lotteries, laser printer support, and room assignment transaction tracking.

At TCU, the decision was made to continue to use the power of the mainframe report generator and editor to organize assignment data and make assignments, but the housing office maintains a separate database containing details on residence hall rooms. When an assignment is entered on a student's record, the information interacts with the student database and the residence hall rooms database to post the rental rate for the assigned room and the room phone number. This information (the residence hall and room number, rental rate, and phone number) becomes a part of the student's University database record, allowing housing status information to be shared easily with other units in the institution (i.e., Dean of Students, Business Office, Campus Police, etc.).

While many universities utilize a mainframe environment to assist with assigning students to rooms and communicating assignments to students through letters generated by a mainframe word processor, all of these functions can also be performed in a PC environment. In a PC environment information is provided to the institution's central student database through electronic data file transfers or "uploading" from one system to the other.

The uploading process requires some form of communications software. A variety are available on the market for PCs, some as communications packages only (such as Carbon Copy) with others as part of an integrated software system (such as MicroSoft Works). Communications software is also available for mainframe environments. TCU uses a communications package called Kermit that supports communications between PCs and various mainframes.

Billing and Collections

After assignments are complete, the system must move from database management environment to the money management environment, namely billing and collectibles. Here, too, the student billing process varies from institution to institution. Some housing departments maintain the complete responsibility for billing and collecting all housing charges from the institution's billing for tuition and fees. Others electronically send billing transactions to a central billing unit or system. This means that some form of data collection (in this case rental rates) is used to create transactions (debits and credits) to be posted to students' accounts. Whether in a mainframe or PC environment, the concepts are the same for posting charges or credits to an individual student's account located in a billing database. The billing system should have the capacity to calculate interest or penalty charges, satisfy general accounting principals, and above all in a service atmosphere, be easily understood by student consumers.

Expenditures

After establishing a system for billing and receiving, the next area of financial management is expenditures, namely accounts payable and payrolls. Whether in a PC, network, or mainframe environment, interaction between personnel data files and payroll files is critical to an efficient personnel system.

Payroll and personnel systems are readily available for the PC environment as most small businesses require the capability of computers to carry out payroll functions such as printing checks, taxes and benefit deductions and payments, etc. One such system is available from Integral (formerly ISI) based in Walnut Creek, California. This is a mainframe based integrated software package that accommodates applicant tracking, personnel records, and payroll functions.

Accounts payable systems are best integrated with a billing and receivables system. These systems are available through a variety of companies for mainframe computers. Many large housing systems use the integrated package from Information Associates (IA) of Rochester, NY. This software accommodates billing, accounts receivables, general financial accounting, and accounts payable requirements. In a PC environment, general database software (i.e., dBase III, Paradox, etc.) could be bought "off-the-shelf" and easily adapted for all of these accounting functions.

Facility Management

Another area of computer automation that has helped housing professionals provide better service for students is the maintenance management software systems. These software systems provide the capacity to organize work requests, special projects, maintenance schedules, and preventive maintenance schedules. Most of these systems are applicable in a PC, network, or mainframe environment. One package, called TMA (The Maintenance Authority) is PC based (either MacIntosh or IBM and compatibles) and offers work orders, inventory control, preventive maintenance schedules, project management schedules, asset management and bar coding options, and graphics interfacing. This package has been marketed to housing professionals through Collegiate Products in Tulsa, OK.

Other maintenance management software systems currently available include Main/Tracker from Elke Corporation, and Chief, from Maintenance Automation Corporation. The improvement of customer service and satisfaction experienced at TCU since installing this software package has been enormous. Preventive maintenance is routinely scheduled and the schedules are forwarded to areas that will be effected by the work so necessary alternative plans can be made. Using a maintenance management system has assured a much faster initial response. Follow up response when the problem spans more than one maintenance area (such as broken pipes that require plumbers first to repair the pipe, maintenance technicians to repair the damage done by the plumbers, and finally, finishing technicians to paint or replace tile) has also improved dramatically. This software system also provides an accounting of a technician's time and provides interfacing with inventory files, thereby maintaining accurate records of stock in inventory.

These systems are another breed of file managers or database programs that also have the capacity to provide a variety of reports. For example, printed lists can be made of all incomplete service orders for any particular residence hall, or how many temperature related service calls there were for any particular period of time in any particular residence hall. These systems also provide an avenue for cost accounting where labor, overhead, and material costs can be calculated for any given service request or service completed. This component has been very helpful in combating vandalism by making available to students details of the institution's actual costs for repairs.

These maintenance management software systems have a scheduling component. But maintenance and housekeeping are not the only areas where scheduling in residence halls is important. Summer conference housing and special repair/renovation projects require schedule coordination. One approach to scheduling is to create a calendar style spreadsheet using any variety of spreadsheet software (e.g., Lotus 1-2-3, MicroSoft Excel). Another approach could be to use Calendar Creator software produced by Power Up. Yet another approach, utilized by TCU, is project management software, specifically Microsoft Project. This software is particularly helpful in allocating resources (such as linen, beds, and supplies).

Other facility management systems include the use of database technology for inventory and asset control. This technology uses bar codes or other scanning devices to create and maintain an accounting for inventories. The applications for this type of technology include inventories of room furniture, appliances, art, as well as repair and maintenance parts. Not only will an inventory system provide information for replacement schedules, but it will also provide financial information regarding the value of assets or asset depreciation.

Facility Planning

For those housing programs with facility planning under their purview, Computer-Aided Design (CAD) software is indispensable. This type of software permits access to architectural "blueprints" of facilities. This enables the user to model structural changes, configure facility space in different formats, determine options for the placement of furniture, and be creative with decorating and design.

Security

Security poses one of the most difficult challenges of the next decade. Residents and their parents are demanding, and rightfully expect, an environment that is safe and secure. The consensus developing in the housing profession is for a card access type of system. These can range from a card with a magnetic strip using readers (similar to an ATM at a bank) to proximity cards using computer chips on a plastic card that will activate a lock when a holder merely gets within a short distance of the reader. Security technology utilizes much of the technology previously discussed. These include database file management and reports, integration with housing records and the student information system, interfacing, via a telecommunications system, with security offices, alarm systems, personnel and maintenance management systems also requiring security consideration.

Security access computer systems using some form of card for access control are readily available on the market. Some vendors include Simplex, HARCO Industries, Honeywell, and Griffin Technology. These systems are quite expensive because they include both the technical equipment (hardware and software), and also the mechanical equipment (door locks,etc.). Considerations for the user include whether a local system (each residence hall stands independent of all others) or a campus-wide system is to be used, where alarm systems will be located, the types of reports to be generated (these can be a listing of all attempted entries, all attempts by unauthorized personnel, or a variety of combinations), and how many doors will be provided with card access equipment. Policy considerations include who will maintain the system, where a student goes when they have lost their card, and who responds to alarms.

The security system for residence halls is a campus-wide issue and can not be decided by housing personnel alone.

Occupancy Forecasting

Planning is clearly one of the most critical items for the housing manager. The use of common spreadsheet programs, such as Lotus 1-2-3, enables forecasting of occupancy by using historical data. The data is manipulated by using historical data, applying any changes in circumstance, and then projecting a result. For example, one could determine the number of new students who live in campus housing over the past five years, discover from the admissions office data the expected number of students, and then ascertain the expected number of residents. This process can be used to forecast by classification, by residence hall or by gender. No special software development is necessary to create a variety of "what if" scenarios.

Computer Labs

Many residence hall programs have established computer labs in campus housing. Most students use computers for word processing. A computer lab can be developed using either IBM or compatible PCs or MacIntosh machines. Many campuses provide software, but students could purchase their own. A common printer for every four or five machines provides the printing capability students need. Security for these areas is a must. To create a computer lab for ten computers will cost approximately $35,000 for computers, room modifications, and security.

Many campuses also have terminals available for students to reach the mainframe. This is especially valuable for those involved in classes requiring computer programming or modeling (computer science, economics, etc.). In this circumstance, it is also necessary to assure that students have access only to those portions of the mainframe that is appropriate. If offering word processing is the goal, however, a computer lab using PCs is most appropriate.

RECOMMENDATIONS

Several recommendations are important for the housing professional considering creating a technology base or expanding an existing base. First, it is important to create a prioritized list of all tasks that could be completed or assisted by the use of technology. The priority should encompass both the elements of importance and the cost. Since it is unlikely that any housing office will be able to accomplish all technological needs in one budget year, phasing the project is common. Without priorities, the phasing will not be accomplished smoothly or efficiently.

In establishing a technological base, the following categories are recommended to help prioritize needs: 1) communication with students on a group basis involving word processing and publishing needs; 2) creating databases for use in assignments, billing, and providing information needs to the university; 3) maintenance, repair, renovation, and purchasing schedules; 4) financial information for building budgets and tracking income and expenses; 5) scheduling special events; 6) building and maintaining personnel files; and 7) establishing a building security program.

Before establishing a program that meets the needs of the housing office, a preliminary step is to determine what is available on the campus and used by other units. It is important that systems be compatible so information can be shared, eliminating duplicate work and effort. The ability to share information electronically is a boon to accuracy and efficiency of information management. Security systems must be in place to prevent changing of data by unauthorized persons, but this can be easily arranged. Failure to share information creates isolated databases and does not provide appropriate service to students who must supply duplicate information to several units.

One of the most difficult decisions is whether to use an institution's mainframe computer, PCs, or a combination of the two. The answer to this depends primarily on the computing environment at the institution. For large computing needs, using a mainframe, if available should be considered. The speed and memory capability of a mainframe make it most efficient. This is particularly true for assigning students to rooms when the number of elements for consideration in the assignment process is large. It is equally true when a communication is being addressed to several hundred students. However, a PC is perfectly appropriate for smaller computing needs. PCs must be connected to a network or mainframe for most effective use. A network must be established, either through the mainframe or a LAN for data to interface.

Frequently one is asked whether to develop software on the campus or to purchase pre-existing software. Our experience suggests that software should be developed locally only if the number of criteria or policy questions make a campus unique from other organizations. For this reason, TCU has developed its own software for room assignments. Our priority values for various criterion in assignments is somewhat unique to our situation. In examining software prepared for market consumption, it appeared that significant modifications would be necessary to meet our purposes. However, new products offering considerable flexibility are becoming available and are worthy of examination.

Many functions of a housing office are not institutionally unique. In these instances, it is appropriate to purchase software from a vendor. Word processing, spreadsheet, maintenance and inventory programs are examples where "off-the-shelf" software is perfectly fine. It is recommended, however, that institutional consistency be maintained in order to share information more easily. For example, at TCU, where WordPerfect is the standard, an institutional license has been purchased, and all offices are expected to use it for word processing.

It is also recommended that all costs be carefully considered in light of benefits. Because technology becomes obsolete so quickly, it is almost impossible to remain "state of the art" for very long. It is important to always buy as much computing power as one can afford, but it is not necessary to upgrade frequently. Unless one is manipulating large amounts of data, memory is more important than speed. Operational costs of adding technology must also be considered. For example, although desktop publishing allows great flexibility in producing printed material and easily allows material to be tailored to specific needs, it is somewhat time consuming. If a determination to produce all publications in-house results in the hiring of additional personnel, it may not be worth the cost. Hence, close examination of the benefits to be derived is crucial. If the operational costs of any new technology can not be assumed within the existing housing budget without an incremental increase in costs, it may not be best to purchase it. Obviously there are exceptions for specific needs, but this general test should first be applied before any large equipment or software expenditures are made.

CONCLUSION

The decision to use computers and other forms of technology has basically been made by the environment in which we live. Computers are a fact of life. Their use can certainly make much of the work of a housing office easier and more effective. Properly used, technology enables resources to be available to concentrate on the educational and developmental aspects of students. But computers can not solve problems merely by their presence. They must be seen as part of the organizational resources and employed accordingly.

The most important first decisions are not to determine type of equipment to be purchased. The primary decisions revolve around policy and the type and variety of services to be offered. Only then can appropriate decisions be made about type and quantity of technology. Policy and service decisions answer the questions about the kind of information needed, the reports that will be used, and the priority of services to be offered. Failure to make these decisions will lead to purchases or development of technology that are a conglomerate of machinery that may not meet student or housing needs.

Finally, the housing professional must constantly remain vigilant against the temptation to view technology as an answer to all organizational problems. The primary aim of any housing operation on a college campus is to support the student's educational endeavors. By its very nature, education is not a precise endeavor. Not all answers can be organized, filed, and printed out. The student will remain as the center of our activities and must, therefore, be seen as paramount in our work. Student affairs is, by definition, an interactive enterprise; technology is a mighty support but not a replacement for the personal interactions between staff and student. Only data files interface. People create the interaction required in a community of learning.

Chapter 8

Counseling Center Programs

William Allbritten

The director enters her office on a Monday morning. Her computer has executed a scheduling program at a preset time shortly before her arrival; the day's schedule of clients is displayed. She quickly checks a database of client files to determine if the scheduled clients require any special arrangements for the client's session. One of her staff administers the Minnesota Multiphasic Personality Inventory; the client completes the instrument at the keyboard. The counselor has results in a few minutes. These results are entered into a computer-to-computer fax of the client's file from a residential treatment facility; the counselor is able to quickly determine changes in the client's profile. The counselor's concern with the profile prompts a search of a remote psychological bibliographic database; the information obtained from the database provides the counselor with a bibliography of current research addressing the issues presented by the client. Later in the day the director must prepare a monthly report. A spreadsheet program, using data extracted from the client database, is used to quickly prepare a graphic representation of the previous month's client load. The director is able to identify emerging trends in client presentations and assign resources accordingly.

This scenario is not fanciful but represents a few of the opportunities that computers present to the modern counseling center. A counseling center is concerned with people; this chapter will examine various possibilities presented by computerization and other high-tech programs that enhance the client/counselor relationship. The focus will be on microcomputer applications that facilitate the helping relationship, assist in administrative functions, and generally make life simpler for the counselor.

ADMINISTRATIVE FUNCTIONS

A variety of options are available to assist a mental health staff with record keeping, billing, client management, service evaluation, and other administrative concerns. Two distinct approaches are available: First, the user may choose dedicated programs specifically designed to accomplish a particular function or series of administrative tasks; second, the user may use a generic product, such as a spreadsheet or database program, and design a custom usage of that program that fits local needs.

Dedicated Mental Health Management Programs

SHRINK: The Practice Manager (MultiHealth Systems) is a comprehensive office management system. Currently available versions provide accounting, billing, expense tracking, and practice analysis functions. Current cost varies between $400 and $800, depending on the version selected. A more comprehensive version canned SHRINK Plus that adds scheduling, clinical records, and progress notes to the other functions is also available for a cost of approximately $1,000. A demonstration disk is available and potential users should avail themselves of these low or no cost demonstration disks whenever possible.

The Plus version provides a comprehensive link to DSM-III-R and other coding systems. This is an extensive practice management package that has been favorably reviewed in the computer press.

For users requiring less complete (and less expensive) computer options, single function software is available. A good example is the Computerized Counseling Center Intake System (Center Systems), which costs about $50. The program allows the user to organize intake and initial clinical assessments into a standard format. Demographic data, current assessment, developmental and situational concerns, and symptomology can be cataloged. A companion program The Computerized Note Taking System provides a summary of clinical notes from a counseling session.

Database Programs

Client data that might be collected which require storage, evaluation, and retrieval are intake and biographic summaries, test data, cost notes, referral information, and termination summaries. Computerized database programs allow the user to quickly organize and retrieve this information. It is the author's view that generic database programs are often preferable to dedicated software in that the former programs provide great flexibility. The trade off against the dedicated program is that greater skill in manipulating the software is required with the general use database program. However, ease of use is a major consideration in current software offerings; hence, skill development in the use of this software should not be difficult.

Many programs provide printed or interactive tutorials in their use; this is a feature that the novice user should seek out. In a university setting, training can often be obtained in database use through course and workshop offerings from computer centers or departments of computer studies. Database software that conforms to existing institutional support and training programs provides the novice user with a well supported tool. The non-institutional user may find that local computer vendors as well as national training institutes offer training opportunities.

With the exception of word processing, database management software is the most prolific field of software types available. However, several general guidelines can be offered:

1. The dBase IV (Borland International) file structure is becoming a de facto standard. While the dBase IV program itself is somewhat costly, the user will find that conforming to the file structure and using less expensive programs that produce the dBase file structure will facilitate data exchange and importation.
2. The program should allow the inclusion of substantial amounts of text in addition to brief address and biographic

type entries in its fields. This facilitates the inclusion of case notes and other textual information.
3. The program should be flexible and allow easy modification in terms of the fields presented.
4. The program should provide robust sorting and search facilities.
5. The program should provide for the importation of data in other formats, such as the Lotus 1-2-3 format, or a variety of text formats.
6. Previously mentioned training and support concerns should be addressed.

dBase IV has a large number of programs installed in business, education and industry, according to software trade journals. It is an expensive program with a retail cost of approximately $450 and, until the revision IV release, was criticized for being difficult to master as the user interface was quite obtuse. The latest version has a menu driven interface that is vastly superior to the simple prompt presented to the user of earlier versions. The program is extremely flexible and allows custom routines to be executed repetitively. This might involve data entry queries, report generation, data export, and like activities.

However, the program can be used without programming knowledge. dBase IV possesses relational capabilities. This permits data in one database file to be linked to another, allowing the user to break massive databases into hierarchal subsets and other applications. One database might contain biographical information, another intake information, another test information, another treatment information and all be linked together by some common element, such as a client identification number. This prevents the need to repetitively enter the same data.

dBase IV will operate on older 8088/8086 machines as long as they are equipped with a hard disk drive. For best operation, machines using 80286 or higher processors are recommended.

Simple report generation is not difficult with dBase IV; however, this author has found that more complex or custom reports require some mastery of the dBase programming language.

PC-File (Buttonware) is a less expensive alternative especially for older machines of pre 80286 vintage. It is currently in revision 6 which supports a graphics oriented interface. The author has found this interface to be slow but not unacceptably so when used on older computers using 8088/8086 processors. Original IBM PCs, Tandys, and so on fall into this category. Revision 5 of PC-File uses a character based interface that functions much faster on older machines.

Version 5 is also available in a version commonly called "shareware." A user may obtain a trial copy of the software and use for a period of time to evaluate it; at the end of this period (variable lengths), the user is expected to purchase the software at its retail price. Both revisions are extensively supported by the vendor. This product allows flexible data entry, easy modification of record structure, database file structure, an outstanding report generation interface, databases to be linked to each other, does not require excessive disk or main memory resources, and is provided with a good tutorial program. It can also run from a floppy disk system.

Spreadsheets

Counseling centers are frequently called upon to provide information concerning client loads, group activity, programming, testing, and other functions to a variety of agencies. As the person responsible for selection of software makes choices, integrating record keeping and reporting functions is important.

Spreadsheet software provides great flexibility in creating numerical and graphic reports of activity. As with databases, a standard is emerging in terms of file structure. The Lotus 1-2-3 (Lotus Corporation) spreadsheet format is accepted by many spreadsheet programs. In addition to Lotus 1-2-3, Borland's Quattro Pro (Borland International) provides compatibility with the Lotus file standard. Both programs are well supported by their vendors, provide built in tutorials, possess adequate manuals, list for about $500 and will operate on 8088/8086/80286 machines. They can also take advantage of the faster speed and extended/expanded memory options that 80386 and 80486 processors provide.

In order to gain maximum efficiency from the use of a spreadsheet to report data extracted from the database program, the rekeying of information should be avoided. This means that the spreadsheet and database program must be able to communicate in a common file structure. Lotus and Quattro both directly import dBase compatible files, thus allowing the user to quickly prepare summaries of client load, presenting problems, session counts, discharge status and other data. Spreadsheets, like general use databases, are recommended over dedicated, single function, software as a result of flexibility and economy. However, a trade off, as previously mentioned, lies in the degree of planning for the use of the software that must take place,

Effectively utilizing these programs requires that the counseling center staff agree on a coding or nomenclature system for describing variables in a client record. The "DSM-IIIR" designation for a problem may be used, or an agreed upon textual nomenclature can be used. However, one should avoid using different terms such as depression and depressed to describe the same problem. This process can have a collateral beneficial effect in that it requires the center staff to give careful thought to how their counseling activities can most accurately be described.

DELIVERY OF SERVICES

The use of computer software to support administrative functions is relatively non-controversial. However, the use of computer software as a direct adjunct to therapy has engendered a substantial amount of debate. This section of the chapter will take a look at some of the possibilities presented by computers as a support for therapy and examine the controversy surrounding computer use in this area. Three basic areas of computer use in service delivery will be examined: direct diagnosis/interpretation, interpretive diagnosis, and test administration and scoring.

Direct Diagnosis

Direct diagnosis involves computer administration of a diagnostic instrument, computer scoring, and computer generation of a proposed diagnosis or analysis of results. The controversy surrounding the use of computers in this function concerns itself with the appropriateness of the interpretive algorithms used. Generally, non-controversial simple issues of quality of presentation, ease of staff/client use, speed, and arithmetic accuracy relate to the administration and scoring of a psychological test. The prospective purchaser should evaluate these items by hands-on experience.

Scoring accuracy can be verified by hand versus machine computation of scores. This latter step is not to be minimized because bugs may exist in some software.

At the point at which a computer actually generates a proposed interpretation or analysis is when the professional must take great care. Guidelines found in the literature emphasize ascertaining the evaluative algorithms used. Many interpretive texts exist for use with psychological inventories; there are variances in these texts' suggested interpretations.

The reputable vendor will provide diagnostic source references in product literature. The user is advised to check interpretive accuracy against manually generated interpretations. Existing protocols can be compared to computer generated protocols for the same item pattern response.

This type of software is costly. Therefore, its potential use should be balanced against manual or a less comprehensive and expensive computer based generation of results. Perhaps the most comprehensive system is the Microtest Assessment System offered by National Computer Systems. A variety of tests offered by NCS are supported. The system allows differing of methods of data entry to be used. A client can complete an instrument directly from the screen, a paper answer sheet can be scanned electronically, and paper answer sheet marks may be manually keyed in by an operator. The cost varies, depending upon scoring options chosen, numbers of administrations ordered, and hardware options required. A base package is offered for about $500 and a trial package is available for about $200. Among the tests and questionnaires supported, according to the vendor, are the Minnesota Multiphasic Personality Inventory-2, Giannetti On-Line Psychological History, Million Clinical Multiaxial Inventory, Million Adolescent Personality Inventory, Automated Child/Adolescent Social History, and the Career Assessment Inventory. The system will operate on older 8088/8086 based 640k pc's. However, the vendor recommends that, to remain compatible with future upgrades, the user acquire an 80286/80386/80486 based machine with at least a 150 megabyte hard drive and 4 megabyte of RAM. The system requires a vendor supplied hardware attachment containing test programming. Additional options include an NCS series 3000 scanner, if optical scanning is desired.

This is a comprehensive system and it provides, from one vendor, a variety of instruments and administration/data entry methods. It offers rapid processing, quick generation of interpretive reports, and the capability to directly integrate results into a word-processor file to speed protocol generation. The system has great appeal for high-volume users who require quick turnaround of results from a variety of inventories.

The initial cost is high but may be offset in terms of staff time saved. Mail-in scoring provides similar reporting options (minus the direct word-processor integration) at a lower cost for low volume users but requires turnaround time of about a week. The reader is directed to vendor demonstrations at conventions and vendor product literature for more information on this efficient system.

There are no computer based alternatives that offer anything approaching the comprehensive set of instrumentation supported by the Microtest system in terms of both administration and scoring. However, many individual inventories are offered in computer form by their vendors. The Psychological Corporation offers the Differential Aptitude Tests in an adaptive, computer administered format. According to the vendor, the test adapts itself to the user's ability level and submits questions that match the client's ability level.

CTB/McGraw-Hill offers a computerized version of the Myers-Briggs Type Indicator. The user can complete the questionnaire and receive results unassisted. Most counseling centers would probably require some staff assistance in the interpretation.

When purchasing a testing package, the user should be cautious that the vendor will be available in the future to support the product with fixes or upgrades. It has been this author's experience as a software reviewer that many testing packages are supported by vendors of limited means. The examples cited are offered by major publishers who have been in the business for years; this is not to necessarily discount offerings from less well known businesses. Perhaps more so than in other areas of counseling practice, "caveat emptor" is an important caution.

Interpretative Diagnosis Programs

Interpretive programs require that the user manually administer the instrument and enter the scores into the computer program. Traditional administration and scoring methods are followed.

Psychologistics, Incorporated, offers report generators for the various Weschler instruments as well as selected intelligence scales. The instruments for assessing children that are currently supported, according to vendor literature, include the WISC-R, WRAT-R, WPPSI/WPPSI-R, Stanford-Binet Intelligence Scale, (4th edition),

Woodcock Johnson Achievement Test (original and R versions), Kaufman Test of Educational Achievement, K-ABC, and the PIAT/PIAT-R. The vendor has indicated that sample interpretive protocols will be provided upon inquiry.

Test Administration and Scoring

Pschologistics Inc. also supports various adult instruments, including the WAIS-R, Stanford-Binet Intelligence Tests, WRAT, WRAT-R, Trail Making Test, Stroop Color and Word Test, Purdue Pegboard Test, Aphasia Screening Signs, Benton Visual Retention Test, Symbol Digit Modalities Test, Woodcock Johnson Achievement Test, and the Kaufman Test of Educational Achievement.

The tests are administered and scored in the routine paper and pencil manner; the results are entered into the program with a proposed protocol being generated. These offerings are available in both IBM/PS versions as well as versions that will run on various Apple computers. Costs vary from $200 for single instrument packages supporting the WAIS-R or WISC-R to about $500 for the multi-instrument packages. If the user requires report generation but does not require machine administration and scoring, these packages represent good value because the number of reports that may be generated is not limited.

Potential professional users should inventory their needs. There are several clear advantages to computerized assessments and inventories if the scale of usage justifies purchase. Advantages include speed of administration, accuracy of scoring, and speed in reporting. The obvious disadvantage is the relatively high cost of the packages if usage volume is low. Old-fashioned paper and pencil administration and hand scoring should not be discarded out of hand in favor of technology unless the conditions exist to take advantage of the capabilities of the automated systems.

STAFF SUPPORT

The competent counselor possesses not only facilitative interpersonal qualities but is up to date on current information, research, and practice recommendations. Books, conferences, and journals have long been the sources of information professionals most frequently turn to assist them in maintaining their professional knowledge base. Often, fast moving research produces new information faster than traditional channels can distribute it. Computers provide a means by which this lag can be addressed.

On-line bibliographic databases provide up to date information as well as easy retrieval and organization of this information. Three methods are available to search bibliographic databases. Two of these are generally based in a central research library facility.

First, library research staff can assist the counseling professional in framing a remote computerized database search. The library staff conduct the search and provide a copy of the results to the professional. The consultative process is repeated if necessary to refine the search. This facility has been available in many libraries for over a decade. Most professional journals are abstracted and accessible through this type of search. Many professional indexes are also accessible through remote searches. There are several shortcomings to using central search facilities.

First, a significant amount of time may elapse between the time each search is framed and results are provided. Second, there is substantial cost involved in addition to the costs required to access the database; the research staff and facilities of the library must also be supported. However, the assistance of a trained professional research librarian can help design a search.

A second method of bibliographic research is based upon CD-ROM technology. Just as music can be stored as digital data on these discs, so can textual information. This is a new technology; new databases are being released on a frequent basis. ERIC, PsychLit, and others of interest to counseling professionals are currently available. Vendor displays at conferences are excellent sources of information on CD-ROM offerings as well as of opportunities to try out this technology.

The requirements to support CD-ROM based bibliographic research involve substantial costs in acquiring and updating CD-ROM discs. Initial costs to subscribe can exceed $10,000. In addition, hardware must be acquired to read the compact discs. Currently, CD-ROM readers are priced in the $600 to $1000 range for popular units.

A third technique of accessing bibliographic databases exists that is fast, relatively inexpensive, may require no additional computer hardware, and allows the counselor to directly interact with the bibliographic database. The database subscriptions available in research libraries are expensive; however, database vendors provide consumer oriented subscription plans. Two of these are offered by Knowledge Index and Bibliographic Retrieval Services After Dark. Many databases of interest to counseling professionals are provided in these services; the disadvantage is that, in return for low cost, access is limited to evening hours between 6 pm and 6 am as well as throughout the weekend. These are low usage times for the database vendors that would otherwise be unprofitable. By offering these low cost options the vendor provides a service to the professional as well as generating revenue during low usage periods.

Knowledge Index charges a fee of approximately $24 per hour (1992 rate) for searching its databases. Periods of time less than an hour are prorated. The author has found that searches yielding 40-50 long form abstracts can be completed in approximately 15 minutes. Time on-line is dependent upon several factors. The user must possess a modem; modems that communicate at high speed (2400 baud) are available at costs between $75 and $200 dollars, depending upon features selected. A communications program is required and these are usually bundled with the modem and do not require an additional charge.

Once accessed, Knowledge Index yields a wide range of resources of interest to the counselor. This author has found the Merck Index Online to be useful in providing drug information. Drug Information Fulltext and International Pharmaceutical Abstracts are also available. For general educational information, ERIC and Academic Index can be searched. This author has found Medline and Aidsline to be of particular value. In the field of counseling practice, PsycINFO, Mental Health Abstracts, Dissertation Abstracts, and Sociological Abstracts have proven of value.

The search process is simple. The user can select either a menu driven approach or a command driven one. The menu driven method walks the user through the framing of the search topic, the retrieval of abstracts and/or full text material, and the display of these materials. The command driven method is faster and is quite simple. Very few commands must be mastered.

After material is retrieved, the user can produce permanent copies of the information in two ways. Hard copy can be ordered; this is expensive with cost dependent upon the length of the retrieval and its source. A second method of preservation of the search results exists in the communications software's ability to open a "capture file" and retain on computer disk all information that is displayed on the screen. The capture file can then be printed.

Bibliographic Retrieval Services After Dark (BRS) and Knowledge Index are similar. BRS has a minimum monthly fee of about $12 in addition to a one time startup fee. This is applied to any searches conducted and is charged even if no searches are conducted. Search costs are based upon specific costs tied to particular databases, the length of access to the database, the number of retrievals, and the length of the output requested. Subscription to BRS provides access to a wider range of databases than Knowledge Index but is somewhat more expensive.

The user will find many of the aforementioned databases available. Additionally of interest to counselors are Alcohol Information for Clinicians and Educators, Medical and Psychological Previews, Medline, Abledata, Alcohol Use and Abuse, Psychalert, Social Work Abstracts, and the Exceptional Child Database. Retrieval can be accomplished in a variety of forms - hand copy from the vendor, short, medium, and long abstracts, as well as, in some databases, full text displays.

The use of these databases utilizes the computer's greatest strength which is speed. When up-to-date research or bibliographic information is required, there is no substitute for an up to date computer based bibliographic databases.

CURRENT ISSUES

The vignette outlined at the beginning of this chapter has been demonstrated to be feasible with current, relatively inexpensive technology. However, new technology places new twists on old professional issues. The need to ensure that scoring and interpretive algorithms are accurate when computer based tests are administered. There is no substitute for hands-on demonstrations of computer based instrumentation. An additional suggestion would be to code a selection of hand scored and manually interpreted instruments into the computer based assessment instrument. A comparison could then be made of the computer generated results to the manually obtained protocol. Research literature and vendor data should be carefully examined before any computer based assessment system is implemented.

A second issue is that of confidentiality. Just as access is restricted to paper documents, tapes, and other artifacts of the counseling process out of respect for the client, access to computer based data must also be protected. The database programs described in this article all provide password encoding. For programs that do not provide secure password access, the author suggests that the user consider any of a number of available programs generically referred to as DOS (disk operating system) shells. These programs provide easy navigation of a hard disk and provide the capability to limit access to specific programs or areas of the hard disk. The reader should contact a computer vendor for a demonstration of these products.

A second means of providing security is hardware based. Most current personal computers provide a key lock that deactivates the keyboard when the machine is locked. The wise user would then secure the keys to the computer just as keys to file cabinets are secured. Similarly, if floppy disks are used to secure client data, physical security should be maintained. The very ease of access provided by computers also creates a new route for the unauthorized access to data.

A third issue is that of client comfort when using a computer. Even after a computer based system of service delivery is implemented, hand administered versions of the questionnaires and instrumentation should be maintained for use with clients for whom computer use is inappropriate. It is important that the focus of counseling, the client, not be lost in the relative glamour and high-tech gloss of computers. The counseling profession is and always will be people oriented. The use of computers should take place in ways that enhance this relationship, not in ways that provide additional blocks to effective development of a helping relationship.

A fourth issue is that of cost. Computerization may be difficult to justify in low volume settings in which traditional manual methods have been found adequate in terms of efficiency. However, the ability of the computer to quickly access massive amounts of data, as in test interpretation, suggests that strong consideration be given to the use of computers for this reason, even in settings in which the volume of activity makes a purely cost based justification difficult.

The counseling staff must also be considered. Are they comfortable with using computers? Would computers inhibit their ability to facilitate client growth? Is adequate training available? All of these are questions that must be answered prior to computerization of counseling services. It is important that enthusiasm for new technology not obscure the need to pursue the type of consensus based decision making that has historically proved effective in working with professional staffs.

The implementation of computerization should flow from needs perceived by the staff, not imposed from management. The human component of counseling, whether it be a consideration for the client or respect for the counselor, cannot be subsumed in a rush to adopt new technology. Once a system has been decided upon, additional considerations must be attended to. Staff training is essential. Again, tryouts of software provide a quick feel for the degree of difficulty likely to be posed in mastering the software. The learning curve to develop a competent, daily usage of software may be steep.

Training may be available from vendors in the form of support media, such as training video tapes. The vendor or a professional organization may also provide site based or regionally based training programs. These should be reviewed and incorporated in terms of adequacy in the decision making process.

EMERGING TRENDS

What does the future hold? Predictions are always problematic. Events have a way of establishing a degree of independence that defies prognostication. However, several trends appear to be emerging. The medical profession has for several years had available diagnostic programs that "learn" from experience to assist with diagnostics. It is likely that the technology of artificial intelligence will migrate to the helping professions. Similarly, a concept called "fuzzy logic" is making its appearance. Traditional programming techniques require that branching to be either/or decision. Fuzzy logic allows intermediate decisions to be made. Combined with programs that "learn" through artificial intelligence techniques, this concept portends great advances in diagnostic capability.

Scanners, keyboards, mice, joysticks, and touchscreens are used with current technology to communicate with computers. Voice input, still impractical for everyday use because of memory and other hardware demands, is becoming more efficient. If this technology can be implemented at a reasonable costs, many of the problems of interacting with a computer can be addressed in a communication mode that is more natural.

Software is available to serve many purposes. Competing packages must be evaluated. As with the "shakeout" of office automation software that took place in the mid 1980s, it can be expected that as the user base expands, a similar focusing of interest on fewer software packages will take place. The base of information upon which to plan purchases will also become more comprehensive. For now, confronted with a wide variety of offerings, the wise potential user must take advantage of resources such as this text, hands-on tryout opportunities, sample versions, and vendor presentations to help determine specific needs.

Software selection should incorporate the extent to which the vendor will support with upgrades of specific products. A revision of the DSM is expected soon; will software providing diagnoses based upon the DSM nomenclature be updated as the DSM is updated? This is but one example of the type of obsolescence upon which the wise purchaser must plan.

High technology can facilitate a "high-touch" environment in the counseling center. This chapter has examined programs that, through their speed, accuracy, and comprehensiveness, provide the counselor with evaluative, storage, and data acquisition resources beyond imagination a few years ago. The counselor can be freed from many administrative/support tasks to concentrate on the client: the past, present, and future focus of all counseling.

Chapter 9

Teaching-Learning Programs

Joan Comas

Faced with the prospect of declining enrollments and subsequent funding reductions, institutions of higher education are increasing their recruitment and retention efforts. Similarly, social realities are spurring institutional commitment to teaching excellence in response to wide-spread concern for the quality of American education. Collectively, the social context of education in the 1990s provides impetus to the growth of campus-wide academic support services for students and faculty. These programs commonly are provided by centers for teaching and learning (CTL). They rely heavily upon technology for the delivery of their services which are primarily designed to enhance the academic performance of students and the teaching skills of faculty and graduate teaching assistants.

The typical CTL offers programs to help students (a) succeed in problem-solving courses, (b) improve study techniques, and (c) prepare for professional and graduate school entrance exams. CTL services are generally aimed toward supplementing the achievement of successful students as well as providing limited remedial assistance. These programs may include free tutoring, study skills workshops and courses, math reviews, entrance exam preparation courses, consultation, and a multimedia resource center.

The resource center or independent study lab, is the cornerstone of most operations. Lab materials, predominantly computer programs and videotapes, provide self-paced instruction that complements all staff-delivered services. In correspondence with CTL objectives, resources are usually concentrated in the areas of study skills, entrance exam preparation, and selected courses. The courses of focus are predominantly problem-solving classes: mathematics, chemistry, physics, statistics, and engineering. These courses are generally selected for supplementary emphasis based upon their (a) difficulty level, (b) adaptability to multimedia presentation, (c) common content across individual instructors, (d) suitability for strategic intervention, and (e) unavailability of other campus support programs.

Materials in the social sciences are usually not targeted. Typically, the content of social science courses is not standardized, thereby demanding the accumulation of different resources for various teachers. More importantly, students usually do not have conceptual difficulties with social science classes; instead, problems reside primarily in the comprehension, synthesis, and retention of massive amounts of material. These skills are fundamentally reading functions and, therefore, are addressed through CTL courses on reading and study skills.

Generally, students who use the materials of the lab are self-referred. While professors may encourage the use of particular resources, student visits are voluntary and do not accrue academic credit. The value of a CTL's resources, therefore, lies in the degree to which students—not staff or faculty—find materials constructive and attractive enough for sustained use. Thus, a routine part of lab check-out procedures, students should be asked to evaluate the helpfulness of each resource utilized by rating the material on a five-point Likert scale. Spreadsheets can be generated regularly that reflect the number of times each item was utilized and the assigned evaluations. These records indicate the true utility of the computer programs and videotapes of the CTL.

The purpose of this chapter is to identify those technologically based resources which can be effectively utilized to support and complement academic instruction on most campuses through centers for teaching and learning. The CTL at The University of Alabama was established as a part of the student affairs division in 1985 as a Learning Skills Center (LSC). Since that time it has been expanded several times and is now known as a CTL serving in excess of 10,000 students and faculty annually.

The resources recommended in the following sections are based upon records of over 45,000 student usages of the CTL resources at The University of Alabama. Only materials that were frequently utilized and consistently rated as "very helpful" are cited.

STUDY SKILLS RESOURCES

One of the most popular computer programs, that provide instruction on study strategies, is the Computer-Assisted Study Skills Improvement Program (CASSIP). The package integrates a study skills diagnostic test and ten study skills instructional modules. The diagnostic test, which may be administered through either a computer disk or a printed edition, measures the student's knowledge of effective study skills and learning principles. Although the 200-item true-false test is untimed, most students can complete the inventory in about 45 minutes. Through pre-testing, areas are identified in which students need the systematic instruction provided by one or more of the ten modules.

The study skills modules provide interactive instruction on the following topics: (a) managing time, (b) improving memory, (c) taking lecture notes, (d) reading textbooks, (e) taking examinations, (f) writing themes and reports, (g) making oral reports, (h) improving memory, (i) improving interpersonal relations, and (j) improving concentration. Each module is self-paced, typically requiring approximately 45 minutes to complete. The ten independent modules can be used in any sequence and any module may be omitted if desired. A check on understanding of concepts and methods is provided through immediate grading and feedback of questions presented throughout each unit. The modules are easy to use, concise, and varied in presentation styles. Combining the diagnostic test and the instructional units provides a sense of relevance and immediacy that is appealing to students.

Students may also respond positively to videotapes in the area of study skills. A 50-minute video entitled *College Success* is particularly useful. The tape presents techniques vital to academic success in college. Demonstrations and exercises are used to teach the skills of (a) time management, (b) notetaking, (c) reading textbooks, (d) test preparation, and (e) test taking. This video is an excellent overview of study strategies and is one of the few resources that truly is directed toward college students.

Focused upon note taking and outlining skills, *How to Survive in College*, a one-hour video, teaches practical systems for classifying different kinds of materials. Note taking methods are explained in the forms of simple lists, compare/contrast, cause/effect, and narrations. Techniques for outlining and taking notes from textbooks also are presented.

The ability to use time wisely is critical to college success. *The Time of Your Life*, a 30 minute film, summarizes the time management principles presented in Alan Lakein's book *How to Get Control of Your Time and Life*. Emphasis is given to determining goals, establishing priorities, constructing "To Do" lists, and utilizing an ABC priority system. A series of six one-hour videos comprise a Time-Life production entitled *Time Management System*. Although two of the six lessons specifically address business settings, each lesson is discrete and of benefit to college students.

RESOURCES FOR STANDARDIZED ENTRANCE EXAMS

Because of the motivational level of students who seek to enter graduate and professional school, materials for standardized entrance exam preparation are in great demand. Among the many resources in this area, the products of four publishers consistently are rated highly by students: Video Aided Instruction, Inc., The Graduate Admissions Preparation Service, Educational Test Service, and Interactive Learning Systems, Inc.

Video Aided Instruction, Inc., produces videocassettes for the following entrance exams: Graduate Management Admissions Test (GMAT), Graduate Record Exam (GRE), Law School Admissions Test (LSAT), Miller Analogy Test (MAT), and Scholastic Aptitude Test (SAT). Generally, two two-hour tapes are available for each of the entrance tests. Each set features an overview of the test format, approaches to each question type, and a cursory review of underlying concepts. Sample questions from each topical area are examined, along with the principles necessary for solving the problems. These videotapes are relatively inexpensive and provide an excellent introduction and concise instruction for each of the entrance examinations.

The Graduate Admissions Preparation Service produces comprehensive sets of audiocassettes and manuals for the Medical College Admission Test (MCAT), Dental Admission Test (DAT), GMAT, GRE, and LSAT. All of the series provide extensive practice tests and instruction in all areas covered by the tests. As audiocassettes, usage is somewhat laborious; and each series is lengthy, ranging from ten cassettes for the LSAT to 38 tapes for the MCAT. However, most students are very conscientious in preparing for entrance exams and find that time devoted to these resources is productive.

Prepared by the staff who produce the actual tests, software from Educational Test Service has the advantage of authenticity. Computer packages for the GMAT and GRE consist of sample tests and three full-length, previously administered exams. Sample tests include sections for each problem type and area. The disks containing actual tests may be taken in either the immediate feedback mode or the test simulation mode. At the end of the test mode, the user's raw score, scaled score, and percentile rank are given. The option of receiving an explanation for any question also is available.

Similar computer programs for the MCAT and the LSAT are produced by Interactive Learning Systems. Each program contains two diagnostic disks which analyze the user's performance. Followup study disks for each test section can be studied in either a test or a tutor mode.

Additional test preparation packages that are substantial and attractive to students include The Perfect Score, a program for the SAT, and Sandra Smith's Computer Review for NCLEX-RN. The Perfect Score consists of five study diskettes and a test diskette covering all SAT scales. The test diskette features a time clock that allows students to simulate actual test periods for each section. Sandra Smith's Computer Review for the NCLEX-RN, the professional licensure exam for nurses consists of a series of clinical situations and multiple choice questions relating to those situations. The program produces a detailed performance summary and a printout of questions answered incorrectly.

In addition to resources designed for specific tests, other generic materials have been beneficial to students in preparing for standardized entrance exams. Two videotapes developed for CLEP exams provide excellent reviews of algebra and geometry that are relevant to the ACT, SAT, GRE, and GMAT. Preparation for the vocabulary and analogy portions of the SAT, GRE, and MAT is facilitated by computer programs developed by Program Design, Inc. (PDI), Hartley, and Davidson. PDI and Hartley's programs focus on instruction and practice with types of analogies and, concomitantly, vocabulary development. Davidson's Word Attack, and Word Attack: Roots and Prefixes provide learning activities in a gaming format that is both entertaining and instructive.

RESOURCES FOR SCIENCE COURSES

Biology

Materials for college-level biology are abundant, particularly in the highly visual area of anatomy and human physiology. The following computer programs are among the best, according to student ratings: (a) Body Language, a series of 16 computer disks that provide instruction and practice in labeling the various systems of the body; (b) The Body Transparent, a program with adjustable difficulty level that uses a game format to provide practice in identifying body parts, learning facts, and determining function; (c) Protein Synthesis, a biology disk that requires knowledge of organic chemistry; (d) Genetic Engineering, a program on recombinant DNA, cloning, isolation of genes, and genetic diseases; (e) Introductory Genetics II, two diskettes dealing with principles of genetics; and (f) The Cell and Cell Chemistry Series, a comprehensive program with questions of varying levels of difficulty.

Additionally, excellent videos that correspond with the content of college biology courses are available. The following titles are examples of the numerous videocassettes released by Coronet/MTI Film and Video: *The Living Cell, The Nucleus, The Plasma Membrane, The Cytoplasm, Cell Differentiation, Decoding the Book of Live, Cancer: A Genetic Disease, Muscular Dystrophy: The Race for the Gene*. Similarly, Harper & Collins, publishers of the textbook, *Principles of Anatomy and Physiology* by Tortora and Anagnostakos, provide outstanding videos. For example *Body Works*, a film that overviews the nervous, circulatory and muscular systems, was filmed by an Oscar-nominated production team, and the film is accompanied by a topic-by-topic cross-reference to the Tortora and Anagnostakos text. Other releases by Harper & Collins were produced as part of the "Innovations" series on the Public Broadcasting System.

Chemistry

Computer-assisted instruction in college chemistry also is well developed. A ten-disk program entitled Introduction to General

Chemistry, provides instruction in basic chemistry concepts: the elements, inorganic nomenclature, chemical formulas and equations, atomic weights, percent composition, gas laws, acids and bases, the metric system, and solutions. Additionally, Chemical Nomenclature, a computer package with exercises in identifying and naming various compounds, is a good supplement to general chemistry courses.

Introduction to Organic Chemistry, a set of eight disks, demonstrates principles of organic chemistry through simulated experiments and animations. Topics covered in this program include alkanes and alkenes, substitution reactions, IR and NMR spectroscopy, arenes, alcohols, aldehydes and ketones, and carboxylic acids. Within this program, Chemrain provides an entertaining chemistry version of the popular Space Invaders arcade game. Chemrain challenges the user to identify fast reacting combinations of organic compounds with a variety of reagents. Another resource for organic chemistry courses is Organic Stereochemistry, an instructional package covering the concepts of stereochemistry as they are applied to organic molecules. The program includes tutorials defining terms by example and a large number of randomly generated problems.

Physics

Two computer programs and a video series are particularly effective with students. General Physics is a complete series designed to accompany an introductory physics course for college students. Topics include vectors and graphing, statics, motion, conservation laws, circular motion, thermodynamics, electricity and magnetism, optics, atomic physics, solar system astronomy, stellar astronomy, and physics games. Physics: Elementary Mechanics tests and evaluates reasoning skills and knowledge of the principles of mechanics. After the presentation of simulated physical situations, students are challenged to find answers by using the least possible system-supplied help and information.

Released by Addison-Wesley Publishing Company, *Video Lessons for Conceptual Physics* deals with qualitative aspects of physics. The 12 videos introduce the concepts of Newton's first law, pressure, Newton's third law, relativity, atmospheric pressure, evaporation and boiling, condensation, waves and sounds, polarized light, electrostatics, and nuclear fusion.

Resources for Mathematics Courses

Of all academic areas, mathematics has attracted the most extensive development of computer and video resources. Increasingly, publishers of mathematics textbooks are creating videos and disks to accompany their books and providing these materials to adopting institutions at no cost. Addison-Wesley and Scott Foresman are major publishers of mathematics texts with such parallel materials.

Student ratings of the videos and computer programs that accompany an Addison-Wesley text, *Introductory Algebra*, by Keedy/Bittinger have been particularly high. A videotape featuring clear, concise explanations of the material is available for each textbook chapter. Disks aligned with the chapters are useful for both instruction and mastery self-testing. Similarly, Scott Foresman publishes a series of textbooks by Miller and Lial: *Understanding Elementary Algebra*, *Introductory Algebra*, and *Intermediate Algebra*. Corresponding videos and computer packages are furnished for these texts. Additionally, W. H. Freeman and Company provides tapes and disks for the textbook *For All Practical Purposes: Introduction to Contemporary Mathematics*.

Among the plentiful computer programs for entry-level mathematics, the following are recommended:

1. Algebra Problem Solver, a set of six disks covering signed numbers, polynomials, equations and inequalities, simple graphing, factoring algebraic expressions, and solving complex equations.
2. Math Lab, a beginning algebra series providing instruction on topics ranging from exponents and integers to quadratic formula.
3. Alge-Blaster, a program presenting algebraic problems in a gaming format.
4. The Calculus Toolkit, a program for graphing functions, generating tables of function values, investigating vector fields, graphing solutions of differential equations, evaluating definite integrals, and exploring limits, conic sections, and complex numbers.
5. Exploring Calculus, a comprehensive calculus program
6. Mathematical Modeling with Math CAD, a package addressing linear algebra, differential calculus, and integral

calculus; allows students to perform complex calculations and mathematical analysis swiftly and easily on a personal computer.
7. Master Grapher, a package containing powerful utilities for graphing functions, conics, polar equations, parametric equations, and surfaces.
8. 3-D Grapher, a program for graphing expressions in three dimensions.

VIDEOTAPES OF CLASSES

To supplement commercial materials, videotapes of selected classes can be produced and made available to students. The courses should be selected for their general curricular relevance and level of difficulty and might be concentrated in the areas of mathematics, chemistry, engineering, and statistics. Participating professors should be selected by departmental chairpersons based on their reputations as outstanding teachers of each course. The videotapes serve three basic purposes by allowing students to (a) review lectures for greater comprehension, (b) benefit from the teaching skills and viewpoints of additional, "master" professors, and (c) view lectures that were missed—physically or mentally!

Three distinct taping methods could be utilized. With all filming procedures, however, each course should be taped live and unrehearsed within regularly scheduled classes. Zoom lens and wireless microphones can be used for minimal disruption to classroom activities. Students can be employed to videotape in-progress classes utilizing portable video equipment. The flexibility of this method outweighs the technical advantages of the tapes produced by professional media experts and is less expensive.

Many universities have state-of-the-art videoclassrooms as training labs for Communication students and these classrooms could be used as production sites. Extraordinarily high-quality videos, thereby, are gathered.

Students generally respond very positively to the locally produced videotapes. In addition to use by students presently enrolled in the courses, the tapes can be used by entire classes when the instructor must be absent. The videos are also useful to students who wish to review particular topics in preparation for standardized exams and to reentering students who need to review entire content areas. Comparative data indicate that students prefer the campus-made videos to commercially-produced, and far more expensive, instructional resources.

TECHNOLOGICAL RESOURCES FOR TEACHERS

To assess and improve teaching effectiveness, the CTL should provide instructional support for faculty and teaching assistants. The use of technology is critical to three of the services for faculty: course evaluation, videotaping of the teacher, and publication of a teaching handbook.

The Teacher-Course Evaluation Process (TCEP) is a computerized system used to obtain detailed feedback from students about their perceptions of the instruction they have received. This information is gathered solely for the teacher's use in instructional improvement. The information is confidential and is not used for purposes of administrative decision making.

Developed and obtained from Northeastern University, the TCEP system consists of a 40-item questionnaire to be administered to students within the class period. The questionnaire surveys three general types of information: Part I is designed to solicit students' perceptions concerning the degree to which the teacher did a variety of things usually associated with effective teaching and high student achievement, i.e., "how often did a particular event occur." Part II probes more general information about the course and the value students assign to its quality, i.e., "how good was it." Part III obtains self-reports and demographic information about the students which can be used to help understand their responses. Administration of the instrument is untimed but classes can be expected to complete the assessment in approximately fifteen minutes.

The teacher also completes an instructors' version of the instrument which calls for self-rating on dimensions that parallel the student questionnaire

A computer-generated profile of the results and an Instructor's Guide to Interpreting the TCEP are provided by the CTL. The results can be paired with CTL resources to address teaching areas which the instructor may choose to modify.

Another effective way to evaluate and improve teaching is to be videotaped in the classroom. Upon request, the CTL can send a videotape technician to record a class period. Consultation with a CTL staff member or with another faculty member is encouraged during the viewing of the tape. If a teacher chooses to critique the performance alone, printed guidelines and checklists should be provided.

Additional support for faculty and graduate teaching assistants may be furnished through a teaching handbook that should focus upon pedagogical skills and issues, as well as summarizing insitituional academic-support services for students and faculty. Through the use of desktop publishing software and loose-leaf binding, handbooks can be updated, expanded, and reproduced frequently, conveniently, and inexpensively.

ADMINISTRATIVE USES OF TECHNOLOGY

Administratively, the CTL can benefit from standard word processing and desktop publishing software for functions ranging from simple correspondence, to extensive resource listings, to the production of flyers, brochures, reports, and course materials. Spreadsheet programs can be used to track resource utilization and evaluation statistics. Electronic calendars can also be used to schedule tutorial appointments, as well as to record staff appointments.

Mainframe connections provide access to student records for purposes of verifying tutors' grades, delivering academic consultation to students, and facilitating registration in study skills courses. Additionally, diagnostic tests can be scored and profiles generated through the use of computer technology.

ADVANTAGES SECURED THROUGH TECHNOLOGY

Administrative efficiency and enhancement are obvious but vitally important benefits of computer utilization. Outcomes of technology include increased speed, accuracy, and autonomy; decreased costs, file space, and staff; and improved procedures, products, and morale.

Most significant, however, are the advantages secured in the delivery of services to CTL clientele. Students can receive significant help from the technological resources of the independent study lab. Students' use of the instructional resources, in turn, allows CTL tutors and professional staff to dwell upon individual needs of student during counseling/advising appointments. Access to test results, grades, and records provides timely information and further individualization in personal contacts. Furthermore, the administrative time that is saved through computer usage, permits more time to be spent in the direct delivery of services to students and teachers.

FUTURE TRENDS

Undoubtedly, the future will be dominated by interactive/multimedia technologies that provide individualized access to compendiums of information. This technology is designed to permit users to interact at their own pace with computer-driven video images and sound. Among the most promising systems are Compact Disc Interactive (CD-I), Commodore Dynamic Total Vision (CDTV), and Digital Video Interactive (DVI).

At The University of Alabama, a DVI mathematics project is being developed through the collaborative efforts of The Center for Teaching and Learning and The Center for Communication and Educational Technology. The purpose of the project is to construct a comprehensive pre-calculus mathematics course delivered exclusively by interactive video-computer technology. By integrating video, computer-managed instruction, electronic assessment/feedback, and carefully developed learning exercises, it is anticipated that students will be able to succeed in pre-calculus mathematics with a minimum of personal assistance. The combination of striking video applications and the immediacy of computer instruction should result in an exciting product for students.

The program is founded on a hierarchy of skills and associated instructional programs designed to teach and reinforce concepts incrementally. Within this individualized process, understanding is checked frequently. Student responses are continuously evaluated and used to generate subsequent operations: feedback, remediation loops, additional explanation, or movement to successive concepts. Student records are stored in program-management files, allowing an assessment of each student's performance and an evaluation of the effectiveness of the DVI program.

DVI and other technologies will redefine the approach higher education takes to instruction and its support services. As a relatively new academic support service in higher education, learning centers can lead the way for the use of technology in the educational process. Small staffs are able to deliver effective programs to large numbers of students that enhance the students' classroom experiences. By providing enrichment and remediation through the use of technology the staff is better able to work with students on problems that require a "high-touch" approach.

Chapter 10

Career Planning and Placement Programs

Steven J. Miller

A 1991 survey conducted by the College Placement Council (CPC) of more than 1500 career center directors identified as their biggest challenge in the 1990's meeting increased demand for services with shrinking budgets. Survey respondents cited computerization as the key way to help meet that challenge.

Computerization of career services has come a long way since its beginnings in the 1970s. With the introduction of the personal computer (PC) in the mid-1980s and the ever increasing selection of career-related software, automating services has become more feasible than ever. Their low cost and ease of installation were also key factors in making the PC the right tool for automating career centers.

Most important of all, the PC opened up new possibilities for exchanging information between colleges and employers using compatible systems. For example, electronic transfer of candidate information from colleges to employers and employment literature and job vacancies from employers to colleges are two ways computers are helping to speed up the entire job placement process.

Eighty-nine percent of career centers use at least one PC, according to the 1991 CPC survey. In addition, many career centers use multiple workstations linked on a PC network to provide broader access for staff and students to enter and search for employment information.

As for software designed to automate career services, many career centers tap the large pool of commercial software packages. There are dozens of commercial programs available which have been designed to perform functions specifically for career center use such as: career guidance, resume development, job search tracking, candidate information transfer, employer searches, and interview scheduling.

In addition, some career centers develop or customize systems in-house to meet their unique requirements. Often students or external consultants are employed to develop these systems, although some centers with large or sophisticated systems employ a full-time computer support person to develop and maintain their system.

According to the 1991 CPC survey, most career centers use computers for word processing (84 percent). Other areas of computerization include mailing lists/labels (83 percent), correspondence generation (74 percent), statistical reports (66 percent), career guidance (55 percent), job vacancy listings (50 percent), employer databases (47 percent), student records (46 percent), candidate databases (44 percent), resume production (44 percent), career planning (39 percent), budgeting (39 percent), employer information/indexing (38 percent), scheduling employer visits (34 percent), library information/indexing (38 percent), alumni files (30 percent), and interview sign-up (22 percent).

COMPUTER-AIDED CAREER GUIDANCE

Historically, career guidance is one of the first areas to be computerized by career centers. Career guidance software helps career centers cope with a high demand from students without requiring a large amount of one-to-one counseling time.

About a half-dozen commercial major career guidance programs are available to career centers and students. Students interact with these programs by responding to a series of self-assessment exercises or true/false questions designed to evaluate the student's skills and interests and type of job and work environment desired. The program analyzes the responses and makes recommendations for careers to explore. Some programs also display job-specific information, including salary range, work duties, and educational requirements. Special modules designed for alumni in career transition are also available.

Educational Testing Service's SIGI Plus and American College Testing's Discover are the two most widely used computer-aided career guidance systems in college career centers.

In addition to offering programs to students who walk into the career center, some colleges use career guidance software in undergraduate credit-courses to educate students early in their college lives about career services and the job search process. The career portion of the course is typically part of a broader syllabus covering college level research or business communication. In addition to traditional students, working adults in continuing education use the programs in special seminars offered by career centers.

JOB SEARCH PREPARATION

A popular area where computer technology can be used to prepare students for the job search is resume development. These software programs identify students' strengths through a series of questions and then suggest an appropriate resume format. Typically, the programs include sample resumes and options for developing cover letters. Among the pioneering programs in this area is Resume Expert, which consists of two modules. Its student module contains a tutorial and guides the student in entering personal information, while the master module converts the student input into a resume. The Perfect Resume Computer Kit, based on Tom Jackson's best selling book *The Perfect Resume*, is another leading resume development program. The program helps users highlight strengths and key skills and create inventories of capabilities and accomplishments. Users may select from a variety of resumes and layouts, and the kit recommends the best format to use.

Of the different types of job search software, the job search skills group has been developed most recently for use in career planning and placement. This type of program tutors students in effective ways to conduct a job search. The Winning Approach to Interviewing, for instance, uses a question-and-answer format to lead students through a mock interview.

Career Navigator combines some of the self assessment features of career guidance systems with job search tracking and tutoring capabilities. The system tutors students in using job search techniques and helps them create a resume and a cover letter. Career Navigator also allows users to maintain a data base of 100 employer prospects and to generate mailings and track responses and contacts.

CANDIDATE INFORMATION TRANSFER SYSTEMS

Electronic transfer of candidate resume information from career centers to employers takes computer generation of student resumes a step further and probably has the greatest potential for speeding up the efficiency of the whole job placement process. These systems got their start in the mid-1980's and are just now beginning to realize their potential.

Some of the more sophisticated systems are designed to allow students to enter their resume information into preprogrammed floppy diskettes. The diskettes are read into the career center's student database. The career center sends a copy of their database to a commercial vendor for distribution to employers. This method of distribution allows career centers to transmit data to all employers that subscribe to the commercial system with one mailing, thus eliminating the logistical problem of having to do separate mailings to each employer.

The largest commercial system is kiNexus marketed by Information Kinetics of Chicago, Illinois and exclusively endorsed by the CPC. The system contains more than 100,000 candidates from some 1500 colleges. The kiNexus career center software is free to colleges. Employers are charged an annual subscription fee. Employers use a CD-ROM system to select candidates based on more than 40 search criteria.

Another candidate-information system, College Recruitment Database collects information from career centers on floppy diskette. Employer subscribers access the database through the Human Resources Information Network (HRIN) using a PC and computer modem. Other systems are College Placement Registry (CPR) available on the Dialog on-line service and Peterson's Connexion offered on CompuServe.

In an effort to further simplify information exchange, some colleges and employers use DASIS, a standard for electronic transfer of candidate data between college and employer computer systems. DASIS consists of a list of data elements (candidate name, address, major, GPA, etc.) and data element sizes and positions within the computer data file of candidate information. DASIS is endorsed by the CPC and the Midwest College Placement Association (MCPA).

Job Listing Services

Computerized job listing services facilitate the transfer of job listings from employers to career centers. The systems increase efficiency and cost savings by eliminating the need for participating employers to call each career center individually. JOBTRAK and JOBLINK are two popular services.

Employers place job listings with all or select groups of career centers participating in the network. Job listings that describe the company, its job opportunity, and the skills required for the position are transmitted to participating career centers' PCs using a modem/phone line linkup. The services are free to colleges. Employers are charged a fee based on the number of listings and targeted colleges.

EMPLOYER DATABASES

In the area of employer literature, some employers distribute software containing information on job opportunities within their organizations. FMC Corporation is one of the pioneers in this area. In 1990, they released a program consisting of two modules. The first module, FMC Story, describes the company's history, products, and business sites. FMC Career Opportunities, the second module, allows students to display descriptions of job opportunities at FMC according to three search criteria: individual interest in an industry sector, educational background, and geographical preference. After accessing job information, the user can also display information that describes the job site.

The Federal Occupational and Career Information System (FOCIS) is a software program available from the Federal government which students use to identify government career opportunities that match their abilities, interests, and preferences. FOCIS contains detailed information on more than 360 white-collar occupations within some 450 federal organizations.

Commercial databases containing large collections of employer profiles are also available. These systems generally do not contain information about career opportunities. However, they do provide a good source for other types of information that students can use to help prepare for an interview or to find employer prospects. For example, Dun's Million Dollar Disc compact disc-based system includes geographic, industry, and other profile information on more than 180,000 public and private companies that have a tangible net worth of $500,000 or more. Students can search and display company profiles based on various criteria, including location, company size, and industry type. Because of the relatively high cost and limited application of these systems, only a small number of career centers have implemented them. Academic and public libraries are the largest users of this type of system. Therefore, it may be more cost effective for career center staff to direct students to a local library where a system is available than to purchase such a system.

ANNUAL/STATISTICAL REPORTS

Statistical reports are often required from career centers by college administrators for tracking annual placement rates. For instance, a career center may need to track the percentages of students who were hired, who are still looking for a job, and who are planning to go on to graduate school. To make the task easier, many career centers enter placement data into a spreadsheet software program to track and manipulate the data. Current-year figures can be entered side by side with data from previous years to track percentage changes. The programs are also used to produce bar or pie charts to further illustrate the college's placement statistics.

Budgeting and accounting is another area where spreadsheet software programs are commonly used for producing cost reports for inclusion in the career center's annual report. Similar to statistical reporting of placement data, current-year and historical personnel and operating cost figures are entered into the spreadsheet program for tracking percent changes in cost from the previous year or for projecting next-year cost estimates.

Career centers are increasingly using desktop publishing to produce high quality annual reports. The ability to merge word processing text with spreadsheet graphics into a finished report make the programs an ideal tool. Desktop publishing can also be used to produce job vacancy newspapers, newsletters, posters, and flyers.

CAREER INFORMATION INDEXING

Career centers can easily use database management systems to allow students to use key words to search through various databases such as: employer literature, bibliographies of job-search publications, graduate school indexes, and career development material. Career centers can use database management indexing systems to more effectively manage the large amounts of information stored in their libraries. Using these systems, students are able to retrieve the specific information they need quickly. A large selection of PC database management software packages are available for building library indices.

INTERVIEW SCHEDULING AND SIGN-UP

Many career centers have developed computer systems which are capable of doing much of the administrative work of on-campus recruiting; including recruiter and interview scheduling and job vacancy listings. These systems range from the simple to the elaborate. One recruiting system may be on a personal computer for career center staff to enter data, such as recruiting schedules and the names of students who want to interview. It then runs a program that decides which students get which interviews and makes time and room assignments. Another system may be run on a campus-wide computer network and allow students to register for interviews from remote campus locations.

1st Place marketed by Academic Software allows career centers to maintain a student database and an employer database. A scheduling module, which compares student information to the employer database, is used to sign up students and compile interview schedules.

Once the interview schedules are set, the computer FAXes the information to employers for confirmation. FAXing can be done using a few keystrokes from any of several computer workstations linked on a PC network. The system also includes a computer-phone job line for students to call. The FAXing and job line are controlled by the PC using anolog-to-digital converter and digital-to-analog hardware.

VOICE MAIL AND TOUCH-TONE TELEPHONE SYSTEMS

In addition to traditional computer systems, career centers have been implementing automated telephone voice mail systems to address the problem of staffing constraints. These systems use a career center PC integrated with appropriate converter hardware and software to manage the phone calls.

Career centers set up job lines that enable students and alumni to call the career center to hear prerecorded job and events announcements. After calling the system, the student hears a menu of categories and can select one of interest using touch-tone phone codes.

One of the most innovative systems is the San Francisco State University (SFSU) award winning Voice Mail Job Line. Employers call the system using a 900 number to place job listings in their own voice. The call costs the employer $5, compared to $72 to place a job listing in a local newspaper. Since the system was introduced, job listings have increased fourfold from 120 to 500 listings per week.

Another feature of SFSU's voice mail system is a career advice network, which allows students to call and receive career advice from working professionals. After calling the system, students select one of nine career areas. The student then listens to messages from professionals willing to provide free career advice. The voice messages includes the advisor's job, career, education, and phone number.

Seventy-five professionals from the private sector, government, and university faculty participate on the network for a term of one year. The system receives 125-150 calls per month, mostly from sophomores and juniors selecting a career path.

In addition to offering job line capabilities, Total Scheduling System (TSS) marketed by Tres-D Corporation allows students to sign up for interviews from any touch-tone phone. The student enters their password and personal social security number. The system uses the information to retrieve the student's resume from the career center data base. The student enters the code for a particular employer and interview time slot. The computer checks the student's resume to see if the student meets the employer's criteria for the position. If not, the student is asked to select another employer.

Modular Voice Application Job Hotline developed by U.S. Telecom International (Joplin, MO) allows career centers to place phone calls to students with prerecorded announcements, such as: reminders regarding changes in a recruiter schedule, to contact students about openings on a schedule that may be filling a bit sluggishly, to remind students of workshops that they have signed up for, to ask students to contact the placement office with more information requested by an employer, and to solicit information for graduate surveys. Career center staff record announcements directly into the PC using a standard telephone. "Call lists" of student phone numbers are stored in the system and used to place phone calls automatically to selected groups of students. These lists, incidentally, can be transferred from existing student data bases, eliminating the need for staff to rekey data. In addition, multiple announcements can be maintained, each designated to go to a different group of students. The system will continue to call students until the call is answered and also maintains statistics on call activity.

The key benefit of touch-tone telephone systems is the enormous amount of time they save staff and students. Staff are saved hours of time required to place and answer phone calls. Students are saved having to make many personal visits to the career centers, which also reduces the traffic through the center. Staff are able to devote more quality time to counseling and managing projects that require personal attention.

ON-LINE NETWORK

Recently, an on-line network was established by a group of recruitment and placement professionals to provide a link between their offices. Called Career Network, the system provides electronic messaging and bulletin board options to allow colleges and employers to keep in touch regarding upcoming events, employer visits, and job fairs. An on-line job listing service allows employers to distribute specific job descriptions as well as detailed profiles to colleges throughout the Network.

VIDEO TECHNOLOGY

In addition to computer technology, most career centers use video to assist students with their job search.

Videotaping practice interviews is a tool many career center counselors use to help students develop interviewing skills. Students approach counselors asking for help in refining their interview skills, or counselors may approach students who have received negative evaluations from recruiters. Video is a powerful tool for helping students identify strengths and weaknesses in their interviewing sessions.

Some career center directors have found other ways to use video in the job search. One use is for secondary education majors presenting employers or school district recruiters with a three-to five-minute video of actual student teaching sessions during on-campus interviews. Another entails sending video interviews to foreign employers to demonstrate language proficiency. Many career centers also make interviewing and job search video tapes available for student viewing.

FUTURE TRENDS

With all the computerization that has already occurred, career planning and placement has surely entered the computer age. Now comes the process of fine-tuning and further implementation.

Development of new technologies along with expansion of existing technologies such as CD-ROM, on-line databases, and touch-tone telephone systems hold many possibilities. These technologies have the potential to vastly expand career centers' information management capacities. As more CD-ROM selections become available, for instance, career centers' will be able to replace large paper files of employment literature with a few CDs. Students would quickly search for the specific information they are looking for and generate a printout copy.

Similarly, the establishment of large on-line databases will provide students with a valuable resource for searching career and employment information. In addition, faster modem standards will make accessing on-line information more appealing.

With the introduction of video telephones on the horizon, use of touch-tone phone systems may become even more appealing. In addition to hearing job listings, students may see a video display of the company location and work environment.

These and other exciting possibilities will certainly keep career centers on the cutting edge and help staff provide fast, quality service to students. Without question, the best is yet to come.

REFERENCE

College Placement Council (1991). *Career Center Director Survey*: Unpublished Survey of the College Placement Council

Chapter 11

Student Life, Student Centers, and Student Activities

Edward G. Whipple
David L. Grady

Although computer technology, as it relates to higher education administrative and program functions, has been in existence on campuses for the last twenty-five years, it only has been in the last decade that student life administrators have taken advantage of it. There are two major reasons why many staff have not yet fully embraced computer technology in the student life area. First, few staff members have had any training or developed expertise in computer use; and second, only a few specialized software packages have, thus far, been developed for student life use. For the most part, staff members have had to adapt software to meet their own particular program needs. However, as computer technology advances, additional software programs designed specifically for student life applications should become available. The increased use of properly written software programs should not only save time for the student life staff member, but will also provide improved services for students. If a computer can do much of the paper work, the time a staff member can spend with students increases; thus increasing time for "high-touch" activities.

Staff members who work in student life must realize that it is not necessary to be a "computer wizard" to effectively utilize modern computer technology in their daily activities. It is no longer very difficult to create or customize a particular software program

148 *Technology in Student Affairs*

to meet the particular needs of a special administrative or program function. All that is required is a basic knowledge of computer systems and standarized word processing, desktop publishing, spreadsheet and database software programs.

This chapter focuses on how student affairs staff members in the student life area can best utilize modern computer and information technology to perform their tasks. Specific areas addressed are student union management, student activities (i.e. student organizations, fraternities and sororities, student government), office publications, student life research, student discipline, and new student and parent orientation programs.

Further, this chapter focuses on specific software which the authors have found to be beneficial in their daily work and the work of other student affairs professionals whom they have surveyed. There are, undoubtedly, other programs used at institutions not surveyed that may also be beneficial. Readers may, therefore, want to further investigate all available programs before purchasing any specific software program.

With the continuing improvement of technology, it is critical that student life staff keep abreast of new developments. Reading various computer magazines, keeping in communication with the institution's computer staff, talking with colleagues at other institutions, and visiting computer stores enable one to become knowledgeable about emerging software programs. In addition, as more software companies realize the higher education market, particularly as it pertains to student affairs functions, it is very likely that they will create and market additional programs which can be readily used by student affairs professionals to help support and complement their daily activities.

GENERAL STUDENT LIFE FUNCTIONS

The first software which many student life professionals have found beneficial pertains to database management. Marketed by the Ashton Tate Company, dBase software provides the opportunity for staff members to quickly develop and manage such information as student organization officer files, students attending an orientation session, and fraternity and sorority membership rosters. Other database software programs which perform the same functions include Microsoft Works for either an IBM or Macintosh computer and FileMaker Pro and 4th Dimenson for the Macintosh. All of these programs work on PC's and cost less than $300 each to purchase.

For financial management in the student life area, Lotus 1-2-3 and Microsoft Excel are top choices. Even though these programs are not designed specifically for student life financial management functions, student life staff members have found it easy to adapt the software to manage budgets in such areas as the student union and student organization administration.

The word processing software boom in the 1980s has also allowed all student life staff members, both professional and support, to better manage their own workloads. The mere opportunity to electronically save and retrieve information (i.e. letters and reports) frees time and provides for convenient organization. Microsoft Word and WordPerfect have become heavily utilized on college and university campuses throughout the country. Microsoft's Word for Windows, a 1989 package, integrates the windows functions with word processing capabilities to allow for graphic document creation and also allows IBM and IBM compatible computers to be operated with the same user-friendly icon logic used by Macintosh computers.

STUDENT CENTER MANAGEMENT

There are several excellent software programs available for student center facility management. The most popular are the Welber Room and Event Scheduling System and Integrated Management Systems' Room and Event Scheduling Software (RESS).

The Welber System is designed specifically for nonacademic and activities scheduling. Most institutions use it primarily for student center event and room scheduling. The system has specially designed screens and graphic displays. These screens provide for reservations entry, updates, space and equipment availability and inquiry. The software takes the user through a series of questions, thus providing a user-friendly atmosphere. In addition, the Welber System provides for two dozen types of management reports (both daily and long term). These reports include such items as scheduling, set-up, food service, equipment, security, and audio-visual equipment requirements. Statistical reports can also be run for a month, specific quarter or semester, or year. These summaries can provide an analysis of room usage by frequency, relative use by group or individual, attendance, or sum totals of income derived or waived for various sponsors or categories. The Welber System comes with a detailed manual. The multi-user version is available for computers using the Novell or Banyan network software.

Integrated Management Systems' Room and Event Scheduling Software (RESS) offers the possibility to design individual printouts and change the length of entry fields within the program. In addition, this software allows the user to schedule facilities, network, book food service, and calculate room and equipment charges. The RESS offers reports for a specific time period. These include operations, audio-visual equipment, tentative reservations, set reservations, cancellation listing, food, and lists of users, events, and buildings. Statistical analyses are available by organization and by facility. This software has the ability to interface with Lotus 1-2-3. Two RESS systems are available: entry level and enhanced. RESS can also be used with the Novell or Banyan network software.

Another excellent software system for student center managers is TicketMaker Professional from TicketStop in Bellevue, Washington. Designed for use on either an IBM compatible or Macintosh PC, this events management software can be purchased for under $500. It allows student center staff to design and print tickets to any sponsored event. The program automatically prints seat and row numbers, varying prices, ticket serial numbers, and allows messages to be printed on the reverse side. For auditing purposes, TicketMaker Professional keeps track of all ticket information, as well as the number of tickets sold.

STUDENT ACTIVITIES PROGRAMS

Student Organizations

At present, there is no commercially available software which is designed specifically for student organization management. As staff who work with student organizations know, keeping track of hundreds of student organizations, their officers, and registration status can be a formidable task. At The University of Texas-Austin, the campus activities area of The Office of the Dean of Students has created a database which tracks over 750 student organizations. The database is located on the university's mainframe computer and accessed through Macintosh computers in the campus activities office. For each organization event registered, information such as purpose, membership requirements, activities/interest, authorized representatives, addresses, advisor, date first registered, and last date registered is entered. With this information, a variety of reports can be produced. Some of these reports include lists of organizations, mailing labels, and demographic data for the authorized representatives.

To aid registered student organizations with financial management and provide for continuity between officers, a student organization bank was established at The University of Texas. At present, approximately 765 bank accounts are active which generate approximately 105 transactions (totaling $26,000) each day. All of these accounts and the transactions are now tracked with a custom program developed using 4th Dimension software on a Macintosh computer. Not only has the use of computer technology reduced errors and speeded up transaction processing time, but it has also allowed the campus activities office to reduce clerical staff members and hard copy file storage requirements.

Fraternities and Sororities

Fraternity and sorority rush is a major challenge at most colleges and universities that host Greek letter organizations. Computer technology has made rush much easier to administer. Many colleges and universities in the 1970s wrote rush programs on their mainframe computers to aid with rush. While some institutions still use systems on mainframes, most campuses today use personal computers (PCs). One of the most widely used rush programs is Compute-A-Rush which was developed and is marketed by D&D Digital Systems. This program requires a DOS-based computer (IBM or IBM compatible), printers, and an optical scanning machine. With this program, party invitations can be issued, parties can be scheduled, and bids can be matched. Chapters with compatible computers can issue invitations and bids using their own computer and then submit the computer disk to the institution's "rush headquarters" instead of filling in optical scan cards.

For chapter operations, Questa Corporation has developed a comprehensive program called the Questa, a membership management software package. This DOS-based program offers a financial function that allows a chapter to manage both accounts receivable and payable. In addition, separate data files for rushees, new members, active members, and alumni can be maintained. From these files, mailing labels, directories, and personalized correspondence can be produced.

For chapter grade computation, no specific software has been designed. Most institutions rely on their registrar's office to provide individual grade information, which is then computed. Some colleges and universities provide a coding system for members and pledges which is automatically handled on the mainframe, thus providing chapter grades with specific populations identified (i.e. active membership, pledges/associate members, and total chapter membership). For example, the University of Alabama-Tuscaloosa's Office of Student Life developed a grade report system which uses data from the Office of the Registrar and a Lotus 1-2-3 program to produce comprehensive Greek grade reports each semester.

Student Government

As with other student organization data management, there has been no specific software designed specifically for student governments. However, most student government offices now use PC based standard word processing, desktop publishing, database, and spreadsheet programs for their internal operations. A few student governments are also trying to find ways to use computers to assist them in running their elections more effeciently. For example, at The University of Texas at Austin, the Student Association, in conjunction with the Office of the Registrar, is utilizing the campus's mainframe computer program used for telephone registration, to also run its elections. To vote in student government elections, students enter their voter ID number (generated for each election) and their personal identification number at phone banks located across campus. Elections results are available within an hour after the polls close.

OFFICE PUBLICATIONS

With a personal computer, the proper word processing or desktop publishing software, and a good laser printer, the need for having publications typeset can be eliminated. Not only will doing publications this way save money by eliminating typesetting and the layout expenses, but it will also reduce the time needed to make changes and allow one to have greater input into the final product.

Simple publications such as handbooks, flyers, and some newsletters, can be produced using standard word processing software programs. Most word processing programs will allow a user to vary font size and type, to format the publication in columns, and to import graphics and tables. Most of these programs also contain a "WYSIWYG" (What You See Is What You Get) feature that allows the user to see the product on the screen as it will appear when printed. Three examples of word processing programs with these features are Microsoft Word, Word for Windows, and *WordPerfect*.

More sophisticated publications, such as multi-page brochures and newsletters, are better if produced on software developed specifically for desktop publishing. These programs provide more flexibility than word processing programs. In these programs, text can be wrapped around graphics and text can be rotated, rules and boxes can be included, color separations can be produced, and special effects can be created. Ten years ago, the cost of these types of programs was prohibitive for most student life offices. Today, however, they are much more affordable. For example, Aldus' *PageMaker*, the most commonly used PC based desktop publishing program, is now offered in an academic version for both IBM compatible and Macintosh computers in most campus computer stores for less than $300.

STUDENT LIFE RESEARCH

The old days of punching computer cards in order to do student life research have long passed. Today, the need for a mainframe computer to do statistical analyses has been eliminated. Statistical analyses can now be done in the comfort of the office or at home on a 4MB/80RAM personal computer costing less than $2,000. Also, some of the most popular statistical packages, once limited to mainframe usage, are now available in personal computer versions. These packages include SPSS and SYSTAT for Macintosh and IBM compatibles and PC SAS for IBM compatibles. Depending upon the software selected, basic statistics (i.e descriptive, crosstabs, t-tests, regressions) and advanced statistics (i.e. discriminant analysis; loglinear, logistic, and nonlinear regression; multivariate analysis) are possible. Data can be entered directly into the program or entered into a spreadsheet program, then imported into the statistical package. In addition to tabular output, these programs also have graphic capabilities. Once the data have been analyzed, the report can be completed using a word processing program. Many of these word processing programs have options that make the creation of tables easy. Charts can be imported directly from the statistical program or produced in a graphic-creating program and then imported.

Before purchasing a copy of one of these packages, check with the institution's computer center to see if the campus already has a multi-user licensing agreement with one or more of the software developers. If so, a complete version of the program can be "leased" for your computer at a cost significantly below that of the full purchase price.

STUDENT DISCIPLINE

Another student life area that can benefit from computerization is student discipline. The volume of cases, the need to store and retrieve archive information, and the need for end-of-the-year statistics are just a few reasons for using computer technology.

The most common use of computers in this area is for database purposes. For example, at the University of Texas-Austin and The University of Georgia, information on each discipline case is entered into a computer database. This information includes student demographics, violation, sanction, disposition, hearing officer, and date the case was received and closed. In addition, a comments field is available for information that does not fit in one of the predefined fields. Once the database is created, searches (by name and/or student identification number) for past disciplinary problems can be done quickly and accurately without having to search through files by hand. Annual statistics can also be produced easily by exporting the data to programs, such as CricketGraph or Harvard Graphics, that produce all types of graphs. The program used at The University of Texas was created using 4th Dimension software on a Macintosh computer, while The University of Georgia uses an IBM computer. To avoid unauthorized entry to the databases, passwords are utilized.

While the paperwork portion of the disciplinary process cannot be totally eliminated through computerization, computers can make the process much easier. Standard letters can be created and saved on a word processing program, then personalized as cases come in. When the same letter is to be sent to several students, the word processor's mail-merge feature can be utilized to save time. If letters vary by type of violation or sanction, paragraphs containing the appropriate language can be created, saved, and inserted in the individually created letters.

NEW STUDENT AND PARENT ORIENTATION PROGRAMS

Keeping track of hundreds of students and parents who attend one of several orientation sessions each summer can be a logistical nightmare. By using computers, this nightmare can be made more manageable.

A sophisticated computerized orientation registration system exists at the University of Texas at Austin. Each summer approximately 6,500 new students attend one of ten orientation sessions. Using the information stored in the admissions database, the Office of the Dean of Students sends each new student a personalized orientation registration form. When the form is returned, basic information (name, session assigned, money paid, housing, placement test reservation, etc.) is entered into the orientation computer program on the University's mainframe computer via a computer terminal in the Dean of Students Office. The day after the information is entered, the student receives a personalized confirmation letter along with additional orientation information. Each week, several printouts are produced for the orientation staff. These printouts include a master list, session lists, a cancel/no show list, and a list by special population (e.g., gender, ethnicity, students older than average). The orientation program also interfaces with the computer programs of other university departments. Through this interface, the housing department prints a master housing list, the testing center prints admission tickets for placement tests, and the registrar's office prints "Registration Information Sheets" for use during telephone registration. In addition, the computer prints a name tag for each participant to wear during the orientation sessions.

At The University of Alabama-Tuscaloosa, computers are also

used to help staff in the Office of Student Life with Parents' Orientation. After reservation forms are received, the parents' names are entered into a database on a word processing program. Using the mail-merge feature of this program, the parents are sent a personalized confirmation letter and master lists and name tags are printed. The evaluation of the Parents' Program is also compiled by use of a computer. On opscan cards, parents "bubble" in answers to questions about their impressions of their orientation program. This information is then scanned into a personal computer using an optical scanning machine and the results are printed. Using this method, evaluation results are available the same day each orientation session ends. Staff members are thus able to make changes, if necessary, in subsequent orientation sessions and receive instant feedback as to whether the changes resulted in higher parent ratings. It is, therefore, no longer necessary to "wait until next year" to try to improve program effectiveness.

DESIGNING ADDITIONAL SOFTWARE

At this time, although there has not be a proliferation of software designed specifically for all student life administrative and program functions, most institutions have designed their own or customized commerically available software to best meet the needs of their program's goals and the college or university's students. The student center management area, Greek affairs administration, and to a degree, student life research, have the most software available, while other student life functions must rely on institution designed programs or customization of standard PC based word processing, database, desktop publishing, and spreadsheet software.

Where, then, does a staff member turn, who has to develop or customize a software program. Based on our experience, the following recommendations are offered:

1. To get the program written there are several options:
    - Hire computer science majors or professors to do the work, or
    - Identify class projects (computer science, computer honors programs) to assist with the development of the program, or
    - Seek help from computer literate staff in the office, or

- Identify data processing professionals on campus, or
- Hire outside programmers to develop the program.
2. Before designing any customized program be sure of the following before beginning:
    - Ensure that all the individuals who will utilize the program have input into the concept of the program. After this process, an agreement should be reached among the staff not to change the idea. Remember, changes cost money and time!
    - Ensure that the programmer has a clear idea of the area where the program will be used and what the final product should accomplish. It is better to spend money initially on concepts and design than to have to make costly changes later.
    - Ensure that the programming agreement provides for adequate technical and operational documentation.
    - Ensure that the contract contains time for training on the product and time for "debugging" after the program is in operation.
    - Ensure that the program is compatible with other systems that related offices might use.
    - Ensure thinking about the future! The program must be flexible enough for future changes. It is better that the program has features that are not currently used than to have a program that does not do enough.

FUTURE TRENDS

So, what does the future hold for the expanded use of computer and information technology in the student life area? First, one can undoubtedly expect an increase in the types of software which will become available for student life use. As more staff become computer literate, the demand will increase for programs designed to meet specific administrative and program needs. With this increased demand should come new software applications to meet it.

Several new uses of communication and information technology most likely will also occur. For example, the same technology used for telephone registration can also be used to disseminate a variety of other information quickly, efficiently, and confidentially to student callers. One such system, called ASKUS, is already in operation at the University of South Carolina. By using a touch-tone phone, members of the university community can call a predetermined number to get information on a variety of topics. This information ranges from student center events to athletic schedules, from information on student services, to information on health related issues such as AIDS and stress. Also by using voice-mail telephone technology, students at the University of Texas at Austin and The University of Alabama - Tuscaloosa can now call up a "voice" computer program to find out their course grades prior to receiving the printed grade report in the mail at the end of the semester.

In another development, to identify special populations, the Office of the Dean of Students at The University of Texas at Austin commissioned an outside programmer to create a generic student query database for use in several different programming areas within the office. The program, written using 4th Dimension software on a Macintosh computer, allows select student records to be imported from the university's mainframe computer. Using these records, the office can accumulate information on student participation in office sponsored programs and events (including time and dates) and staff contacts with students (meetings, phone calls, and correspondence). In addition, staff time and correspondence can be tracked. Currently, the program is being used in the retention services area. For example, by using the student data, the effectiveness of programs sponsored by the office can be evaluated by comparing the retention of those minority students who take advantage of these programs to those who do not. Future plans call for this program to be used to track retention of students with disabilities and to collect data for student activities transcripts.

Finally, as budget difficulties necessitate personnel reductions, the reliance on computers to do much of the work previously done by staff, will certainly increase in the future. It is, therefore, critical that student life staff members take the opportunity to learn as much as possible about computers and modern information technology in order to more fully utilize their potential in the student life area. What better place to learn than the campus setting? By taking advantage of classes available to staff and the expertise of other members of the campus community, student life staff members can more readily develop software programs designed to meet their various administrative, program, and student needs. Through the increased use of technology, student life professionals should be able to devote more of their time to "high-touch" activities with individual students and student groups.

Chapter 12

Recreational Sports and Wellness Programs

Craig Ross

Recreational sports and wellness programs are an integral part of campus life and are experiencing a period of rapid growth on college campuses across the country. Participation in sport for fun and fitness is a very popular leisure-time pursuit for students, faculty and staff. As a service component of the university's mission, recreational programs strive to meet the sport and fitness needs and interests of the university community by providing diverse opportunities where health and wellness goals may be cultivated and satisfied during leisure time.

Recreational sports involves a broad spectrum of sports programming encompassing four general program areas: (1) informal sports, designed to make university sport facilities available for casual, self-directed participation to coincide with the individual's sport and fitness interests and time schedules; (2) fitness/wellness, which promotes fitness and well-being through various fitness sessions designed to enhance cardiorespiratory endurance, muscle endurance, muscle strength and flexibility; (3) intramural sports programming ranging from highly organized and competitive tournaments to casual programs designed entirely for the sake of fun and enjoyment with minimum emphasis on winning; (4) and club sports, groups that organize because participants share a common interest in a sport while providing the benefit of member involvement in organizing and implementing club functions.

How successful recreational sports professionals are in providing quality programs to their student, faculty and staff constituents depends to a large degree on the staff's management and organizational skills. Therefore, technological advances in the past few years offer great potential and promise for recreational sports and wellness programming.

The age of computerized recreational sports operations is rapidly becoming a reality. With the price of computer hardware and software continuing to decrease, it is now feasible for every office to have access to a system. The recreational sports professional can no longer ignore the benefits of this powerful management tool.

Generally, the computer applications in the recreational sports area can be broken down into two broad categories: (1) commercially available software which has been custom designed by software companies for specific use in a program area (i.e. tournament scheduling and fitness management programs), and (2) special applications which can be designed using standard personal computer software programs (i.e., word processing, spreadsheet, database and desktop publishing).

This chapter will first discuss specialized software which is commercially available for the recreational sports professional and then discuss applications of standard personal computer software specific to recreational sports programming.

SPECIALIZED SOFTWARE

Tournament Scheduling

One of the greatest computer needs expressed by recreational sports staffs is tournament scheduling software. There are a number of software scheduling programs currently on the market ranging in price from $80 to $3,000. They include, but are not limited to, the following: Auto Scheduler (about $250), League Scheduling (about $1,000), League Scheduling System (about $3,000), League Scheduler Plus (about $150), The Robin Tamer (about $185), Sports Data System, Sports Log (about $1,000), Sports Scheduler (about $100), 20,000 Leagues (about $100), and Tournament Director (about $200). The wide range of prices reflects the diversity and complexity of the features of each software package, and the number of teams which can be scheduled.

When considering purchasing a tournament scheduling program, there are a number of features that should be considered. However, what is best for each particular organization will depend to a large degree on the number of teams entering tournaments, the tournament formats chosen, existing computer hardware, and budget limitations of the department. This author recommends that the following program features be studied before purchasing any scheduling software:

1. The program should check for scheduling overlaps as well as allow for re-scheduling of game dates due to team conflicts, weather cancellations and other programming concerns.
2. The program should be able to schedule for round robin, double round robin, single elimination and double elimination meets and the various challenge tournament formats. With each of these formats, the ability to seed teams and assign handicap scores is important.
3. Depending on the tournament needs, make sure the program can handle the upper limits in terms of teams, leagues, divisions and the number of different facility sites that could be used.
4. A valuable feature of a computerized system is that it allows for the creation of master schedule reports that can be viewed on-screen or on a printed report for the entire master tournament schedule in advance for a particular date, facility, league or team. Being able to view these reports lends great flexibility to the staff for rescheduling games, preparing sport facilities, and monitoring the number and the skill level of game officials, supervisors and other employees.
5. It is very important that the staff have the capability of deciding whether the selection of teams and the creation of both leagues and divisions will be established through an automatic random selection by the computer, or by a set of staff-defined criteria.
6. Because a computerized system can create detailed reports that are specific to the sports program, it is probably the

most important component of the scheduling program. The design and actual print-outs of reports and team schedules should be flexible enough and resemble those that were being used when scheduling was done manually. Game times should be printed in standard am/pm format rather than military time in order to avoid confusion among students not familiar with military time. Dates should also include the day of the week and facility sites should be represented by the name of the facility rather than a code. Printing of individual game scoresheets, including eligible players, is also very beneficial. Facility schedules and reports by specific sites, by court and field and by either a range of dates, times, divisions, or leagues can all be useful when managing sport tournaments.

7. The program should provide a means of generating and maintaining team listings and rosters by sport, division, and leagues as well as an alphabetical phone list with addresses of team captains for mail-merging of form letters.

Other features, while not essential, but which can be very helpful to the staff include: optical scanning for mass data entry of team information, league standings with won-loss records for the various leagues, point tracking for team and individual participation and performance, employee scheduling of officials and supervisors based on a pre-determined rating scale for each game, and sportsmanship ratings of teams and individuals throughout the season and year.

If a system is wanted that can perform all of the above features, the League Scheduling System (INFO 2000, approximately $3,000) is recommended. While the most expensive, it will do everything listed above plus more. Another high-end system that is very good is League Scheduling (Programmed for Success, Inc., about $1000). If all that is needed is a program to schedule tournament games, the 20,000 Leagues (Sports Stats, Inc., about $100) would be a very good choice.

An effective computerized sport scheduling system can save many hours of routine yet tedious work. A computerized scheduling program can help to eliminate the human mistakes that are inevitable with scheduling. It has enabled many departments to do more complete and accurate scheduling in much less time than they previously spent with their manual system.

FITNESS AND WELLNESS PROGRAMS

As the fitness boom accelerates, it is quite evident that computer technology has also spread into what was once considered weightroom dungeons. Fitness software is becoming more and more sophisticated with customized programs for practically every aspect of fitness conditioning and assessment.

Not only are the machines and management techniques becoming more sophisticated but so are the participants. And as they get more involved and accustomed to computer advances in everyday living, they are also expecting the same in their fitness work out. Participants who use the local health club or YMCA, which has several computerized services, also expect the same from university campus facilities. In order to attract and retain these participants, university recreational sports professionals must keep pace with technology.

Research has also shown that a key to the success of any fitness and wellness program is participant motivation and retention. For participants to adhere to a fitness program requires a sense of satisfaction which comes from constant positive feedback highlighting achievement and progress to date. Because feedback is so critical, computers are becoming excellent tools for motivating participants by providing instant comparison reports of personal goals and accomplishment.

Among the most popular fitness software packages are those that provide fitness assessment or a screening tool to measure one's progress. These assessment software programs will measure and record body composition, flexibility, abdominal strength, upper body strength, body fat and aerobic capacity. After the results have been analyzed, an individual, customized week-by-week exercise program or prescription print-out can be given to each participant.

Another popular program is a daily exercise log. Exercise logging allows individuals to record their daily workout figures immediately following the exercise workout. For example, E-Log (Institute for Aerobics Research, about $300) designed by Dr. Kenneth Cooper, is a microcomputer based software program that calculates calories and aerobic points for over 30 activities. E-Log can perform daily, weekly, and monthly monitoring of different types of workouts, workout pace, aerobic conditioning levels, heart rate, blood pressure, weight body measurements, and other physical data. Some programs will also analyze eating habits or diet and suggest modifications, if needed. Users can receive a daily, weekly or monthly "report card" to show their progress to that point. These reports truly provide incentives, feedback, and reinforcement motivation to the participant and help keep participants coming back to the facility.

Some of examples of software programs for fitness/wellness related needs include the following:

- Fitness Assessment: HealthCheck;
- Exercise prescription: Alternate Computer's Computer Fitness Evaluation and Exercise Prescription;
- Computerized exercise tracking log: JennWare's FICIS;
- Exercise training: Body Logic's Training System;
- Body composition: MacClub's Body Comp;
- Fitness/lifestyle profile: HMC Version 5.0;
- Personalized exercise program for fitness equipment: MacClub's Fitness Trainer;
- Turnkey fitness management systems that include membership tracking, financial management reports; and other features are: ATA's Club Computer System, MacClub's Control, and Computer Outfitter's Club, Management Plus.

While several software packages offer a low cost alternative to an educated fitness instructor, there is no adequate substitute for a well trained fitness professional. However, proper software can be a way of providing support to the professional in making decisions about a participant's fitness program. If used properly, computers can be a means to providing an overall cost-effective and efficient fitness program as well as a tremendous motivational tool by its ability to create and maintain participant awareness of the benefits of fitness and wellness activities.

INSTRUCTIONAL SPORTS PROGRAMS

In order to have an enjoyable experience in any recreational sport, it is important that the participant develop the interest, basic knowledge, and fundamental skills associated with that sport. The manner in which instruction takes place depends to a large degree on the need and purpose of the participant, as well as the setting that it takes place. The recreational approach to instructional sports is much more informal and "fun" than the academic classroom but, nevertheless focuses on the learning process and improving the student's skills and knowledge of the sport.

With the recent advances in technology and the low cost of personal computers, there has been a significant impact on the instructional aids that are available for an instructor or coach to use. These aids include such items as audio-visual equipment, i.e. video cassette recorders, overhead projection display panels, cassette recorders, and special computerized equipment for the various sports, to name just a few.

The now obsolete 16 mm film/projector has been replaced with the VHS videotape which is both cheaper to purchase and is available for viewing immediately after being taken. Using a video tape recorder and a personal computer, an instructor can now provide immediate feedback by "breaking-down" in slow motion a student's swing (tennis, golf, etc.) into specific segments allowing for an analysis and critique of incorrect movement as well as visually showing proper techniques and form. Videotaping, used in this manner, can serve as a very tangible and positive form of motivation. Commercially available videotapes such as Sybervision's golf, tennis, and racquet ball series can also be used to enhance learning by using a "how-to" approach. With these tapes, the student watches and is instructed in the proper techniques for that particular sport.

Advances in technology have also provided for specialized equipment for teaching sports such as golf and tennis. In golf, for example, a student can "hit" into a video screen image of a famous golf course hole and immediately be given the distance, trajectory and accuracy of the ball based on the spin of the ball detected by sensors within the screen.

While high technology will never be a replacement or substitute for instruction, it is a very valuable resource and supplement to the education process. These aids are excellent devices that can be used to motivate and encourage students and can make the learning process much more interesting and fun for both the participant and instructor.

CUSTOMIZED USE OF STANDARD PC SOFTWARE

Equipment Inventory

Campus recreational sports programs are no different than any other business in terms of organizing and tracking inventory lists of sports equipment, facility equipment, and the various pieces of office furniture and machinery. Because of the large number of part-time employees and the amount of equipment needed to support a recreational sports program, it is important that the staff maintain equipment inventory lists that are accurate and current to ensure accountability and inventory control. The type of equipment inventory system that is developed and implemented depends primarily upon the needs of the department.

Since university recreational sports programs are different on every campus, there really is not one particular commercial software package that is specific enough for every institution. However, an equipment inventory system, using a database management program is very easy to develop. Key components should include: (1) modules that would link the actual equipment database, vendor database, staff database, and facility location database together; (2) easy-to-update and modify any item; (3) an automatic tag numbering system so each piece of equipment can be given a unique tag number for identification purposes; and (4) reporting capabilities that produce the following reports: master inventory of all items by tag number and an alphabetical listing of items, inventory summary by grouping of items, inventory summary by vendor, inventory report by vendor and purchase price, inventory report by facility location, and inventory by lost, stolen or discarded equipment.

When developing and implementing a computerized inventory system, there are several points that should be taken into consideration. Make a list of equipment items that have a life expectancy of over two years which may include items such as basketballs, soccer balls, softball bases, table tennis tables, volleyball nets and poles, and so forth. Softballs, clipboards, pens, table tennis balls, and other expendable supplies would not be appropriate to include in this inventory list. Their frequent loss or damage would require constant updating of the computer inventory that would not be cost-efficient.

Maintain staff accountability for the equipment for which they are responsible. This accountability can be emphasized by distributing an itemized location report to each staff member for verification purposes on a monthly basis.

A tag numbering system for each item which uses a metal tag with the departments' name imprint and computerized equipment item number on each tag is also very helpful. This will assist in locating lost or stolen equipment.

For larger programs with significant amounts of equipment, developing a computerized equipment maintenance program will be cost effective in the long run. A typical computerized maintenance system consists of a maintenance service history, budget planner, cost/use analysis, and maintenance due schedules.

Interest Surveys

Computer technology can be a valuable staff resource in determining participant interest levels for the various sport programs that are offered. Targeting a promotional campaign to specific participants whom are known to be interested in the programs well in advance of actual starting dates is a key to the success of any program and increases the campaign's effectiveness. A computerized interest survey questionnaire completed by participants at the beginning of the academic year or semester provides the staff with an instant source of individual names and corollary interest in particular sports. The survey should include: a personal data section including housing unit, affiliation, address, phone and class status; leadership positions that are available; and all of the sport offerings that are currently being offered as well as sports that could possibly be offered if facility space were available.

After the survey is developed, it could be distributed in a number of ways, including the use of a registration booth, residence hall orientation, freshman orientation, newspaper clip and mail, office counter, club sport meetings, team captain's meetings, unit manager meetings, and/or employee meetings.

Once the data is gathered and entered into the computer, the staff may query specific information that will be useful in program delivery. Typical uses would be to find possible teammates for major team sports, partners for individual sports, as well as provide a mailing list of potential participants through direct mailings. When developing a new event or preparing to begin an existing event, contact participants who have expressed an interest in that particular sport. For example, four weeks prior to the deadline for an intramural basketball deadline, search the database for individuals who have indicated an interest in basketball on the survey form. Once this is completed, print the list of the individual names on mailing labels, place a label on an information flyer/entry form and deliver via campus mail. Using this process provides an opportunity to promote the upcoming programs to those who have expressed a genuine interest.

The computer gives the staff the capability to market the various sport and wellness programs to individuals that are known to be "interested" participants. The system saves time and financial resources as well as allowing staff members to personalize their marketing approach. By knowing in advance who the market is, one is sure to see an increase in participation figures as well as providing a valuable service to the students, faculty and staff on campus.

Facility Scheduling

Successful scheduling of recreational facilities is dependent upon a number of factors that are unique to each student affairs department. Every organization will have specific needs and program interests that are specific to their particular situation. Some departments will be solely responsible for scheduling recreation facilities that serve the entire student body, faculty, and staff while others will share facilities between athletics and recreation and will need to prioritize building needs using preferred and agreed upon scheduling time blocks. In this scenario, a mutual understanding, communication, and cooperative spirit between departments are a must if the scheduling and management processes are to be effective.

With this in mind, the computer can be a very valuable aid in assisting with the assignment of facility reservations for all sport programming areas. Block schedules and reservations for the facilities can be computed for daily, weekly, seasonal or yearly time spans. With a computerized facility scheduling program, it allows the staff to: (1) develop a block schedule months in advance; (2) reserve specific times for individual program areas within each block; (3) eliminate double "bookings" for facilities; (4) issue reservation confirmation forms to each user; (5) develop reports that include master schedules by semester or year, daily schedules of reservations including contact names and any special set-up needs and daily facility/room schedules for posting at the site; (6) effectively monitor a facility counseling checklist for each user group; and (7) cancel and reschedule a facility reservation at a moments notice.

Much of the detail work associated with routine facility scheduling is ideally suited for a computerized system. It is a system that reduces the bookkeeping chores for the staff, while at the same time, increases their ability to provide on-site facility management.

Accident Reporting

Because of the very nature of sports and the risks involved with the various programs, accidents are going to occur. The responsibility of the sport programmer, is to minimize the number of these occurrences through proper facility maintenance and to take every precaution possible. Computers have a valuable role in assisting staff in this decision-making process. Data that is gathered for each accident is vital in providing staff with an overall view of how safe the actual event is. Statistical cross-tabulation analysis of this data provides a correlation between various factors involved and enables the staff to develop possible causes for the accidents and necessary measures to reduce their frequency. Typical factors include: (1) actual playing field/court and the frequency of accidents/injuries occurring at each site; (2) types of injuries by sport; (3) demographic background of each individual injured including gender, age, and other factors; and (4) the number of accidents in a sport by the type of accident.

By having this type of information immediately available either in numerical or graphic form, the staff can make educated decisions on why accidents might be occurring and what can be done to prevent them in the future.

Statistical Applications

As with any program, event statistics provide valuable information to the recreational sports staff in student affairs. Sport programs in particular require a significant amount of time for calculation of the volume of information that pertains to each program offered. Some of the statistics that the staff should review would include: (1) the actual number of entries or enrollment figures in comparison with previous years' totals; (2) the number of times a participant engages in a sport activity (this is useful for comparison purposes as well as a predictor for future growth patterns); (3) the number and percentage of games scheduled, forfeited, and actually played in comparison to the previous years' statistics, thereby allowing the staff to identify potential factors affecting participation; (4) facility usage levels revealing changing use patterns and interest levels among participants; and (5) the number of intramural sport protests, disciplinary action, and accident reports (this information may give an indication of how well the game officials are controlling the game environment).

Another important role for using the computer in statistical analysis is program evaluation reports and demographic statistics. Assessing how effective each of the programs are in terms of participant satisfaction and whether the stated goals and objectives were achieved are very important. The computer can play a vital role in data collection and interpretation of these results.

The staff may wish to solicit responses on demographic information or opinions and attitudes participants might have about the program. The usefulness of the data collected lies in being able to fully appreciate, interpret, and make necessary recommendations for improvement. Typical software packages provide a large number of options to analyze data. Most provide descriptive statistics which include sum, mean, minimum, and maximum calculations as well as frequencies and cross-tabulation tables. Being able to evaluate each program with valid information based on participants unit of participation, class standing, age, gender, and other factors allows the staff to constantly improve the delivery of each program event. Because of the growth of the programs over the past few years, an effective evaluation process will only be accomplished through the use of sophisticated computer systems.

In terms of financial analysis, recreational sport programs are not unique from any other business. As budgets are being reduced and scrutinized even more than in previous years, the computer is becoming an essential tool for administrators to perform year-to-date cost analysis and income target analysis, as well as forecasting budget trends.

Miscellaneous Applications

There are a variety of other applications of customized standard microcomputer software which can be helpful in recreational sports and wellness. For example, computers can also be used for: recording event registration fees and charges, including demographic information, financial records and receipts, mailing lists, billing statements, enrollment rosters and waiting lists; performing personnel scheduling and assignments of hourly wages for game officials, activity supervisors, lifeguards, and other personnel for each facility site and program area; completing word processing tasks such as producing sport rules and regulations, manager manuals, form letters for forfeits, rescheduled game notices, press releases, annual reports, agendas, and announcements.

Computers can also assist in calculating up-to-date intramural sport point standings by units of participation and by individual sports as well as developing publicity and promotional informational material such as sport flyers, newspaper articles ads, and monthly activity calendars. Project management tracking software assists the staff by helping to visualize each sporting event or project through graphically illustrated PERT and GANTT charts. Employee database programs maintain and track hourly wage employee rates, positions of employment held, start dates and salary, wage and frequency of raises, and other personnel related information.

In terms of fiscal control, computers can assist with budget management by monitoring and maintaining supplies and equipment purchases, payroll entry and reports, income reports, accounts payable and account receivables entries, and similiar functions.

Other miscellaneous software applications that are beneficial for the recreational sport professional can include: staff organizational charts, needs assessments, cost projections for maintenance of sport facilities, personal desk organizers, golf handicapping, voice mail, and electronic bulletin boards. This is only a small sample of the numerous applications that are pertinent and can be adopted for recreational sports. How effective a computer is really depends on each specific setting and the staff involved.

SUMMARY

Recreational sports and wellness programs will continue to grow in response to participants' desires, needs and interests. The use of the technology in everyday programming and administration is giving student affairs administrators opportunities to provide, improve, and expand recreational sports programs in ways that were not possible ten years ago. However, it is important to remember that as technology plays a greater role in sport management, it will not build physical fitness nor will it automatically make a department operate the way it should. While it can provide the necessary incentives and a foundation to build upon, success still rests with the individual and staff.

The expanding use of high technology promises many benefits to both users and professional staff alike. It is becoming very apparent that as technology increases, so too will program effectiveness, efficiency, and financial savings. This, in turn, will increase the time professional staff members will have to advise and teach students about the benefits of health, wellness and life-long fitness programs.

Chapter 13

Student Health Centers

Thomas S. Strong
William Mark Whitson

Student health centers across the nation began embracing computer technology and other high tech equipment in the administration of their programs and services with the availability of the personal computer in the early 1980s. Prior to that time, only a few student health centers used the college's mainframe computer for limited administrative functions such as student billing.

This chapter discusses hardware and software applications, operating systems, and the future of automation in patient care in today's modern student health center. It also offers the results of a national survey of selected student health centers showing the current extent of utilization of computer technology in the administration of student health programs.

High-tech instruments are used to diagnose and treat illnesses, to run tests, and perform non-invasive surgeries. Indeed, the future of medicine lies in its ability to harness and use effectively the technology that is advancing so rapidly. It is necessary therefore, to point out that this chapter will limit its discussion of the high-tech applications to only the administrative functions in a student health center. These applications include record keeping, pharmacy programs, business functions, and medical clinic applications.

Such programs provide for more informed decisions. Medical

records have the ability to track a patient's medical history and review that history electronically as well as via the traditional written medical chart. Business managers can automatically bill insurance companies and private patients. Accounts receivable balances can be updated and maintained as a result of daily work flow and not as an addition to the work load. Physicians can track trends in diagnosis and maintain specialty board certifications by utilizing statistical data. School policy requirements for immunizations can be tracked by admissions and records offices.

In February of 1991, the Russell Student Health Center at the University of Alabama conducted a national survey of thirty comprehensive student health centers. Usable responses were received from eighteen universities where the respective size ranged from 7,000 to 49,000 students. The survey was done to measure the extent to which computer automation and other technology is currently being applied in university student health centers.

The survey found that typically the larger the student population (and generally the more comprehensive the student health center), the greater was the use of information and computer technology. Although most systems presently are personal computer (PC) based, the general trend is toward multi-user, multi-tasking minicomputer based systems. As staff members gain experience, confidence and dependence on an automated computer system, the need to share information, and thus the need to increase computing power, grows proportionately.

TECHNOLOGICAL ADVANCES

The greatest stride in technology for student health center applications has been in the advance of lower cost computer hardware. This has led to two results; first, powerful minicomputer systems capable of handling the requirements of the large databases and workloads common to student health centers are now widely available; second, with each technological advance, prices of the computer hardware suitable for use in student health centers has come within the reach of more student health center budgets.

With the introduction of personal computers in the early 1980s, the general population became more computer literate and dependent. As demand for application software grew, the demand for more powerful hardware also grew. Users wanted to share database in-

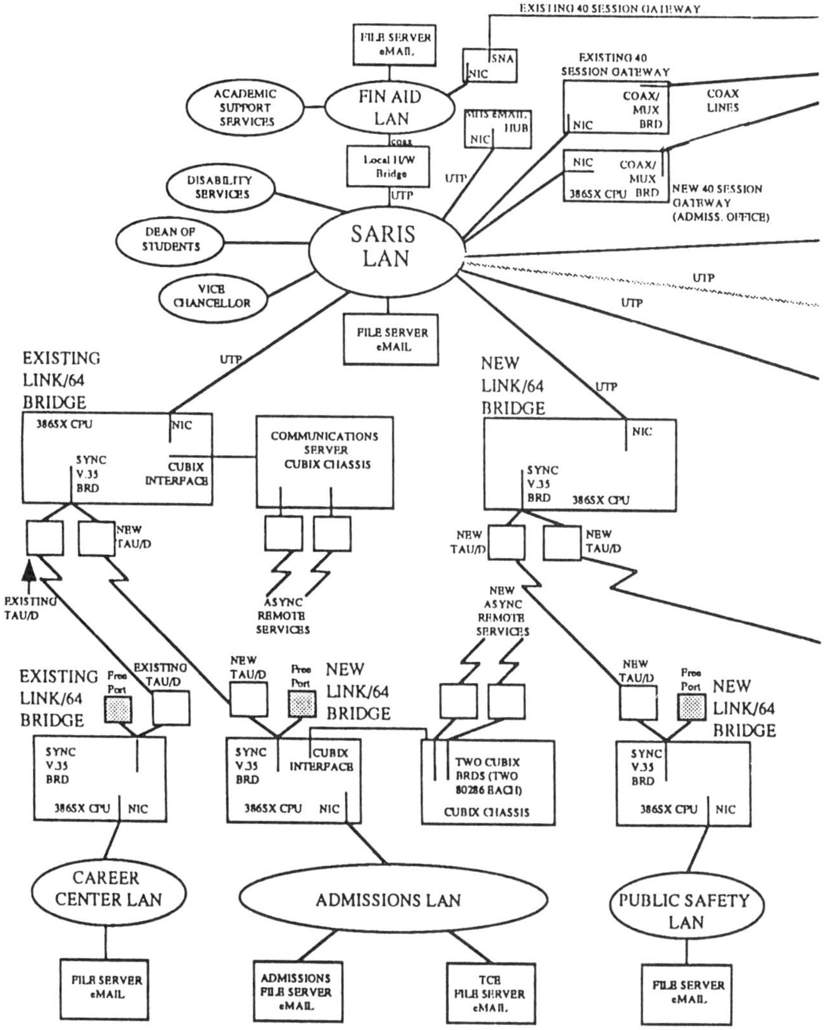

EXISTING 40 SESSION GATEWAY
FILE SERVER eMAIL
SNA
NIC
ACADEMIC SUPPORT SERVICES
FIN AID LAN
EXISTING 40 SESSION GATEWAY
COAX/ MUX BRD
NIC
COAX LINES
HUB
NIC
coax
Local H/W Bridge
UTP
NIC
COAX/ MUX BRD
386SX CPU
NEW 40 SESSION GATEWAY (ADMISS. OFFICE)
DISABILITY SERVICES
DEAN OF STUDENTS
SARIS LAN
VICE CHANCELLOR
UTP
UTP
FILE SERVER eMAIL
EXISTING LINK/64 BRIDGE
UTP
NEW LINK/64 BRIDGE
UTP
386SX CPU
NIC
SYNC V.35 BRD
CUBIX INTERFACE
COMMUNICATIONS SERVER CUBIX CHASSIS
NIC
SYNC V.35 BRD
386SX CPU
NEW TAU/D
EXISTING TAU/D
ASYNC REMOTE SERVICES
NEW TAU/D
NEW TAU/D
NEW ASYNC REMOTE SERVICES
EXISTING LINK/64 BRIDGE
Free Port
EXISTING TAU/D
NEW TAU/D
Free Port
NEW LINK/64 BRIDGE
NEW TAU/D
Free Port
NEW LINK/64 BRIDGE
SYNC V.35 BRD
386SX CPU
NIC
SYNC V.35 BRD
CUBIX INTERFACE
386SX CPU
NIC
TWO CUBIX BRDS (TWO 80286 EACH)
CUBIX CHASSIS
SYNC V.35 BRD
386SX CPU
NIC
CAREER CENTER LAN
ADMISSIONS LAN
PUBLIC SAFETY LAN
FILE SERVER eMAIL
ADMISSIONS FILE SERVER eMAIL
TCE FILE SERVER eMAIL
FILE SERVER eMAIL

formation and share hardware. This has led to growth in the area of minicomputer markets and networking of personal computer based systems. A minicomputer typically supports 16 - 32 users within the same environment or on the same computer. These computers have large capacities for user memory and for disk storage and have very fast processing units or even multi-processors within the same computer. This environment has allowed for the sharing of information about patients which needs to be continually updated and revised.

Software vendors have been caught in a dilemma because there are so many different manufacturers of hardware and customers wanting software to function properly on all makes of hardware. This has caused a move toward a generic or universal operating system. More and more, UNIX, an AT&T and Bell Laboratories product, has been offered as that standard for student health related operating systems. This will make shopping for both hardware and application software much easier. Competition among vendors of both hardware and software should encourage the development of even better products throughout the next decade.

Application systems have been developed for almost every function necessary for the management of most student health centers. However, because most of the software was designed for use in hospitals or health clinics where an emphasis is placed on money, billing and profits, and most student health centers function on a prepaid basis where most services are provided with little or no charge to students, modifying commercially available systems and programs is generally required. Therefore, for most student health centers, the emphasis shifts from dollars to statistics. While it is very important to track any charges incurred, it is equally important to track numbers of visits, lab tests, x-rays, and so forth. Most systems written for use in the private sector fall short in capturing, tracking, and reporting these statistics effectively. This has forced many student health centers to develop their own software.

The general rule with software pricing is that the larger the computer on which the software runs, the higher the price of the software. This typically applies to software developed by vendors. Thus, most mainframe based systems were developed in-house by campus computer centers' programmers.

An application system developed in this manner may have the tendency to stagnate over time since the only need for change must come from only one user. On the other hand, systems developed by a vendor which supports many users will, by demand, change to meet the needs of all the users. Vendors usually upgrade their software periodically based on emergency needs and ideas received from their clients or users.

Unfortunately, though, there are currently no large commercial systems on the market that meet all of the special needs of college student health centers. Therefore, current needs must be met by developing systems "in-house" on-campus, or by contracting with a vendor to modify a hospital/clinic type system to meet the needs of a particular campus environment.

There are, however, several administrative functions where commercially available PC type software can be readily modified for student health center administrative functions. These functions include records management, pharmacy operations, medical clinic operations, and business affairs. A discussion of each follows.

Records Management

Federal law and many state laws call for the retention of medical records for 7 to 22 years. The exact length depends on the type of service that is recorded in the records. For many years the only form of records management and storage was to build rooms large enough to hold paper files that were generated by health care providers. Then came microfilm and microfiche. This reduced the size of the rooms needed to store the volumes of information but was very expensive to maintain. In addition, retrieval and reproduction was cumbersome and very time consuming.

With the type of medical services provided at most college health centers, most state laws require record retention in the 7-10 year range after the last entry to the record. Also, college students seem to "go and come" from school over the course of their lives. This creates the need to store and reproduce their medical record over and over.

The latest technology in the area of record storage and retrieval is called digital or optical imaging. This process applies photo imaging technology with computer technology and makes a "copy" of the record in digital format. Storage is made possible by digital disc technology (CD-ROM). Images can be displayed or printed by a laser printer producing an almost exact image of the original record. Currently start-up costs for this technology are high, but long-term costs are very attractive when compared to other types of medical record storage and retrieval systems.

Pharmacy

Pharmacy applications seem to be the most widely utilized within college health centers. The nature of the pharmacy business lends itself perfectly to computer automation. By typing on a keyboard, a myriad of functions take place in the same amount of time that it previously took a pharmacist to attach a typewritten label to a bottle or vial.

Pricing of the drug takes place as a result of the prescription filling. This is based on pre-set drug pricing and a quanity prescribed entered within the prescription filling process. Inventory controls are updated as a result of normal work flow. This gives management drug usage analysis, re-order information, and built-in controls for DEA/FDA controlled medications.

Interactions between prescribed medications can be checked for prescriptions filled up to one year earlier that may have residual traces left within a patient's system. This information can be updated monthly by national data banks that gather and distribute the information furnished by the DEA, pharmacy governing boards, Health and Human Services, and drug manufacturers.

For example, in the area of prescription insurance coverage, technology is now in use to do just that. Not only does the computer fill the prescriptions written by physicians but, through a modem, will "call" a clearing house for pre-paid drug companies and report the claim, tell the pharmacist how much will be paid on the prescription, how much is due from the patient, and when payment will be sent to the pharmacy. This happens in a matter of seconds and saves all the parties involved a tremendous amount of time, effort, and frustration. This is called "on-line adjudication". The practice is spreading to other providers of care services and goods as well.

The decision to begin the process of computerizing the pharmacy is a major step requiring a commitment of time for planning, implementation and training as well as funding for the purchase of the software and required hardware. The following describes the process that The University of Alabama went through in computerizing its pharmacy.

The University of Alabama's student health center pharmacy was one of the first to computerize in the South. An informal survey of major southern universities in 1985 revealed that none had computerized their pharmacies up to that point in time.

A follow up survey of software firms revealed that no commercial software systems designed for student health centers on college campuses were available. Of the forty vendors contacted, only one ultimately was willing to modify its existing commercial pharmacy package for a university student health center. This package designed by the Condor Corporation, called RX-80 (an updated version, RX-90, will be available soon) proved so successful on the University of Alabama campus that it has since been purchased by many other student health centers around the country.

It provides the standard pharmacy information including billing, insurance claims, inventory control, printing of labels, creation of patient records, statistical reports, drug to drug reactions, drug allergies, and patient summary reports.

An additional feature of this package addresses one of the unique problems faced with a college population, namely the influx of new "customers" in the fall of each year. The manual loading of demographic information on each student would overwhelm the proposed system in the early weeks of the academic year. The solution presented by this software is to merge all new students into the pharmacy programs by pulling information from the general student records system. This is an excellent program and works well in a campus setting.

For tracking purposes a unique data element was required for each student. The social security number was chosen since no two numbers are alike. Further it tracks initially by the last four digits of the social security number since they are more unique than the first five digits of the number. This allows it to scan initially only four numbers rather than nine numbers greatly speeding up the searching operation. When it finds the four number match it then performs a more discreet search within all of the four number matches that are the same until the exact match is found for all nine numbers.

A minicomputer is required to run this software effectively. A powerful PC could handle the program if the student body were in the 7500 range and the total number of prescriptions written per year were less than 25,000.

Medical Clinics

Clinic management systems seem to be the second most automated area. This term covers a wide range of departments that either input data to the system, generate transactions to be recorded, or utilize the data once captured. The medical records department is an area where all three of these take place. Typically information is gathered from areas providing care to patients and retained in some form of medical record storage. In the past, most records were kept solely in traditional, written medical charts. With the use of automated application systems, more readily accessible information is at one's fingertips. With the push of a button the patient's diagnosis history, diagnostic testing data, and immunization history can all be displayed. Currently, the most practical use for computerization in the area of medical-clinic records is for the generation of statistical reports for the student health center. A program that works well is the Medical Practice Management System from Business and Professional Services which costs approximately $16,000. This program can generate a wide variety of daily, monthly and annual statistics.

Some examples of the kinds of reports available include: number of students seen in the clinic, categorized by type of illness; insurance claims generated; pharmacy charges; fee for service charges; admissions, discharges and home to bed names and numbers; and numbers seen by departments such as clinic, physical therapy, mental health, and gynecology.

The program can also provide comparative data for month by month comparisons with the previous year and year to date totals. This allows for the tracking of epidemics or other fluctuations in usage which may signal the need to change strategies in the delivery of medical services. This kind of information serves as a valuable tool as decisions are made concerning services at the student health center.

Some student health centers have begun achieving record storage and access with the use of video imaging. As this technology advances, written medical records will become a thing of the past. Utilizing this technology, a physician or nurse simply types patient notes into a computer terminal and the system stores the data along with digital copies of diagnostic testing results, x-rays, and prescriptions for medications which can be integrated with pharmacy application systems. Pieces of this technology are already in place. Total package design is currently in process and should be completed in the near future.

Laboratories now receive orders for testing by computer generated request slips that double for reporting of results and permanent storage of these results. This can also be accomplished electronically on display terminals within the various departments. Results are then keyed back through the system for reporting and updating a patient's electronic medical history. Even reference laboratories now install printers and displays for reporting of referred laboratory testing back to referring physicians and clinics.

Information for billing and collection purposes can be accessed within the accounting or business office. Again, all this occurs simultaneously with providing health care to students, not as an addition to the work load. As long as systems are designed with this in mind, installation and utilization of computer application systems will continue to assist health providers to help insure the health of the student population at the lowest possible cost.

Business Applications

Payment for services and goods has become a major consideration for all involved with health care. Patients want insurance coverage that will pay for all services and reduce their out-of-pocket expenses. Providers of care, services, or goods want quick payment of insurance claims filed or statements mailed directly to patients. Insurance companies want contracted, agreed-upon pricing for services. These are called preferred provider agreements or preferred provider organizations. Although it seems impossible to meet the goals of all these parties, vendors of hardware and software technology are finding ways to bring all of these goals together.

The Medical Practice Management System described in the medical clinic section of this chapter can also be used for business applications. The package is used for both clinical and business applications. The records generated by the medical clinic are used for insurance and billing and have the capability of saving thousands of hours of labor for a comprehensive student health center at a major university. Prior to the availability of this software, most billing was done by generating hand written bills used for batch processing by the university's mainframe computer. These charges were then processed by the University's mainframe directly to the individual student bills.

This software also has the capability of recognizing students who are not currently enrolled but who plan to be in school the following semester. For example, a student may remain as a resident in the same community as the university but may plan to work in the summer and still needs access to the student health center. This program can bill the student on a fee for service basis during the summer as a non-student and return the student to active status in the fall when the student is once again enrolled.

Another important application is the processing of insurance claims. Student visits generally do not result in an insurance claim since most services are provided at no cost. For those items that do generate an additional charge, insurance claims can be processed automatically. Each student record indicates if the student has insurance and then automatically generates the claim request where applicable. No longer is it necessary to process insurance claims by hand, significantly reducing clerical time.

The program employs the national standard coding system adopted by the insurance industry for diagnosis called International Classification of Diseases (ICD) and procedure called Current Procedural Technology (CPT). By using this code and comparing it to the benefits allowed by the student's private health insurance policy, claims can be denied or processed accordingly.

One drawback the program has, however, is that credits must be done manually. This occurs when a student pays for a service and reveals later that insurance was available to cover part or all of the costs.

FUTURE TRENDS

There is a promising future for expanding the use of modern technology in student health centers. For example, in the area of patient care, systems are now on the market that offer bedside recording of nurse's notes, vital signs, and doctor's notes and orders which can then be typed directly into computer terminals and directed to central computer systems which share the information with other appropriate departments such as the pharmacy and laboratory. There are also experimental systems in place that, through voice recognition technology, can transcribe this same input and accomplish the same distribution of information when a doctor or nurse simply speaks into a microphone. Because there is a need to document all services provided due to the litigious society in which we live, "paperwork" takes a major portion of every health care provider's time. Therefore, by using modern technology to reduce the time spent on documentation, health care providers should have more time for direct patient care.

In summary, the advances in technology have given the providers of health care and related services more time to spend with patients. They, thus, can provide more comprehensive services to students in a more timely fashion without increasing personnel costs. There is no greater waste than to have highly trained and skilled medical professionals performing unnecessary repetitive or clerical tasks. Technology has allowed the shifting of those duties to machines so that the professional staff can better utilize their medical training and skills. This should result in improved medical practice at reduced costs.

Chapter 14

The Office of the Chief Student Affairs Officer

Molly Lawrence
John L. Baier

As the role of the Chief Student Affairs Officer (CSAO) increases in complexity and scope, it is critical that the CSAO possesses as much accurate, current, and timely information as possible for effective decision making and policy analysis. Modern computer and information technology can support and facilitate these needs regardless of institutional size or breadth of responsibility. It is, therefore, surprising that typically one of the last offices to utilize and embrace computer technology has been the office of the CSAO. The actions of the CSAO and his/her immediate staff set the tone for the rest of the student affairs division. If the CSAO is perceived to be computer shy, then the rest of the division will likely be slow to take advantage of the benefits of technology. On the other hand, if the CSAO is technologically literate and leads by example, the division is likely to properly embrace technology and use it to enhance student affairs' historical "high-touch" activities.

The purpose of this chapter is to describe ways that technology can be utilized to improve student affairs administrative, communication, and management functions within the office of the CSAO. Specific areas which will be covered include budget management, personnel management, word processing, desktop publishing, and networking.

BUDGET MANAGEMENT

One of the first applications of personal computers (PCs) by most CSAOs was probably in the budget management area. The financial accountability of most CSAOs is usually comprised of numerous funding sources: state or institution funded budgets, auxiliary enterprises, endowment income, grants, and hybrid budgets. The tasks include not only being able to contemporaneously manage existing budgets, but budget planning and allocation functions as well. Special projects such as capital financing and financial modeling are also important tasks. A brief description of how computer technology can be used for each of these tasks follow.

Current Budgets

The CSAO has a critical need to know the current status of all budgets under his/her authority. The institutional financial accounting department usually provides the CSAO with a monthly statement which shows current monthly activity (for reconciliation purposes) and year to date totals. This information can easily be entered into a standard spreadsheet program (i.e. Lotus 1-2-3 or Excel for either IBM compatibles or Macintosh PCs) which will allow comparison with the same period from previous years. Depending on the accounting system used by the institution's financial accounting department it might be possible to download the previous financial history either directly onto a PC computer's hard disk or on several floppy disks. This would save considerable staff time in loading the information manually. The most recent three years would be adequate history for most comparison purposes. Maintenance could be accomplished monthly by entering the information from the monthly institutional financial statements.

Current year expenses can be analyzed by comparing current year-to-date with current budget. The resulting percentage will alert one to trends that are unusual when compared to the same information from previous years. The information can also be used to project expenses by comparing current year-to-date with actual experience in previous years. Budgets can be reviewed individually or summarized by budget type. The entire division's budgetary accountability can also be summarized.

The purpose of current budget tracking is not to simply restate information presented on the institutional monthly reports but to develop management reports for use by the CSAO. The comparison and year-to-date information would be useful in identifying changes in fiscal patterns. Also, if a department has several accounts, a consolidated report would give the CSAO a larger picture of current operations. The specificity on institutional monthly reports needed for reconciliation purposes is not necessary for CSAO reports. The intent of these management reports is not micromanagement but to keep the CSAO informed regarding his/her fiscal accountability. The management reports can stimulate the need for additional information and provide a basis for discussions with department heads.

The CSAO has the complete picture of divisional fiscal needs. Temporary and permanent reallocation of funds can be explored without causing high anxiety among staff. Areas for possible program expansion or perhaps the need for restriction of services can also be identified.

Future Budgets

The annual budget building process can be initiated from the same spreadsheet monitoring current budgets. To ensure the current spreadsheet will not be altered, it is recommended to copy the needed data into another spreadsheet. Modeling can be accomplished to illustrate various reallocation strategies, student fee rates, housing or board rates, interest rates, impact of known expenditure increases, and so forth. While it is useful to have the input of department heads in final budget determination, it is of great value to the CSAO to be able to model the impact of various scenarios before the process actually begins.

The effectiveness of long term budget planning is also enhanced by computer spreadsheet analyses. Nearsightedness has proven to be fatal on numerous occasions. While department heads are basically concerned with short term impacts, the CASO must be consistently vigil on focusing on the next five years. Increases in various student fee rates or increases (or decreases) of other incomes can have a significant impact not only on the student affairs division, but also the entire institution. Strategies must, therefore, be orchestrated so that if significant changes occur, the institutional impacts can be measured and considered. The benefit of long term fiscal planning is especially evident when capital financing is required to fund new facilities. Funds to service debt do not usually appear overnight and sometimes must be built to the appropriate amount over a period of many years.

Enrollment Management and Fiscal Planning

Enrollment management is a crucial element of institutional planning. Depending on the divisional organization, some CSAO's will be more involved than others in enrollment management. Regardless of whether the student affairs division has total or partial responsibility for admissions, advising, records, financial aid, new student orientation, and other areas traditionally involved with enrollment managment, student population and demographics cannot be ignored. Along with long term fiscal planning, enrollment modeling is essential. Student body characteristics should be entered into a spreadsheet for at least the previous five years. Some assumptions should be made for the student body composition for the next five years. Long term fiscal plans should be reviewed with enrollment projections. Opportunities can be identified and strategies developed. Projections must be reviewed periodically as new information is collected.

Enrollment demographics impact every facet of student affairs. From the counseling center to the student union, characteristics of the student body should be considered. The average age of students can be changing, as well as the racial composition, male/female ratio, and married student percentage. All of these factors play a role in the programs and services offered by Student Affairs and, thus, in the fiscal requirements to meet student needs.

Fiscal Analyses

Spreadsheet analyses can be useful in numerous other decision making areas. For example, when trying to decide whether to lease or purchase equipment, modeling the annual lease cost over a period of years versus the impact of drawing down fund balances for a purchase can be compared. Another example would be a feasibility study for a new residence hall. Expenses can be estimated at various number of bedspaces resulting in the income generation requirements. Depending on the bedspaces, the room rates can also be calculated. Because most spreadsheets have an automatic calculation feature for such formulas and can generate different scenarios in a matter of minutes, other fiscal analyses spreadsheet applications are limited only by the creativity and needs of the CASO and his/her chief fiscal assistant.

Some other applications might be a breakdown of the percentage of each dollar of residence hall rates of debt service, maintenance, programming, resident assistants, and central housing administration. The same analysis could be applied to each dollar of student fee income for the union, student health, recreation, student publications, student government, student programming, and similiar programs.

Charts and Graphs

Spreadsheet data can easily and quickly be transformed into graphic presentation. Charts or graphs can facilitate readability and comprehension of numbers. An entire complex comparison spreadsheet report can be transformed into a line, pie, bar, stacked bar, or combination graph which can faciltate understanding. One goal of spreadsheet management reports is to make communication of fiscal information to the CSAO and president a task not overly time consuming or taxing. Because time management is important to every CSAO and president, as much information as possible should be presented in the most effective manner possible.

PERSONNEL MANAGEMENT

Without question, the most important resource available to a CSAO is personnel. The recruitment, selection, orientation, training, and evaluation of staff is a primary responsibility of the CSAO and one in which computer technology can play an important role. The other aspect of personnel management, using staff time to its greatest efficiency, can also be enhanced through computer technology. Following are a few examples of how this can be done.

Employee Database

By using a standard PC based database management software program (i.e. dBase), it is possible to quickly establish and maintain accurate employee data. Appropriately formatted employee databases can be of valuable assistance to the CSAO.

The flexibility of databases depends on the forethought in format design. While it is not impossible to modify existing databases, the process can be cumbersome and time consuming. Therefore, as with all software designs, it saves time and money if proper planning is done before installing a personnel database management system on an office computer.

Based on considerable experience, it is recommended that the following fields should be included in any employee database:

1. employee's name (place last name as a separate data item for alphabetic sorting purposes);
2. prefix (Mr., Ms., Dr., etc. for labeling and individualizing communications);
3. department or area (keep descriptions consistent; again to facilitate sorting);
4. birthdate (list in reverse order of year/month/date so sorts will be by year);
5. service date (again use year/month/date order);
6. employee classification or position code (professional, clerical, maintenance, technical, etc. to facilitate selecting by classification);
7. employee status (full time or part time; temporary or permanent);
8. race;
9. sex;
10. job title.

Other information might also be useful, based on a review of the capacity and speed of the computer. Other limitations of available software should also be reviewed before expanding the employee database further. Baseline data can usually be provided by the institutional payroll or human resources management department. Through networking computers, this database can be massaged and used by the CSAO's office with little difficulty. Maintenance of additions and deletions can be done through the routine CSAO approval of personnel action forms. As a double check for accuracy and completeness, it is advisable to ask each department head to edit a printout of his/her departmental personnel database at least twice a year.

An employee database has many uses. It can be used during annual planning cycles for anticipating staff retirements due to age or years of service. It can also be used in times of staff expansion or contraction for quickly identifying employees by part time or temporary status. Progress toward achieving affirmative action goals can also be routinely monitored on a periodic basis. Anniversary of service dates or even birthdays can be recognized. Communications can be facilitated by division wide dissemination or to select groups. Undoubtedly, additional uses will evolve as the CSAO recognizes the value of maintaining an accurate employee database in his/her office.

Other items that might be considered in an employee data base are salary history, date of last time position description was reviewed, or degree level achieved. Databases can interact with spreadsheets. Short term and long term planning can be enhanced by incorporating current salaries into a spreadsheet and projecting salary costs. Other database variables could also be copied into a spreadsheet format and modeled.

Staff Recruitment and Hiring

The staff recruitment and hiring process can also be facilitated by PC usage. Using word processing and database software, position announcements can routinely be prepared and disseminated to other student affairs offices, placement centers, faculty of schools with appropriate degree programs, professional associations, and other groups that facilitate informing potential candidates. Equal opportunity and affirmative action procedures can also be supported through routine notification to predominantly minority or women's colleges, placement networks targeting women or minorities, and minority or women's professional associations.

A recruiting database can be built which accommodates the widest dissemination for any recruitment strategy. The recruiting database can be merged with a word processing program to generate individualized letters. The dissemination can be tailored to meet the specific position being recruited by adding or deleting notification as appropriate.

The recruiting database can either be one database or a combination of several databases with various uses. The multiple database approach might combine the following databases: other CSAOs and prominent student affairs professionals and faculty in the region or nation; university placement center directors; and individuals and groups concerned with supporting the advancement of women or minorities in student affairs.

Tracking of applicants is yet another process which can be supported by the use of computer technology. For some positions, receiving over 200 applications is not uncommon. An applicant database can easily be developed as applications arrive. Again, merging the database with a word processing program on a modern PC with a high quality laser printer can create individualized letters to notify applicants of receipt of their application; routine requests for references, transcripts or other information; notification of search process if progress is taking longer than expected; and informing applicants of the conclusion of the search.

Determining hiring rates can also be facilitated by information in the employee database. A proposed salary can be reviewed relative to comparable positions in the division or to ascertain "fit" with a department. Salary compression is a concern in higher education institutions. Unfortunately, information in a database cannot alleviate the concern but it can at least make the CSAO aware of the impact a salary offer or hiring salary could have within the division.

Staff Development and Evaluation

Depending on the staff size and scope of staff development activities, it is also possible to develop a staff training transcript for each employee. Several student affairs' staff development programs are instituting "core curriculums" that require staff to complete a minimum level of training and/or professional development activities each year. Again, a database approach would provide for an accurate, easy to retrieve summary of not only an individual's professional development history, but could also provide summaries by program, employee classification, and other database variables.

A golden rule to remember when using computers is that information produced from a computer is only as good as the information entered into it and the software program that operates it. The old adage of "trash in - trash out" still holds true. But with the proper design of an employee staff development transcript program and the right software, it is possible to utilize the transcript for both merit pay and promotion evaluation decisions.

Numerical values of annual evaluations can also be built into databases. Comparison between evaluations and proposed salary adjustments could be quickly analyzed if such information was loaded into a database format. While the CSAO's goal would not be to set individual salary adjustments, there should be some comparability within the division. Sorting variables included in a database would facilitate identification of possible concerns.

WORD PROCESSING

While much of the written communications developed by the CSAO are individualized, some are repetitive in nature. But regardless of the nature of the document, whether it is a research paper with footnotes and tables or a one page memo to a single individual, PC's can facilitate the process.

Individual communications can be produced through various word processing packages and easily edited. The most commonly used software programs are WordPerfect and Word, although there are several other excellent ones. By using a good quality laser printer, the final product can be enhanced greatly over typewritten copy. Correspondence that is repetitive can also be individualized through mail-merges and "inserts" from other databases to make it more personal and complete.

Depending on the software package, most have a variety of options that increase usefulness. A spell check dictionary is especially helpful. Some dictionaries allow the addition of acronyms, professional terms, and other words not found in the standard dictionary. Depending on the amount of creative original work that is actually composed on the PC, a thesaurus and word count feature can also be of great assistance. Some word processing programs additionally have options to assist in grammar usage and can evaluate the reading level of the document. There are also "readability" programs that can compare documents to a specific writing style. Depending on your particular word processing needs, there is likely a software program currently available to meet them.

Some word processing programs are "programmable" with macros. Macros can be designed to eliminate keystrokes of most often performed functions. The complexity of programming macros is

196 *Technology in Student Affairs*

variable between software programs. The sophisticated user will find it well worth the time and effort to master macro development. Macros are stored in a macro library and evoked through function keys or a combination of control keys (alt, Ctrl), and letters or numbers.

Presentations can also be supported through the development of transparencies, computer monitor slide shows, and slides for slide projectors. These outputs are not only professional in appearance but they are easy to produce. Visuals add so much to the quality of a presentation and can pictorially portray what is sometimes difficult to articulate. The use of a computer screen slide show does not necessarily need to be limited to a small group able to view a monitor. Most institutional audio video or educational media centers have a projection device which allows a computer screen to be projected onto a standard room screen.

Hence, by utilizing all of the features of word processing software and reproduction equipment, the office of the CSAO can reduce costs, time, and staff required to produce routine reports, correspondence, and presentation materials.

DESKTOP PUBLISHING

One of the newest applications for personal computers in most offices is desktop publishing. New desktop software packages like Aldus's PageMaker are extremely user-friendly and can produce in-office camera-ready copy of very high quality. This saves time, reduces printing costs, and allows the final product to be seen before sending it off to the printer. Following are a few specific examples of how desktop publishing software can be used in CSAO offices.

Newsletters

The primary use of desk top publishing software in most CSAO offices is for the publication of "in-house" newsletters. Through a regularly produced newsletter, divisional staff can be kept abreast of activities in other student affairs departments and receive notice of upcoming training or other professional development activities. Staff accomplishments can also be recognized through this vehicle.

Including staff profiles in each issue is also an excellent means of team building. Newsletters can also be an effective method of disseminating information on new or revised policy or procedures. Depending on the graphics involved and the design layout, some newsletters can be accomplished through the use of sophisticated word processing programs, but most are produced using desktop publishing software. Excellent software programs are available for both IBM compatible and Macintosh PCs. Because desk top publishing permits the production of inexpensive but high quality newsletters, most student affairs divisions can produce one with minimum expertise, staff committment or expense.

Certificates of Appreciation

Another method of staff recognition that is meaningful and also inexpensive to produce with desktop publishing software are certificates of appreciation. The choice of font style and paper used can make a significant difference in the appearance of a certificate. For example, most of the national honorary societies are no longer having the name of new initiates entered on certificates with calligraphy but are using the "olde English" type font now available on most higher quality laser printers. Institutional seals, logos, mascots, and other marks can also be scanned onto a disk and used in the desktop program. Most institutional publications or printing departments have such scanning devices and will offer scanning services to other departments for a very modest cost.

Organization Charts/Directories

Desktop publishing software is also ideal for producing organization charts for individual offices or departments, areas, and the division. The size of the boxes can be varied, relational lines can be drawn at will, boxes can be moved freely, and shadows or shading can be put on selected boxes. Organization charts can now be produced within a fraction of the time it once took to produce them with a typewriter.

It is also very easy to produce and update attractive divisional and departmental staff directories each year. Personnel data from the employee database can be imported into the desktop software program and merged into an attractive, but inexpensive, "directory".

Once again, the clerical staff time required to produce such documents with a PC is about one tenth the time of a document.

NETWORKING

The capability of being able to communicate with other computers is fast becoming not only common place but a necessity. The full benefits of using computer technology cannot be obtained if microcomputers are not fully networked to each other and to the central campus mainframe computer. Networks allow for on-line interactive communication with any other connected computer. Files can be transferred from computer to computer in seconds. Files can be accessed in a "read" or "view only" mode, where no one but the file originator can revise the file. A code word is another means for maintaining file integrity. Files can also be accessed with update capability so that it can become a progressive work by many authors.

Electronic mail (E-mail) is also possible with networked computers. With many student affairs offices spread across the campus and providing increasingly expanded service hours to meet the needs of students, electronic mail is a fast, accurate means of communicating between departments when all staff are not immediately accessible.

The integration of databases, software packages, hardware sharing, and common calendars are also advantages of networks. Network versions of software can be purchased (called site licenses) with a minimum additional amount paid for each work station. In addition, every office does not have to have all of the peripheral devices, such as scanners, plotters, wide-carriage printers, color printers, and tape back-ups, that make computers work more effectively. Therefore, the proper development of Local Area Networks (LANs), which link computers within a single building or portion of a building, and Wide Area Networks (WANs), which link computers between buildings and/or between campuses, are very important to the effective and efficient use of computer databases, software programs, and electronic communications in student affairs. Each student affairs division should carefully develop appropriate networking systems to meet the particular needs of their campus, and every CSAO should be networked to each student affairs office, as well as the campus' mainframe computer. A complete discussion of how this can be achieved is provided in the Part III of this book (Chapter Sixteen - Managing Computer Systems and Networks).

SUMMARY

In summary, many of the functions performed in the office of the CSAO lend themselves nicely to computer technology. By using standard word processing, database, spreadsheet, and desktop publishing software, it is possible to more efficiently and effectively generate and update organization charts, personnel records, student fee schedules, budgetary data, policy documents, and similiar materials; produce high quality publications; respond to routine correspondence; and coordinate staff recruitment and staff development activities. Through networks (both LANs and WANs) it is also possible to be "on-line" with the campus' student database, fiscal information system, personnel system, alumni office files, security department, and other student affairs office, thus enabling almost instant communication with other departments and key campus personnel.

Finally, because utilizing technology is not inexpensive, it must be considered very carefully and with a broad perspective. The impact on staff effectiveness, time savings, improved final product, student services, and ability to make more informed decisions is considerable. But careful consideration must be given to planning and managing hardware, software, and network purchases to match both current and anticipated future needs in order to realize the full benefits of technology. A number of recommendations concerning these matters are provided in the concluding chapter of this book.

Part III

Administrative Considerations and Implications for the Future

This part examines some important issues that face the administrator who is considering the technological transformation and computerization of his/her student affairs programs and/or offices. These issues include legal liabilities, ethical questions, and the purchase, updating, maintenance, and networking of computer and information systems. Finally, the implications of the technological explosion on the future of student affairs are discussed.

Chapter 15

Legal Liabilities and Ethical Issues

Patricia A. Hollander

Computer technology has permitted some remarkable improvements in the administration of student affairs during the past decade. The use of this technology, however, has also exposed institutions of higher education and student affairs administrators to new types of legal liability. For example, when an employee in a student affairs office makes illegal copies of a computer program, not only is the individual employee legally responsible, but in addition, the head of the office or department where the individual works, along with the governing board, may also be held responsible on grounds that they did not provide to the individual employee either proper training or adequate supervision. It is, therefore, very important that all student affairs administrators, and especially chief student affairs officers (CSAOs), be aware of the legal liabilities concerning the use of computers and computer software in educational settings.

Legal liabilities include possible allegations of the following: copyright infringement through impermissible copying of computer programs; wrongful claims of ownership of computer programs developed by campus employees or students; negligent use of computers resulting in personal injuries, incorrect records, improperly programmed computers, and inadequate security causing breaches of privacy and confidentiality; and criminal acts, such as unauthorized access, fraud, and destruction of data.

Ethical issues, too, arise from the presence of computer technology on campus. Ethical issues include: determining whether hacking is a playful act, a criminal act, or something in between; determining whether there is equitable access to computers and to training; and determining whether there is equitable policy for the sharing of revenue from the development and marketing of new computer products.

The purpose of this chapter is to briefly discuss these areas of legal liability and ethics, and, then, to offer a few suggestions on ways to manage risks and reduce legal exposure.

LEGAL LIABILITIES

Copying Computer Programs

There are any number of occasions when it would be convenient to have available some extra copies of computer programs. There may be a temptation simply to make additional copies rather than purchase them. Resist the temptation. The liability for infringement is too great. The law of computers is, for the most part, the law of copyright. Today's courts are applying copyright law to computer-related matters with increasing frequency.

Is it legal to make a copy of a computer program? Generally not. It may be helpful to think of a computer program as though it were a book. Would one think it legal to make a copy of a book? Of course not. There is one exception set forth in the Copyright Act which allows the copying of a computer program. A back-up or archival copy is permitted. That is, when a computer program is purchased the copyright statute permits the owner of a purchased copy to make a new copy for archival or backup purposes in case the purchased copy accidentally is damaged or destroyed. The copyright law goes on to state that the archival copy must be destroyed in the event that the purchased copy is no longer in the possession of the purchaser (Copyright Act 1980, Sec. 117).

Of course, a purchaser of a computer program may negotiate a contractual agreement with a seller permitting the making of copies. Such an agreement may provide for copying up to a certain number of copies per mainframe or per site, for example. The buyer and seller can make whatever arrangements for copying and payment for copies that suits them. What is important to remember is that a computer program is a commercial product, and when it is used, its copyright owner wishes to be compensated.

"Fair use" of computer programs is permitted by the Copyright Act. When a use is a "fair use," permission of the copyright owner generally is not required. "Fair use" is defined as use for purposes such as criticism, comment, news reporting, teaching (including multiple copies for classroom use), scholarship, or research (Copyright Act 1976, Sec. 107).

Four factors are set forth in the statue to determine whether a particular use is a "fair use":

1. The purpose and character of the use, including whether the use is for a commercial purpose or for a nonprofit educational purpose;
2. The nature of the copyrighted work;
3. The amount and substantiality of the portion used in relation to the copyrighted work as a whole; and
4. The effect of the use on the potential market for or value of the copyrighted work.

Note that it is no protection against a charge of copyright infringement to say that copies of a computer program were made for a non-profit organization such as a college or university. Most computer programs are made for sale, so when copies are needed they should be bought. As was mentioned earlier, contracts between a buyer and seller may provide for site licenses or similar arrangements.

Regarding the amount and substantiality of the portion used, Congress contemplated "reproduction by a teacher or student of a small part of a work to illustrate a lesson" (House Report, 1967). Generally an excerpt would be defined as a small part of a work used, for example, to illustrate programming techniques or to show what is source code as compared to object code. Clearly, it is not fair use to copy a whole computer program.

A recent court case involving the copying of materials for inclusion in anthologies for sale to students is instructive. In that case, a federal court found there was infringement of publishers' copyrights where a photocopying firm, Kinko's, worked with faculty members to identify and copy excerpts of material without permission of the copyright owners for sale to students (Basic Books 1991). There is concern that unless academia finds ways to discourage perceived infringement related to copyrighted computer programs, similar legal action may be forthcoming.

In summary, under the "fair use" section of the law it is permissible to:

- make one back-up or archival copy;
- transfer a copy of a purchased computer program from floppy disk to hard disk for use with one's own hardware;
- lend a purchased copy of a computer program to students in serial fashion, as one would lend a book;
- purchase twenty copies of a computer program for use by students in one class and then use the same copies for a subsequent class; negotiate a purchase contract permitting the copying of a computer program for use at an entire site, or with multiple machines, etc; and make copies of those computer programs that are not protected by copyright, that is, that are in the public domain, because they were created with public funds under government research grants or because their creator did not copyright them.
- It is not permissible to purchase one copy of a computer program and use it to make twenty other copies for use by students or others.

Put in other words, most legal commentors believe the owner of a purchased computer program may do the following with it: (1) "copy" it by using it in a computer's memory; (2) make one backup or archival copy; (3) make adaptations in order to use it in a particular machine; (4) lend it; (5) sell it (in which case the backup or archival copy must be destroyed); and (6) copy very brief excerpts to distribute in a classroom for an educational purpose such as demonstrating a programming technique or illustrating the difference between object code and source code.

Penalties for copyright infringement can be quite severe. They include: (a) injunctions against further infringing use; (b) impoundment and destruction of the infringing articles; (c) actual damages and profits attributable to the infringement; (d) statutory damages of $200 per incident for an innocent infringer and $100,000 per incident for a willful infringer; (e) costs and attorney's fees; and (f) criminal prosecution fine and/or imprisonment and seizure of infringing articles (Copyright Act 1976, Secs. 502-509).

Plagarism, of course, is an additional charge that may be made when one person copies another person's computer program and passes it off as his or her own work without proper permission and attribution.

Ownership Of Software Developed On Campus

Does a college or university own the copyright on software created by its employees (faculty and staff) and by its students? The answer is, generally no. Software usually is deemed to be a literary work, and traditionally at most educational institutions, literary works belong to the author of the work. Thus, just as the copyright on books and articles usually belongs to the person who wrote the work, the same may be said regarding those who write computer programs. The exception would be where a person is hired specifically to write such works as part of his or her job, and in those cases, the employer is deemed to be the author.

There are instances where computer programs that are integral parts of manufacturing and similar processes are protected by patent rather than by copyright laws. In those cases the traditional patent rules at colleges and universities applies, and usually the patent is assigned to the college or university with arrangements for revenue sharing of sales or license fees. Educational institutions should, therefore, have written policies regarding the ownership of computer software or hardware created by employees or students.

Selling Computer Software and Hardware at a Discount

Colleges and universities sometimes negotiate with computer companies to purchase software or hardware in bulk for resale at a discount to students, faculty, and staff. Local computer merchants may challenge such arrangements. There may be state laws that prohibit colleges or universities from interfering with private enterprise; or federal statutes, such as the Robinson-Patman Price Discrimination Act, may be involved. It is important that the college or university legal counsel be consulted before any discount arrangements are put in place.

Personal Injuries - Health and Safety Hazards

Video display terminals (VDTs) have been of some concern. Eye strain caused by use of VDTs may result in eye fatigue, flickering sensations, shooting pains, double vision, blurring of vision, itching and burning eyes, and headaches. There also are as yet unconfirmed reports of miscarriages and other pregnancy-related complaints said to be related to exposure to radiation when working with VDTs. Any electrical equipment, including computers, may present shock hazards. Also, fire is a great risk since computers involve the use of materials such as plastic in the construction of both hardware and software which may produce toxic fumes when burned.

Damages Caused By Incorrect Records

When records are computerized there sometimes is an unwarranted assumption that they are correct. Relying on incorrect records may result in damages to students for which a college or university may be liable. For example, a student may offer proof that a tuition bill was paid even though the computer record shows it outstanding. In such a case, were the student to be expelled based on the incorrect records, the institution may be liable for damages to the student's credit rating.

Improperly Programmed Computers

If a computer program is meant to remove an "F" when another grade is substituted for it, but is programmed improperly and the "F" remains, and then, for instance, should that result in a student's being refused admission to a medical school, the institution may find itself sued for damages.

Liability For Inadequate Security

Computerized records that are meant to be confidential must be adequately protected by such methods as proper training of personnel and the requirement of special codes for access to confidential information. Thus, personnel who handle academic transcripts must be trained as to who may have access to that information. Access to computerized academic files should require special codes.

Criminal Acts

Colleges and universities must make clear to students and employees that those who are found guilty of criminal acts related to the use of computers will be prosecuted, and that in addition to punishment by courts there may also be campus-based sanctions such as suspension or expulsion. Two federal statutes apply to federal crimes involving the use of computers: the Federal Comprehensive Crime Act of 1984 and the Counterfeit Access Device and Computer Fraud and Abuse Act of 1984. These statutes make almost all computer-related fraud, theft, tampering, or destruction federal offenses. Legislation has now also been passed in most states regarding criminal acts specifically involving computers.

Conduct deemed criminal includes: deceiving a machine; computer fraud (with and without intent to deceive); altering computerized credit information; computer damage or destruction; offenses against computer users; unauthorized use; modification or destruction of programs or data; use of computer to commit embezzlement, disposition of personal property, larceny, larceny by conversion; tampering or alteration of computer; unauthorized access; denial of computer services; altering or destroying programs; computer trespass, removing data, causing malfunction, or altering, creating, or erasing data; extortion via threats to damage computer; theft of computer-related materials; theft of computer services; computer invasion of privacy such as unauthorized examination of personal or financial data; personal trespass by computer; offenses against computer data programs; and offenses against computer equipment and supplies. Criminal penalties range from ninety days to twenty years of imprisonment and from $100 to $150,000 in fines.

The unauthorized use of computers is one of the most common forms of criminal conduct on campus. In fact, many perpetrators do not even think of this conduct as a possible criminal act. They may never give a second thought to logging on to a computer to practice their programming skills, or logging on during lunch hour to do a little personal business. Indeed it may be difficult to prove criminal intent in such instances. Deliberately altering or destroying data, of course, generally indicates clear criminal intent.

Colleges and universities must, therefore, be careful to set forth in their policies how they will respond to criminal conduct. For example, will all such conduct be reported to the police without exception? Will some possibly criminal conduct be "excused" as a "first offense"? The campus policy should be clarified.

ETHICAL ISSUES

Hacking

What should colleges and universities do about hackers? There are two schools of thought. The first views hackers as playful experimenters. The second views hackers as dedicated destroyers. Whatever the institution's view, make it clear in policy documents and rules.

Equitable Access and Training

Favoritism in supplying computers and training has been charged from time to time. In public institutions under certain circumstances, charges may be made that individuals are being deprived of their rights under the Fourteenth Amendment to the Constitution which provides for equal treatment under the law. Private institutions, of course, would not be subject to charges of constitutional deprivation, but there may be contractual promises regarding access spelled out in catalogues or handbooks.

Revenue from Development of New Programs

In order to prevent litigation over who owns computer programs created by employees or students, colleges and universities should establish policies that indicate who owns what, and, regardless of ownership, how revenue derived from a commercially successful program is to be shared. This will reduce possible litigation in the future. Also, if "ownership" is shared between the employee and university, both may be motivated to create and market new products.

RISK MANAGEMENT

Managing the risks of liability regarding computers on campus includes the following: putting in place clear policies and rules, training personnel properly, and shifting the risk to insurance when possible.

The first two have been emphasized earlier. The third matter, shifting the risk by acquiring appropriate insurance coverage, requires comment.

Property insurance

General business insurance may consist of an "all risks" policy that covers all risks except those specifically excluded. Covered in most situations would be accidental damage caused by fire, water, storm damage, explosion, theft, malfunction of other equipment, vandalism, and in some cases malicious damage.

Special computer insurance policies are available in addition. They specifically cover computers, terminals, peripherals, programs, data, and storage media. Experience has taught that it is important to make inquiries such as whether such insurance provides only for replacement of disks or includes the costs of reentering the data on new disks. Another important question is whether the insurance covers earthquakes and floods as well as electrical and mechanical failures. One should also inquire about coverages for erasure of data by magnet or electricity and programming errors.

Personal liability insurance

People who do programming are well-advised to consider personal liability insurance should they be found personally liable for programming errors or for omitting data from a program or a database. Certainly programmers who are employees of a college or university should find out from their employer whether they are covered for mistakes made within the scope of their employment and for what kind of errors they are not covered. Also, are their defense attorney fees and court costs covered? Student programmers who may be found culpable for errors also need to know how the institution's insurance covers them, if at all, and if not, they should seek personal liability insurance.

RECOMMENDATIONS

In summary, the following recommendations are made to all student affairs professionals and organizations who currently use, or plan on using, computer technology in their daily activities.

1. Copyright infringement

Make clear to employees and students that copying of computer programs, if any, is only permissible under the provisions of the copyright laws. Be sure to seek permission from copyright owners or negotiate site contracts whenever using copyrighted programs.

2. Ownership of computer products created by employees or students

Develop policies as to who owns what products and how revenue is to be shared. Also be certain to make staff and students aware of these policies.

3. Negligence

Take reasonable care under the circumstances to: (a) provide safe and healthful conditions for working with computer equipment; (b) see that procedures are in place to allow appropriate and timely correction of computerized records; (c) assure that computers are programmed properly; and (d) provide adequate security as to privacy and confidentiality.

4. Criminal acts

State how and when the institution will inform state and federal authorities about possible crimes involving computers. Also be certain that all forms of criminal acts are included in student conduct codes and employee handbooks along with a listing of the possible penalties to be imposed if found guilty of violating any of them.

5. Risk management

Review regularly what possible exposures to liability exist and what steps, including insurance, are being taken to protect each staff member and the institution against the exposures.

6. Hacking

Decide whether to treat hacking as a mere playful act or as a crime, or something in between. Inform employees of the institution's policy on hacking and consistently enforce these regulations.

7. Equitable access to computers and to training

Try to assure that all relevant groups are provided appropriate access and training to avoid charges of unfair or unequal treatment and educational opportunity.

8. Sharing of revenues from technology research and development

State what help will be offered to bring new products up to marketable quality and what arrangements there are for sharing of profits when products are sold.

By doing these things, student affairs administrators and organizations should be able to effectively utilize all of the computer and information technology available to them without infringing on the legal rights of others and without incurring unnecessary legal liabilities and risks. Modern technology offers much to improve the efficiency and effectiveness of higher education. One need not fear its use, but must take care to use it within the law.

LIST OF CASES

Copyright Act, Sec. 107. 17 U.S.C. 107 (1976)
Copyright Act, Sec. 117. 17 U.S.C. 117 (1980)
Copyright Act, Secs. 502-509. 17 U.S.C. 502-509 (1976)

REFERENCES

Basic Books, Inc. v Kinko's Graphics Corp., 758 F. Supp. 1522 (S.D.N.Y. 1991)

Computer Law Monitor (1983). Asheville, N.C.: Research Publications, Inc.

Hollander, P.A. (1986). *Computers in education: Legal liabilities and ethical issues concerning their use and misuse.* Asheville, NC: *College Administration Publications.*

Hollander, P.A. (1984). An introduction to legal and ethical issues relating to computers in higher education. *Journal of College and University Law.* Fall, 11, 2, 215-232.

Hollander, P.A. (1983) University computing facilities: Some ethical dilemmas. In M.C. Baca and R.H. Stein (Eds.), *Ethical principles, problems and practices in higher education* (62-73). Springfield, IL.: C.C. Thomas, Publishers.

House Report (1967). U.S. Congress, House Judiciary Committee, 90th Congr., 1st Sess., 1967, H.R. Rep. No. 90-83 ("1967 House Report") at p. 65.

Chapter 16

Managing Computer Systems and Networks

Gary D. Malaney

As noted in the previous chapters of this book, student affairs is no stranger to the use of computer and information technology. In fact, in many respects, student affairs has been a leader in developing computer applications in the field of higher education. For example, many of the student-related systems for advising, financial aid, registration, scheduling, billing, student health, and housing described in this book were developed or initiated by student affairs administrators.

Various aspects of computerization dealing with both mainframe and personal computing have been discussed in the student affairs literature for the past 25 years. For example, the *NASPA Journal* has been a source of numerous articles relating to computerization. Topics have included job placement (Menke, 1966; Pyle & Stripling, 1977), decision support systems in enrollment management (Beeler, 1989), management information systems (Mac Lean, 1986), and telecommunications (Allbritten & Bogal-Allbritten, 1987). A few technical computer journals have also discussed student affairs issues (e.g., Mullen, 1990); however, there has been very little written anywhere about how to manage computer resources within student affairs.

In addressing the computer management issue in student affairs ten years ago, Sampson (1982) noted that "almost every area of student personnel is relying on computers in some way to enhance available services" (p.40). He also noted several standard problems with which administrators must deal, such as lack of adequate software, staff anxiety and negative attitudes toward computing, access and privacy issues, incompatible hardware and software, and waste of resources. Sampson indicated that "it is the task of resource management to minimize problems that limit the effectiveness of computer applications as well as maintaining control of how the resource is used" (p. 42). These points were also reiterated by McCredie (1983), Masland (1985), and Kalsbeek (1989).

While many of the issues concerning computer management have not changed since Sampson's article, other authors have expanded on the issues. More recently, Green (1988), Hawkins (1988), and Ryland (1988) discussed several computer management concerns. While their writings do not directly discuss student affairs, the issues they raise are directly applicable. Those issues include planning and budgeting for computer resources, decentralized versus centralized control, and distributed computing, all of which are discussed in this chapter.

Many changes have occured in the computing industry in the past two decades, and administrators who deal with computerization within the student affairs enterprise must be more informed about the computer environment today than ever before. Twenty-five years ago, student affairs managers involved with computing simply had to learn the campus' mainframe environment and the specific application(s) involving their area. And, while that may have seemed difficult then, it appears relatively simple now, given that today's student affairs administrator is likely to have computer applications in each of the following environments: mainframe, mini, micro, and local area networks (LANs). A particular administrator may need to understand only the environment storing a particular application, but someone within student affairs should have command of the larger scope. That person must know how all of the applications interact within the multiple environments and how to maintain compatibility. This takes some vision as well as a broad understanding of computing trends and technology.

The different environments compound the normal problems associated with managing any computing system such as hardware and software selection, compatibility issues, costs, vendors, installation, cabling, maintenance, expansion capabilities, and upgrading and replacing systems. The purpose of this chapter is to explore these issues and provide recommendations for student affairs administrators. Examples will be drawn from the University of Massachusetts at Amherst (UMA) which is heavily involved in computing within student affairs.

The chapter begins with a look at how centralized management and support can play a crucial role in addressing all of the issues noted above. Following that discussion, the focus turns to the current software and hardware technology of local and wide area networks (LANs and WANs) which give divisions of student affairs new computer power. The discussion of the development, use, and management of the WAN, in this case, a series of connected LANs within the Division of Student Affairs at UMA, will show how greater computing continuity is achieved throughout the Division. That discussion should prove beneficial to student affairs divisions at other campuses as they proceed into this type of computerized environment. Following the WAN discussion, the chapter focuses on the necessary personnel and committee support for continued management and planning.

CRITICAL MANAGEMENT ISSUES

Centralization and Distributive Computing

Perhaps the first key issue for a Chief Student Affairs Officer (CSAO) to consider when looking at computerization is the topic of centralization. With the proliferation of small, powerful personal computers (PCs), it is not unusual, especially in large institutions, for some departments in student affairs to develop computer databases and applications for their own needs without discussions with the central student affairs administration. This process is analogous to the computer revolution of recent years where individual academic colleges and departments established their own small computer centers separate from the campus' centralized data processing center (Kissler, 1988; Ryland, 1988). Kissler noted that in a specific institution these minicomputer centers are likely to spread to various sites, and "the central campus mainframe will shift from being the primary provider of computing to a fast computational tool that serves a network of distributed machines" (p. 50). In fact, this scenario has already occured on many campuses.

While this approach can and does work, and there are certain advantages, it also can be problematic by allowing isolation of those departments from each other and central administration. This isolation can be particularly disadvantageous within a student affairs operation where sharing of resources and knowledge is extremely important for good service to students. While an independent computer operation can provide autonomy for a particular department, thus providing control over its computing environment, such operations can be costly in terms of duplicating hardware and software as well as staffing within the division of student affairs as a whole. This approach can also be problematic in terms of future compatibility issues as student affairs or the campus decides to network departments.

Another alternative is to have some form of centralized organization for planning computer activity within the student affairs area. In 1984, the Division of Student Affairs at the University of Massachusetts at Amherst recognized the need to centralize computer support for both mainframe and personal computing. The CSAO delegated that responsibility to the Research and Evaluation Office which reported directly to him and already had staff members who were very familiar with most of the aspects of the campus computing environment. In time, systems coordination became a major responsibility for that office, and the name of the office was changed to reflect that importance, becoming the Office of Student Affairs Research, Information, and Systems (SARIS).

The primary responsiblility of the SARIS systems staff is to assist in all forms of computer activity throughout the division and serve a coordinating role in the collection and distribution of information pertaining to computer systems. Any office or department needing computer assistance is supposed to utilize the resources within SARIS. It is important to note that SARIS's role is not to infringe on the autonomy of departmental computer activity. The purpose is to provide a central resource for collecting and distributing information regarding such issues as hardware and software technology, applications development, personnel, funding and resource allocation, and division-wide computing standards. SARIS recognizes the need and advantages of distributive computing for the individual student affairs departments but also provides a common linkage for sharing among those departments.

System Design and Expansion

One important reason for centrality relates to system design, especially if a student affairs division decides to pursue the design of a Wide Area Network as depicted later in this chapter. The design of a major computer network takes extensive cooperation among the participating units. Even if such networking is not already in place at an institution, it is likely to occur in the future. Therefore, it is important for departments to communicate regarding computer issues. Communication about standards of compatibility and information about which hardware and software departments should utilize will make the network system design easier later. A centralized office or individual who is responsible for working with all departments will improve the likelihood of success.

Resource Allocation

The funding process for computer systems will vary depending on the institution. At UMA such operations as housing, health services, and student activities are semi-autonmous units which generate their own fundings through student fees, and thus, can make their own decisions about how to spend their money. But those units must check with SARIS before actually purchasing computer equipment for reasons which will be explained shortly.

The State-funded operations such as admissions, financial aid, dean of students, career center, academic counseling center, and public safety are funded centrally from the CSAO's accounts at the beginning of the year. However, funding for computer equipment funding is maintained centrally and not allocated to the departments. During the Fall semester, departments must turn in to the CSAO all requests for computer equipment for that year, and those requests are turned over to SARIS for review. SARIS staff members contact departments regarding their overall computer plans for the year to see if their requests will meet their plans, and requests are often altered based on those discussions. Therefore, the equipment funding process becomes an important part of the on-going planning and resource management for the entire Division.

Selection and Purchase of Hardware and Software

With the increase in available vendors for hardware and software, including a large contingent of mail-order companies, the selection and purchase of these items can be a major undertaking, especially if one is interested in finding the lowest price. However, price should not be the only criteria; service should be an important consideration, especially if a department does not have the necessary in-house technical expertise. Often, it will be worth paying a little extra for the convenience of having a local vendor who can provide quality and timely service.

Because pricing seems to change daily, new vendors appear continuously, and service reputations come and go, it is important to have someone in student affairs who stays informed about current market variables. In addition to the above issues, public institutions often have to deal with State educational contracts where vendors have been approved by the State to do business with its agencies. However, the best deals are often found outside the State contract, so someone on the staff has to be aware of the process to put out bid requests for vendors not on the contract. It is very easy for departments to simply pick a vendor who is local and on the contract without investing the time necessary to find a great deal. An individual department may save only a few hundred dollars on a PC by going out to bid, and the paperwork can be extensive and the process time consuming. However, if all PCs being purchased in the entire Division are packaged together, the potential for savings is great. For this reason, at UMA all computer hardware and software requests must go through SARIS where staff members keep up on the latest prices and negotiate deals with vendors. SARIS acts as the central agent for purchasing, receiving, and delivering all computers for the State-funded departments in the Division.

Another reason for having a central clearinghouse is to ensure compatibility within the Division whether it be for hardware or software. Software compatibility is crucial because, there must be limits regarding the number of different types of PCs and software packages if there is to be appropriate support centrally. For instance, when everyone in the Division is using the same wordprocessing or spreadsheet packages, staff support for training and troubleshooting is much simpler. Given that most of the PCs used are either IBM-compatible or Macintosh equipment, the concern over PC compatibility is not as extreme today. Of course, when one is dealing with local and wide area networks, then hardware compatibility is a greater concern. PCs must be purchased which will fit into the existing networks, and staff members must be concerned about such things as cabling, network cards, and printers. These concerns will be discussed later in the section on networking.

Installation and Maintenance

Installation and maintenance are two areas of concern for most purchasers of computer equipment. Some departments opt to pay a vendor to do everything, while others prefer to do everything themselves. The latter option is fine if the department has existing expertise on staff, but it probably makes most sense to do some combination. It is not uncommon for a local vendor to deliver and set up a PC at no additional charge, and a manufacturer's warranty will be in effect for a limited period. Some vendors will also offer annual maintenance contracts after the warranty period. The question becomes whether this is cost effective. SARIS does not have maintenance contracts on individual PCs, but machines which are crucial to the functioning of the WAN are covered. These include fileservers, bridges, and gateways, which are explained later in this chapter.

Since these machines are relatively inexpensive today and their lifespans can be from three to five years (or longer), if a major problem occurs the machines can be replaced. Today's machines are also fairly easily repaired by repair shops at relatively low cost, because the PCs consist primarily of plug-in boards which are simply replaced. Since the life span of a PC is limited and more powerful machines are developed each year, it is important to set aside funds for replacing machines. Rather than spend a great deal of money on maintenance contracts for PCs, departments would be well advised to consider pooling that money for individual repairs as needed and for a systematic replacement-and-upgrade program for existing machines.

Internal Support

While a department can find a vendor who will perform almost any service for a price, internal support is generally more cost-effective. More in-house expertise for the division means more services can be performed for the departments without spending extra money for external services. In-house training programs in both hardware knowledge and software applications can be very cost-effective, especially in the area of LAN technology.

Internal system design expertise is also very important. Someone on staff should keep up with the new technologies by reading the latest trade magazines, journals, and books. It is crucial to be able to know which vendors are not fully informed. Often a vendor is more interested in selling a particular product than in caring whether it is the best product for your needs. Someone on the student affairs staff needs to stay current to help prevent vendor sales pitches from leading to waste. If this staff member is centrally located in the division, the person is more readily available as a resource for the whole division.

Protecting Data

In-house expertise is especially critical in terms of protecting data from destruction, theft, or inadvertent loss. Damaged and lost data have been discussed more often recently in terms of the impact of viruses within computer systems, but in fact, loss of data can come from a variety of sources, including natural disaster, floppy and hard disk destruction, and theft. While data loss can result from many different means, permanent impairment on a system can be avoided generally through proper backup and archive procedures. Systematic procedures should be developed and maintained by an in-house computer staff person in each department.

When designing backup procedures, all users within a department should be encouraged to backup their own data onto floppy disks. Even though a departmental staff member may be backing up departmental data on a regular basis, users also should backup their own data to provide extra protection and individual security. Actually, if departments are working in a non-LAN environment, this individual backup procedure is the best means of insuring that users' data are protected.

In a LAN environment, a department also should designate one individual to be in charge of backing up on a nightly basis all data on the fileserver. Large capacity tape drives which fit into the hard drive slots of PCs are available to perform this task. On some LAN systems the backup procedure can be preset to run at night, thus avoiding the need to have someone actually monitor the backup process. The designated staff person then simply must load a tape before leaving the office and take it out upon returning the next day.

Proper storage of tapes and disks is also important in providing protection from inadvertent loss of data. Disks and tapes should not be stored next to any magnetic device, including electronic devices since they generate magnetic fields. Any form of magnetism has the potential to destroy stored data, so disks should not be stored next to a PC. It is also very important to store a complete set of data in an off-site location, meaning in a different building. This step is designed to prevent loss of data due to fire; although, a fire-proof safe would be a viable alterntive. Of course, many people do not take precautions against fire, because people generally believe that such destruction is never going to heppen to them. And when it does happen, there is no way to recover the data. Without off-site storage or fire-proof safes, years of work can be permanently destroyed by fire.

Turning to virus protection, there are many virus protection programs which can be purchased for individual PCs and LANs. Each day the departmental designee should run a virus software check to see if any known viruses are detected. If detected, viruses can be deleted. Of course, the key word here is "known." Many existing protection programs search for known viruses, so protection programs need to be updated as new viruses are discovered. Software developers usually provide new releases of their protection software for a nominal fee. To protect against viruses, users must be very cautious about what data to install on a PC. Virus programs are often imbedded in other software which is copied and circulated. Users should only load purchased software onto their PCs. Shareware is a common source of viruses. The cost of purging viruses from a contaminated system can be quite high, so every precaution should be taken to prevent such occurrences.

In the LAN environment, users must also take special precautions against providing remote access to the LAN. LAN dial-up capabilities from external locations provide not only other potential sources of virus contamination, such capabilities also provide another source of hacker intrusion to the system. Many student affairs offices are already vulnerable to large contingents of student employees, some of whom are hackers by hobby. While it is very difficult to create a fool-proof system against hackers, it is important to provide as much security as possible. Obviously, if remote dial-up access is prohibited or limited, one more security threat is eliminated.

No matter what steps are taken to help prevent the loss of data, invariably data are lost in every office. If proper backup and archive procedures have not been followed, some data will be irreplaceable. Protecting data should be a vital concern to everyone in the computer business. In student affairs, administrators cannot afford to lose student records. Imagine the loss of all financial aid records after awards have been determined but before distribution. Imagine the loss of all admissions application data or all posted grades for a semester. Preventing permanent data loss is of crucial economic interest to all student affairs departments.

WIDE AREA NETWORKING: THE KEY TO THE FUTURE

The movement at UMA

In the early 1980s, the Division of Student Affairs at UMA began a movement away from centralized mainframe computing with the purchase of a Wang minicomputer primarily to serve the word processing needs of student affairs staff in the Administration Building. While that system functioned fine for years, in 1988, the staff opted for the more powerful and flexible PC environment. The process of slowly replacing the minicomputer workstations with PCs escalated, and soon the minicomputer was scrapped.

In 1989, the Admissions Office developed the first large-scale LAN within the Division. The LAN design was prompted by the impending move of the Admissions Office out of the Administration Building where Admissions had direct hardwire connections to the administrative mainframe for data entry and look-up purposes, and there were direct connections to the Wang minicomputer for word processing needs. Also, a small LAN had just been installed in Admissions in order to run the new transfer credit evaluation software that had been developed by SARIS (Walter & Malaney, 1991). After a complete business analysis, it was decided that a large LAN would most effectively handle all of the computer needs of the new Admissions Center.

SARIS staff members were integral in the design and installation of the Admissions LAN, and the experience gained in that effort was utilized in the design of SARIS's LAN within the Administration Building. The major impetus for the SARIS LAN was the decision to replace the Wang minicomputer which had an annual maintenance cost exceeding $18,000 and was considered inefficient relative to the power of a LAN.

With the implementation of these LANs, it became obvious that tremendous computing power was available in a LAN environment, and soon other student affairs offices wanted to employ the technology for their own uses. Toward that end, SARIS staff members, in conjunction with a local vendor (Systems, Software, Support, Inc.), designed a system of interconnected LANs which comprise the Student Affairs WAN, depicted in Figure 1. While the design continues to evolve, all student affairs departments are depicted, even if some connections are not currently in place.

Local and Wide Area Network Terminology

A discussion of how individual student affairs offices use the technology is provided later, but prior to that discussion it is important for the reader to have an understanding of a few basic terms, such as LAN, WAN, fileserver, bridge, and gateway. It may be helpful to picture a LAN as a group of PCs, their associated peripherals, and printers physically connected by cables. Additionally, network interface cards (NICs) are required within each PC to enable the connections to be established physically. Also, specific network software is required to allow the connected hardware to function together logically. This structure allows many PC users to share information and various resources, such as hardware and software. The shared hardware might include a central data storage facility, commonly known as a fileserver, printers, and devices (bridges, gateways, and communication servers) which allow users to connect to other LANs or computers outside the local office environment. This system of interconnectivity, as depicted in Figure 1, is referred to as a WAN.

The heart of a LAN is the **fileserver** which is a PC dedicated to storing systems data and all of the software needed to run a LAN. The fileserver machine generally is utilized solely to accomplish these tasks and is not used for any other means, for instance as a workstation to do word processing. The type of machine needed

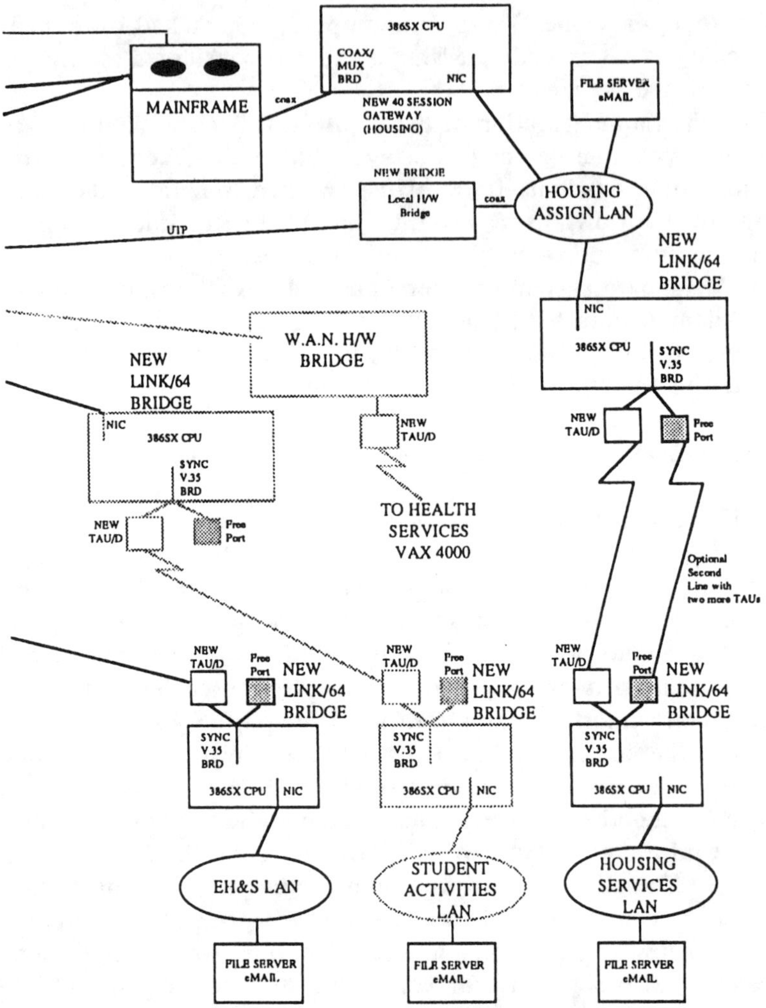

386SX CPU
COAX/
MUX
BRD
NIC
MAINFRAME
coax
NEW 40 SESSION
GATEWAY
(HOUSING)
FILE SERVER
eMAIL
NEW BRIDGE
Local H/W
Bridge
coax
HOUSING
ASSIGN LAN
UTP
NEW
LINK/64
BRIDGE
NIC
386SX CPU
SYNC
V.35
BRD
NEW
TAU/D
Free
Port
W.A.N. H/W
BRIDGE
NEW
LINK/64
BRIDGE
NIC
386SX CPU
SYNC
V.35
BRD
NEW
TAU/D
TO HEALTH
SERVICES
VAX 4000
NEW
TAU/D
Free
Port
Optional
Second
Line with
two more TAUs
NEW
TAU/D
Free
Port
NEW
LINK/64
BRIDGE
SYNC
V.35
BRD
386SX CPU
NIC
EH&S LAN
FILE SERVER
eMAIL
NEW
TAU/D
Free
Port
NEW
LINK/64
BRIDGE
SYNC
V.35
BRD
386SX CPU
NIC
STUDENT
ACTIVITIES
LAN
FILE SERVER
eMAIL
NEW
TAU/D
Free
Port
NEW
LINK/64
BRIDGE
SYNC
V.35
BRD
386SX CPU
NIC
HOUSING
SERVICES
LAN
FILE SERVER
eMAIL

depends upon the size and use of the network. Most of the LANs in the Student Affairs WAN use 386 machines housing 180 meg hard drives as fileservers. Once installed, the fileserver basically sits in a corner, continuously running the network, and is never touched by the users.

The **bridge** is typically a hardware board that plugs into a PC for the purpose of connecting two similar networks. A bridge board in a PC is required at each network site and the connections can be of two different types: remote or local. The remote bridge link is made typically via a telephone line with communications equipment such as a modem at each site, and a local bridge link utilizes a dedicated cable pulled between two LANs within the same building. Again, as in the case of the fileserver, the PCs used for bridges are dedicated to this one task. The remote bridges in the Student Affairs WAN operate with 386sx cpu machines with V.35 boards and TAU-Ds (terminal access units) which are high speed modems. This hardware provides for 64K baud rate connections between the SARIS LAN and the remote LANs: Career Center, Admissions, Public Safety, Environmental Health and Safety, and Student Activities. The local bridges use a dedicated cable and can be seen in Figure 1 as linking SARIS with the Financial Aid Office and with the Housing Assignments Office.

The **gateway** is a combination of hardware (a PC) and software that connects two dissimilar computer systems (e.g., an Ethernet network and a mainframe computer) via a dedicated line. Networks with a gateway can allow up to 64 nodes (PCs or dumb terminals connected to the network) access to a mainframe at one time. Remote LANs that are bridged to the LAN housing the gateway also share this access via the bridge. Use of the gateway allows an office to stop renting 3270 machines and direct lines to the mainframe computer and replace them with networked PCs. As can be seen in Figure 1, all remote LANs have high-speed access to the mainframe through their bridges to the SARIS LAN which in turn is linked to the mainframe via the gateways.

Another item commonly found in a network is a **communication server** which is a dedicated PC with appropriate software connected to a pooled set of modems for the purpose of sending and receiving data over telephone lines to and from other computer systems both on or off campus. In SARIS, the set of pooled TAUs at the communication server allows multiple users to access any available TAU. This cuts down on the cost and necessity of having a TAU for each PC and tying up a telephone line, which is especially important if a campus has only voice lines available for this type of activity. This kind of access could be used for tying into the campus' mainframe computer to utilize global academic networks like INTERNET or BITNET.

While it is not the intent of this chapter to comprehensively explain LAN terminology, it is important for the reader to understand that the above description does not address the many technical aspects of LANs. For instance, one technical point to consider is the different types of physical layouts: Ethernet, arcnet, and token ring, for example (SARIS has adopted the Ethernet topology). Also, there are various types of LAN protocols, or software that enables the PCs to transmit and receive data. There are several types of cable which can be used to connect the hardware, such as coaxial, unshielded and shielded twisted pair, and fiber optic. There are different network interface cards which vary by type of cabling used and PC size and speed. There are also many types of LAN operating systems (SARIS is running Novell Netware 386) which are software programs that function much like PC operating systems (e.g. DOS) except a LAN operating system runs a network (not a PC) and serves as an interface between applications and the network. This section has provided just a sampling of the terminology used in the LAN world. For further information, several good reference sources are available, such as the many LAN trade magazines that have developed in the past few years: LAN Times, Networking Management, and LAN Magazine.

Practical Applications of LANs

The many offices depicted in Figure 1 have widely ranging uses for the LAN and WAN technology, but most of the offices with LANs use them for several standard applications, including word processing, spreadsheets, and mainframe access via the bridges and gateways. Several offices also utilize desktop publishing applications, graphics software, and small database applications for record keeping.

A few offices have unique functions depending upon the type of service they perform. For instance, as mentioned earlier, the Admissions Office has a LAN-based software application which was programmed by SARIS staff to assist in transfer credit evaluation. With this application, courses from the transcripts of transfer student applicants are entered into the computer, course equivalencies tables are accessed, and course equivalencies are assigned to a student's record electronically (Walter & Malaney, 1991). This process allows the Admissions Office to provide transfer applicants with a list of the UMass course equivalencies for the accepted transfer courses at the time of notification of admission. The Admissions Office also enters all of the data from student applications via the LAN and then transmits the data to the mainframe student data base in large batches. This process increases the control that the Admissions Office has over the data before the data go to the mainframe data base.

Housing Services has developed an on-line disciplinary system in which disciplinary records are entered into computers located in the cluster offices of the residence hall system and then sent electronically to the central Housing Office. When necessary, the files also can be transferred electronically to the Dean of Students' Office for further action.

The Career Center will soon be using another LAN-based application developed by SARIS staff to assist in matching student job candidates with prospective employers. With this application, data regarding job openings from specific employers are obtained and entered by the Career Center staff in conjunction with data from graduating students seeking employment. Items including type of job, required skills, and location are run through a computer matching program. The resulting matches then can be displayed for the Career Center staff to be used in counseling students.

As mentioned earlier, SARIS has utilized the LAN to develop and test LAN-based software applications for other offices within Student Affairs. In addition to coordinating computing activity for Student Affairs, SARIS also coordinates the research operation for Student Affairs, so the office has some unique computer needs pertaining to its research function. One of the most common uses of the SARIS LAN is by Project Pulse, the telephone survey research operation, which uses a software package that allows data entry during the survey process via electronic questionnaires (Thurman & Malaney, 1989). Once these raw data are collected, they are built into a data file using SPSS-PC. Analyses are run, graphs and charts are prepared, and text is written. The whole report is prepared through desktop publishing software and is then printed for dissemination.

One of the primary reasons for the development of the WAN is to allow paper-free communication within the entire division of student affairs. Some of the offices with LANs are already utilizing electronic mail packages to communicate. As soon as the entire WAN is completed, the entire division will be able to communicate via electronic mail. Simple messages, memos, letters, and entire documents will be easily transferred across the WAN.

Costs and Benefits for Other Institutions

LAN and WAN usage in student affairs is continuously expanding. The benefits of a LAN over the use of several stand-alone PCs are many. With a LAN, resources are utilized more efficiently because users can share hardware and software. Also, individuals can work more easily on common projects (e.g., papers, graphs, spreadsheets) by accessing the same document without leaving their individual PCs. A LAN also increases the ability of users to communicate by simply sending messages via electronic mail. With the use of a LAN gateway, users can replace out-moded, usually rented, uni-dimensional 3270 machines with PCs that can provide necessary links to the mainframe while simultaneously being used for various personal computing needs.

A primary benefit of the WAN environment lies in the connectivity it provides among offices all over campus. This is especially advantageous to a student affairs enterprise which is housed in several different buildings. With enough money, it is possible to connect almost any type of computer system to the WAN.

While LAN and WAN usage at colleges and universities is increasing, only about ten percent of all PCs on campuses have been networked (Caldwell & Perry, 1990). One of the reasons so few networks are in place is because of cost. Available resources both in terms of money and personnel are likely to play important roles in student affairs administrators' decisions about moving into the LAN/WAN environment. The up-front equipment costs to install a LAN can be considerable, depending upon how many PCs are already owned. However, since maintenance rates for fileservers, gateways, and bridges (PCs need not have maintenance contracts) are generally relatively inexpensive compared to the maintenance of a minicomputer, some savings are possible. As mentioned previously, it is also possible to save money in mainframe rental charges by using a LAN gateway instead of direct lines to each PC or 3270 machine.

Another cost factor relates to software. As Corbitt (1991) noted, networks often utilize special versions of software. Many software programs such as dBase and Lotus 1-2-3 are available in network versions, but many packages are not. And, while it is possible to actually run a non-network version of software on a network, careful attention must be paid to licensing agreements (see Chapter 14 on Legal Liabilities). Most likely additional charges will be required by the software firm to run such programs on a network.

Corbitt (1991) also mentioned the increased problem of security in the LAN environment. When more users have access to a system, there is more danger in having unauthorized access. Fortunately, most network operating systems have good security systems where each user's rights can be limited according to specific needs. If a network has a communication server which allows dial-in access from outside the system, further risks must be addressed. The risks come in the form of unauthorized users as well as system contamination from viruses. Each LAN should be swept for viruses at least daily. Virus contamination of a network can cost thousands of dollars to correct.

Another important and costly issue in networking relates to the personnel needed to manage the system. The LAN world still represents relatively new technology on most campuses, and even on campuses where LANs are being installed, there often are no experienced technical staff members to serve as LAN managers. As Bates and Leclerk (1990) indicated, there are many day-to-day problems which arise once a LAN is installed, such as defective hardware, problematic software, and memory deficiencies, and resolving these problems requires a LAN expert. Vendors are willing to help for a price, but clearly the most efficient and productive answer is to have in-house expertise.

Therefore, before any departments or offices within institutions of higher education become involved with LAN and WAN technology, they should be willing to provide funds for both equipment and personnel. At UMass, the Division of Student Affairs was in a perfect position to succeed in this venture because SARIS had built up a great deal of knowledge and expertise about personal computers before entering the LAN environment. Using existing personnel who are knowledgeable about personal computing is a viable alternative to creating new positions. Accompanied by an expert staff, LANs and WANs should prove profitable to student affairs divisions at most colleges and universities.

THE IMPORTANCE OF CONTINUED MANAGEMENT AND PLANNING

In their writings, Kissler (1988) and Powell (1988) discuss the use of computers by academic deans and college presidents, and their discussions highlight an important point: proper use and management of computer resources is much more likely to occur if the top managers are involved in computing. Today, it is still far too often the case that CSAOs and student affairs department heads do not use computers themselves which makes their abilities to manage computer resources very limited. They cannot relate to such issues as costs and personnel. Regardless of how involved top managers are, the management and planning process must have their endorsement. If the CSAO chooses not to be directly involved then a designate must be appointed to handle computer-related issues within the entire division.

Since 1984, the director of SARIS has been the CSAO's designee on computer issues, providing student affairs representation at university and campus levels as well as within student affairs. The director has tried to ensure that at least three missions have been covered by computer groups within the division: purchasing, planning and system design, and troubleshooting. Historically, many of these functions have been performed on an ad hoc basis, but some permanent committees were established. For years, the Student Affairs Computer Acquisition Committee (SACAC) reviewed computer requests to purchase equipment, but that committee was finally replaced because it consisted of mainly budget personnel and not computer experts.

Most of the planning and system design has also been ad hoc with a few knowledgeable individuals planning systems for specific, interested departments. Little thought was given to the broader needs of the whole division. When the LAN technology was initiated in 1989, the reality of an inter-linked division of student affairs began to materialize. The Wide Area Network plan was left up to SARIS and while constituencies in all of the student affairs departments were brought in for discussions, there was no formal structure or committee. This worked at UMA because of the historical recognition of SARIS as the centralized representative of the CSAO. Most likely at other institutions, someone would need to be designated as chair of a division-wide computer planning group to prepare a systems plan.

It should be noted that a permanent committee (or users group) was established as a result of the informal planning process described above. When SARIS staff members were working on the plan for the WAN, they contacted various departmental computer experts within student affairs. As these discussions persisted, it was decided to formalize the group and call it the PC/LAN Users Group (PLUG). This group also became the informal consultants to SARIS regarding computer purchases, replacing the functions of SACAC.

PLUG continues to meet on a monthly basis to discuss the ongoing changes with the WAN. Topics of discussion include bridging from LAN to LAN, utilization of the gateways to access the administrative mainframe computer, and simple troubleshooting regarding the LANs and PCs. While each department has specific representatives, any individual within student affairs may attend the meetings and solicit advice and information. The meetings have even begun to draw interest from the rest of the campus community which deals with Novell networks. Such a users group is highly recommended as means of disseminating knowledge throughout the division of student affairs.

With the WAN design in place, the CSAO decided that student affairs computer systems should have a formal review, so the Vice Chancellor's Systems Study Group was established to investigate what was happening and where and how the division should proceed. It is interesting to note that this was the first computer systems group that consisted of some department heads who reported directly to the CSAO. As a result, among the various recommendations to come out of this group was a desire to have an on-going student affairs computer planning committee.

Given the continually changing computing environment, it is important to establish an on-going planning group. The student affairs division should prepare short-term and long-term plans. One of the efforts of the UMA planning committee will be the preparation of a five-year systems plan for the Division. Even if the plan is likely to change during that period, it important to have people thinking about long range plans. It is also important to have the

CSAO and the department heads involved so they are aware of computing trends and can apply them to their long range policy plans.

CONCLUSION

As this chapter shows, managing the high-tech computer systems within student affairs is not a simple task, nor is it without cost. Depending on the size of the student affairs operation and the extent of the computer system, that management is easily a full-time job for at least one individual if not an entire staff. Centralization is a key factor, as is the committment of the CSAO. Coordination of the activities among departments and an overall systems plan are important factors in cost-effective resource management which, in turn, should assist in improving services to students.

It is the very nature of the student affairs enterprise to try to provide the best possible services to students. This is often interpreted as personalized," high-touch" service, but it is also important to provide services in a timely manner. Without computerization, such activities as admissions, financial aid, and registration would take considerably longer than they do now. Before the existence of extensive computerization, staff members spent more time interacting with paper than with students. Through the enhancement of high-tech computer systems, student affairs actually has enhanced the "high-touch" aspect of student services.

Acknowledgement

Acknowledgement is due Maarten P. Walter, former associate director for systems and development of SARIS, for his help in the design of the wide area network detailed in this chapter. Also recognized are Rosio Alvarez, Judy Connelly, Joe Fitzgerald, Noel Yu, and SSS, Inc. for their continued assistance in developing and maintaining the WAN, and Judy Connelly and SSS, Inc. for their work in preparing Figure 1. A special thanks is due Elizabeth Williams and Joe Fitzgerald for their comments on earlier versions of this chapter.

REFERENCES

Allbritten, W. & Bogal-Allbritten, R. (1987). Computer telecommunications in student affairs. *NASPA Journal*, 24(3), 57-61.

Bates, J. & Leclerc, G. (1990). Reaching the promised LAN. *Managing information technology: Facing the issues: proceedings of the 1989 CAUSE National Conference*, 349-355.

Beeler, K. J. (1989). Decision support systems and the art of enrollment management. *NASPA Journal*, 26(4), 242-247.

Caldwell, L. & Perry, J. (1990). Providing an environment for campus connectivity: Novell's programs for higher education. *Managing information technology: Facing the issues: proceedings of the 1989 CAUSE National Conference*, 598-599.

Corbitt, T. (1991). Net gains. *Educational computing and technology*, 12(4), 47-48.

Green, K. C. (1988). The new administrative computing. In K. C. Green & S. W. Gilbert (Eds.), *Making computers work for administrators*, (pp. 5-11). New Directions for Higher Education, no. 62. San Francisco: Jossey-Bass.

Hawkins, B. L. (1988). Administrative and organizational issues in campus computing. In K. C. Green & S. W. Gilbert (Eds.), *Making computers work for administrators*, (pp. 13-26). New Directions for Higher Education, no. 62. San Francisco: Jossey-Bass.

Kalsbeek, D. H. (1989). Managing data and information resources. In U. Delworth, G. R. Hanson, & Assoc.(Eds.), *Student services: A handbook for the profession*, 493-512. San Francisco: Jossey-Bass. Kissler, G. R. (1988). A new role for deans in computing. In K. C. Green & S. W. Gilbert (Eds.), *Making computers work for administrators*, (pp. 47-55). New Directions for Higher Education, no. 62. San Francisco: Jossey-Bass.

Mac Lean, L. S. (1986). Developing M.I.S. in student affairs. *NASPA Journal*, 23(3), 2-7.

Masland, A. T. (1985). Administrative computing in higher education. In J. C. Smart (ed.), *Higher education: Handbook of theory and research* (Vol. I), (pp. 173-212). New York: Agathon Press.

McCredie, J. W. (1983). *Campus computing strategies*. Bedford, MA: Digital Press.

Menke, R. F. (1966). Electronic data processing in placement. *NASPA Journal*, 3(4), 10-12.

Mullen, R. W. (1990). Networked "dorm of the future." *Tech Trends*, 34(6), 20-24.

Powell, J. L. (1988). The computer as presidential factotum. In K. C. Green & S. W. Gilbert (Eds.), *Making computers work for administrators*, (pp. 57-69). New Directions for Higher Education, no. 62. San Francisco: Jossey-Bass.

Pyle, K. R. & Stipling, R. O. (1977). Counseling vs. computer in career development. *NASPA Journal*, 14(4), 38-40.

Ryland, J. N. (1988). Distributed computing. In K. C.Green & S. W. Gilbert (Eds.), *Making computers work for administrators*. New Directions for Higher Education, no. 62. San Francisco: Jossey-Bass.

Sampson, J. P. Jr. (1982). Effective computer resource management: Keeping the tail from wagging the dog. *NASPA Journal*, 19(3), 38-46.

Thurman, Q. & Malaney, G. D. (1989). Surveying students as a means of assessing and changing policies and practices of student affairs programs. *NASPA Journal*, 27(2), 101-107.

Walter, M. P. & Malaney, G. D. (1991). A transfer credit evaluation system for a stand alone personal computer or a local area network. *College and University*, 66(2), 95-104.

Chapter 17

Implications for the Future

John L. Baier
Thomas S. Strong

Because the benefits to be gained from the use of modern computer and information technology in the delivery of student services and the administration of student affairs functions are so great, it is necessary that all student affairs administrators not only continue the present use of such technology, but also prepare for the future.

The computer will continue to play a key role in the instructional programs and management of our colleges and universities, as will video, CD-ROM, THOR-CD, interactive multimedia and other technological systems not yet invented or perfected. All technology is likely to become both more sophisticated and easier to use. Exactly how these technological advances will impact our lives, education, and student affairs is unknown. Forecasting is difficult, but the successful student affairs administrator must be ready for change and prepared to take advantage of every opportunity.

One example of this is the emergence of a new technology called "virtual reality". Currently it is being used to make motion pictures such as *Terminator 2*. Basically, it uses computer generated images of non-existant things and then allows those images to be merged or "fused" with actual screen images to create the illusion of reality. Most of the special effects in *Terminator 2* were created using this computer imaging technique. Many campus computer experts believe that "virtual reality" will soon find its way onto college campuses because of its unlimited potential for use in design and engineering modeling. Undoubtably, several applications of this technology will in time also develop for student affairs functions.

Another example is the dramatic increase in the use of interactive multimedia during the past year. Interactive multimedia technology combines speech, enhanced music, video images, animation, and computer capabilities into a unified system (Brady, 1989). It lends itself to instruction based on the very diffferent ways students learn because it can access and produce information using a variety of media in a coordinated nonsequential way.

One way to illustrate the potential of interactive multimedia technology for student affairs is to look at an example of how it can be used in instructional programs. In 1990, the National Foundation for the Improvement of Education (NFIE) released a report entitled "Images of Potential" in which it developed six scenarios of what public schools might look like with the use of integrated multimedia technology in the 21st century. Following is a portion of the report's view of what a technologically advanced high school might be like during the next decade.

> "Diana's Social Sciences class is studying about past civilizations and cultures. Diana's class is using telecommunications to search data bases on topics and artifacts they have discovered. She has just sent a message through her laptop computer at her student workstation to a student in the foreign language class to help translate a script found scrawled on one of the objects. She then calls up the interactive videodisc surrogate field trip of Cancun. She travels through the ruins, choosing many different paths. She selects indepth information on digging techniques. Diana's math class is working on designing the three-dimensional computer graphics simulation of the dig site. They are working closely with the science class to determine the appropriate dating techniques to ascertain the age of the artifacts. They are also studying the site's geological formations to incorporate the appropriate physical and chemical characteristics into the simulator, which will allow them to manipulate the environment . . . Diana finishes class by sending a picture of the dig site to Mario, who is home with the flu. Mario has been keeping up with classwork through the curriculum database connection" (Bruder, 1990, p 29).

This illustration reflects the level of technology which will soon be used in many of our nation's high schools and the "technological literacy" levels of tomorrow's high school students. Is there any doubt that higher education and the student affairs profession has to also become more technologically literate and comfortable so that it can properly take advantage of and use the tremendous instructional benefits (for both staff and students) accorded by advancing technology?

RECOMMENDATIONS FOR THE FUTURE

With these thoughts in mind, the following ten recommendations are offered to ensure the success of the student affairs profession in the 21st century.

1. Keep Focused

Continue to keep the focus of the student affairs profession on students, student learning, and student development. Don't let technology dominate our work. Instead, use technology to enhance the quality of our work with students. It is imperative that student affairs professionals keep mindful that student affairs is a "helping" profession with a century old tradition of providing understanding, nurture, and supportive services and programs to a constantly changing student body which is made up of unique individuals with their own special needs, goals, gifts, and personalities. Simply stated, student affairs is a "high-touch" profession living in a "high-tech" world.

2. Plan Strategically

In consideration of the above issue, the mass of information which technology makes readily accessible, decreases in funding, requirements for accountability and total quality management, legal liabilities, and the rapid advances in technology, it is very important that student affairs organizations develop a sound plan for both applying and maintaining the use of modern technology, in all of its areas of responsibility. It must, therefore, develop, implement, and update plans for using modern technology by using strategic planning methodology; establish a strong central authority to coordinate the planning process, networking and access to computers and data bases; involve as many staff members in the planning and decision making process as possible; and develop an infrastructure which supports the use of technology (i.e. staff training programs, equipment repair, and replacement accounts). Because student affairs organizations have such limited budgets, it is critical that they give very careful consideration to proper planning, implementation, and usage policies before they purchase any equipment or software in order to avoid wasting very limited resources.

3. Provide and Require Staff Training and Development

Having access to modern computer and information technology is of little value if staff members are not available who know how to use it properly. Student affairs organizations must, therefore, continue developing the technological literacy, comfort, and competency levels of all current staff members. All of the methods discussed in Chapter Two (i.e. short courses, workshops, technology related newsletters, tutoring programs, self-paced video learning modules) should be carefully considered and utilized if appropriate to the campus environment and policies.

4. Encourage CAS Standards Compliance

To ensure that new people who enter the profession are technologically literate, student affairs organizations also need to encourage each of our graduate training programs to follow the Council for the Advancement of Standards (CAS) Master's Degree Level Preparation Standards and Guidelines which call for the inclusion of a computer literacy and applications component in each student affairs graduate preparation program, regardless of the program's emphasis. This will help ensure the future computer literacy of the profession. The profession should also consider requiring that all employees stay current and up to date on new technological applications for student affairs in order to be eligible for merit increases and/or promotions.

5. Develop New Applications

The profession must continue developing new computer assisted ways to collect, maintain, manage, and use pertinent data more effectively and efficiently on students, programs, facility usage, program impacts on learning and student development, retention, financing operations, and similiar tasks whenever possible and appropriate. This will help ensure that the student affairs profession stays up to date and on the cutting edge of technology.

6. Continue Networking

The full benefits of using computer technology cannot be obtained if computers are not fully networked to each other and to the central campus mainframe computer. Networks allow for on-line interactive communication with any other connected computer. The proper development of Local Area Networks (LANs) and Wide Area Networks (WANs) are very important to the effective and efficient use of computer databases, software programs, and electronic communications. Therefore, it is imperative that student affairs organizations carefully develop appropriate networking systems to meet the particular needs of their campus and to enhance communications with students, faculty, staff, and other administrators wherever possible.

7. Balance Student and Institutional Needs

As student affairs professionals should try to utilize technology in all new program development and administration, they need to be certain that its use will be good for both students and the institution before proceeding. Before a new technology is purchased the following questions should be asked: (1) Will it be good for students? (2) Will it save time and/or money? (3) Will it be good for the institution? If the answers to all three questions are "yes", proceed with all deliberate speed. However, if the answer is "no" to any one of the questions, especially the first one, it would be wise to defer proceeding until the economic conditions or technological advances warrant further consideration.

8. Make Technology Transparent

Make the expanded use of technology "transparent". By this it is meant that student affairs professionals should design new administrative tools with the use of modern technology as an essential design criterion. Too often administrators have applied technology to existing administrative functions thereby creating systems that are cumbersome and ineffecient. Professionals should apply new technology as an integral part of the design process rather than as an add on to traditional administrative practice.

9. Stay Abreast of Legal and Ethical Issues

In today's litigious society everyone must be concerned with the legal liabilities that are incurred as a result of specific acts, omissions, and decisions. Over the past decade, a considerable amount of case law specific to the use of computers has accrued. All student affairs organizations, in conjunction with their institutional legal counsel, should develop written policies for the student affairs area which deal with the legal and ethical issues related to computer use at their institution. Programs designed to develop an awareness and working knowledge of computer law and the institutions specific computer related policies should also be offered as a part of the division's on-going staff development program.

10. Continue Serving as Guardians of Student Rights and Responsibilities

Student affairs organizations should continue serving as custodians and guardians of student records to ensure against their misuse by others, and should also ensure that student codes of conduct contain prohibitions (and appropriate sanctions) against the misuse and/or theft of computer equipment, systems, files, software, and others' work by students. Toward this end, the college's legal counsel should routinely review all current and planned technological applications and policies to ensure that they are in full compliance with existing laws.

In conclusion, by doing these things, the student affairs profession should be able to derive the enormous benefits that can be gained from technological advances without sacrificing its traditional roots as a "helping profession" interested in meeting the ever-changing educational and developmental needs of college students. The profession need not fear technology, but instead, use "high-tech" to enhance its "high-touch" mission.

REFERENCES

Brady, H. (1989) Interactive multimedia: The next wave. *Classroom computer learning*, 10, September, 56-61.

Bruder, I. (1990) Visions of the future, *Electronic learning*, 10, January, 24-30.

Appendix A:

Listing of Resources by Program Area*

ACADEMIC ADVISING PROGRAMS

Commercially Available Software Systems

ActionTrack, Noel/Levitz Centers for Institutional Effectiveness and Innovation, Inc., 902 East Second Avenue, Coralville, IA 52241, (319) 337-4700, FAX (319) 337-5274.

Teams 2000, P.O.Box 1184, Harrisonburg, VA 22801. (703) 432-5269, (803) 768-7090.

In-House Developed Software Systems

Enterprise State Junior College, P.O.Box 1300, Enterprise, AL 36331, (205) 347-2623. Contact: Dr. Nancy Smith, Betty Bierbaum, or Betty Cully.

Florida Community College at Jacksonville, North Campus, 4501 Capper Road, Jacksonville, FL 32218-4499. Contact: Dr. John E. Farmer.

---

* The American College Personnel Association (ACPA) does not endorse any of the products listed. Also, the editors and chapter authors are not affiliated with any of the software companies or products listed. The purpose of providing this information is solely to make the reader aware of many of the resources that are currently available for use by student affairs professionals.

Florida Community College at Jacksonville South Campus, 3939 Roosevelt Blvd., Jacksonville, FL 32205-8999, (904) 646-2009. Contact: Jerry Patterson.

Massachusetts Bay Community College, 50 Oakland Street, Wellesley Hills, MA 02181. Contact: Donna Green or Cholthanee Koerojna.

Montgomery, College, Germantown Campus, 2200 Observation Drive, Germantown, MD 20874. Contacts: Thomas S. Price or Richard H. Miller.

Northwest Mississippi Community College, Highway 51 North, Senatobia, MS 38668. Contact: Dr. Barbara Jones or Mary Beth Sealy.

Pennsylvania State University, 304 Grange Building, Penn State University, University Park, PA 16802. Contact: James Kelly.

Poise, Campus America, Regency Business Park, Suite 205, 900 Hill Avenue, Knoxville, TN 37951-2523, (615) 523-9506.

Robert Morris College, Narrows Run Road, Coraopolis, PA 15108-1189. Contact: Dr. Don L. Fox, Jr., or Jim Leone.

Solar Program Information, 1340 Florida Education Center, Tallahassee, FL 32399-0400. Contact: Ms. Sandy Fleck, or Ms. Connie Graunke.

University of Wisconsin System Administration, 1656 Van Hise Hall-Rubin, 1550 Van Hise Hall-Bergman, 1220 Linen Drive, Madison, WI 53706. Contact: Larry Rubin or Gail Bergman

Valencia Community College, 1800 South Kirkman Road, Orlando, FL 32811. Contact: Len Burry, Carolyn McKinney, or Marquita Anderson.

CAREER PLANNING AND PLACEMENT PROGRAMS

Career Navigator, Drake Beam Morin, Inc., Order Department, 100 Park Ave., New York, NY 10017.

Career Network, 640 North LaSalle St., Suite 560, Chicago, IL 60610.

Career Placement Registry, Career Placement Registry, Inc., 3202 Kirkwood Highway, Wilmington, DE 19808.

College Recruitment Database, Executive Telecom Systems, Inc., 9585 Valparaiso Court, Indianapolis, IN 46268.

Connexion, Peterson's, 202 Carnegie Center, P.O. Box 2123, Princeton, NJ 08543-2123.

DASIS, NCCSRP, 50 Lind Hall, 207 Church St. S.E., Minneapolis, MN 55455.

Discover, American College Testing Program, P.O. Box 168, Iowa City, IA 52243.

Dun's Million Dollar Disc, Dun's Marketing Services, Three Sylvan Way, Parsippany, NJ 07054-3896.

Federal Occupational and Career Information System (FOCIS), National Technical Information Service, 5285 Port Royal Rd., Springfield, VA 22161

1st Place, Academic Software, P.O. Box 158429, Austin, TX 78745-8429.

JOBLINK, 12062 Valley View St., Suite 239, Garden Grove, CA 92645-1739.

JOBTRAK, JOBTRAK Corp., 1990 Westwood Blvd., Suite 260, Los Angeles, CA 90025.

kiNexus, Information Kinetics, Inc., 640 North LaSalle St., Suite 560, Chicago, IL 60610.

Modular Voice Application Job Hotline, U.S. Telecom International, Inc., 211 Main St., Joplin, MO 64801.

The Perfect Resume Computer Kit, Permax Systems, Inc., 5008 Gordon Ave., Madison, WI 53716-2627.

Resume Expert, Resume Expert Systems, 10500 Barkley Ave., Overland Park, KS 66212-1838.

SIGI Plus, Educational Testing Service, Rosedale Rd., Princeton, NJ 08541.

Total Scheduling System (TSS), Tres-D Corp., 2144 Yellow Creek Rd., Suite 200, Akron, OH 44313.

Winning Approach to Interviewing, Resume Expert Systems, 10500 Barkley Ave., Overland Park, KS 66212-1838.

COUNSELING CENTER PROGRAMS

BRS After Dark, BRS Information Technologies, 1200 Rt. 7, Chatham, NY 12110.

Computerized Note-Taker, Center Systems, Inc., 128 Front Street, Binghamton, NY 13905.

246 *Technology in Student Affairs*

Counseling Center Intake System, Center Systems, Inc., 128 Front Street Binghamton, NY 13905.

Dbase-IV, Ashton Tate, 20101 Hamilton Avenue, Torrance, CA 90509-9972.

Differential Aptitude Tests, Computerized Adaptive Edition. Psychological Corporation, 555 Academic Court, San Antonio, TX 78204-2498.

Knowledge Index, DIALOG Information Service, Inc., Palo Alto, CA.

Lotus 1-2-3, Lotus Development Corporation, 55 Cambridge Parkway, Cambridge, MA 02142.

Microtest Assessment System, National Computer Systems NCS Professional Assessment Services, P.O.Box 1416, Minneapolis, MN 55440.

MMPI-2 Adult Interpretive System, Multi-Health Systems, Inc., 908 Niagara Falls Boulevard., North Tonawanda, NY 14120-2060.

Myers-Briggs Type Indicator and Software, Publishers Test Service, 2500 Garden Road, Monterey, CA 93940-5379.

PC-File, Buttonware, Inc., P.O.Box 5786, Bellevue, WA 98006.

Shrink, The Practice Manager. Multi-health Systems, Inc., 908 Niagara Falls Boulevard, North Tonawanda, NY 14120-2060.

WAIS-R, WISC-R, WPPSI-R Microcomputer Assisted Interpretive Reports, Psychological Corporation, 555 Academic Court, San Antonio, TX 78204-2498.

WISC-R, WRAT-R, WPPSI/WPPSI-R, Stanford-Binet Intelligence Scale, (4th edition), Woodcock Johnson Achievement Test (original and R versions), Kaufman Test of Educational Achievement, K-ABC, and the PIAT/PIAT-R. Psychologistics, Inc., P.O.Box 3896, Indialantic, FL 32903.

FINANCIAL AID PROGRAMS

AID, Software Research Northwest, Inc., 17710-100th Avenue SW, Vashon Island, WA 98070.

FAMS, Information Associates, Inc., 3000 Ridge Road East, Rochester, NY 14622.

Perkins Loans by Greentree Software, Greentree Software, P.O.Box 1003, Cashiers, N.C. 28717.

SAFE, ACT SAFE Office, 5601 La Jolla Boulevard., La Jolla, CA 92037-7524.

SAM, Sigma Systems, Inc., 650 S. Cherry St., Suite 1035, Denver, CO 80222-9870.

SARA or Network SARA, American College Testing Program, P.O.Box 168, Iowa City, IA 52243.

Student Loan Counselor - Plus, Educational Testing Service, College and University Programs, MS-18V, Princeton, N.J. 08541.

HOUSING PROGRAMS

Arts & Letters, Computer Support Corporation, 15926 Midway Road, Dallas, TX 75244.

Cadvance (Computer Aided Design), ISICAD, Cadworks, 4322 North Beltline, Suite B110, Irving, TX 75038.

Calendar Creator Plus, Egghead Discount Software, 14679 Midway Road, Suite 101, Dallas, TX 75244.

Carbon Copy, Egghead Discount Software, 14679 Midway Road, Suite 101, Dallas, TX 75244.

Chief, Maintenance Automation Corporation, 3107 W. Hallandale Beach Boulevard, Hallandale, FL 33990-5104

DataPerfect, WordPerfect Corporation, 1555 North Technology Way, Orem, UT 84057. Entre Computer, 4620 Bryant Irvin Road, Suite 516, Fort Worth, TX 76132.

dBase III, Ashton Tate, 20101 Hamilton Avenue, Torrance, CA 90509-9972.

Financial Accounting System, Information Associates Inc., 3000 Ridge Road East, Rochester, NY 14622

Harvard Graphics, SPC Software Publishing Corporation, 1901 Landings Drive, P.O.Box 7210, Mountain View, CA 94039-7210.

Housing Information System, Applied Collegiate Systems, A Division of Griffin Technology, Inc., Hills of Decker Court, 100 Decker Court, Suite 101, Irving, TX 75062.

Main/Tracker, Elke Corporation, P.O.Box 41915, Plymouth, MN 55441.

Microsoft Works, Microsoft Corporation 16011 NE 36th Way, Box 97017, Redmond, WA 98073-9717.

Paradox, Egghead Discount Software, 14679 Midway Road, Suite 101, Dallas, TX 75244.

Payroll/Personnel System, Integral Systems, 2185 N. California Boulevard, Walnut, CA 94596.

PF Write, Egghead Discount Software, 14679 Midway Road, Suite 101, Dallas, TX 75244.

SSH (The System for Student Housing), Softech Associates, Inc., 19 Revere Road, Suite 1B, Piscataway, NJ 08854.

TMA (The Maintenance Authority), Collegiate Products, Inc., 8212 South Harvard, Tulsa, OK 74138.

Waterloo Script, WATCOM, 414 Phillip Street University of Waterloo, Waterloo, Ontario, Canada N2L 3G1.

WordPerfect, WordPerfect Corporation, 1555 North Technology Way, Orem, UT 84057.

INTERNATIONAL STUDENT AND SCHOLAR SERVICES

SOFTWARE

Data Perfect, Word Perfect Corporation, 1555 North Technology Way, Orem, Utah 840587, 1-800-451-5151

International Student and Scholars Management System, Education Catalysis, Inc., 186 South Street, 4th Floor Boston, Massachusetts 02111, (617) 482-8982

IVYSOFT Foreign Student Database Management System, Ivysoft International, P. O. Box 241090, 1393 Ivy Road, Memphis, Tennessee 38124, (901) 763-2956

PC Automated International Student Records System, Dr. Gregory A. Kuhlman, Director, Brooklyn College Career Services, 1305 James Hall, Brooklyn, New York 11210-9966 (718) 859-6932

Q & A, Symantec Corporation, 10201 Torre Avenue, Cupertino, California 95014 (408) 446-8958

University of Michigan (student/scholar database software), Jon O. Heise, Director, International Center, 603 East Madison, University of Michigan, Ann Arbor, Michigan 48109-1370 (313) 747-2256

ASSOCIATIONAL SUPPORT

Institute of International Education (IIE), Statistical Research Division, 809 United Nations Plaza, New York, New York 10017 (212) 984-5347

MicroSIG (NAFSA's Microcomputer Special Interest Group), John D. Hopkins (Chair), American Language and Culture, Program, Department of Translation Studies, University of Tampere, Box 607, Tampere SF-33101 Finland (31) 156-828.   Bernard E. LaBerge (Co-Manager of INTER-L), Assistant Dean and International Student Adviser, Office of the Graduate School, Virginia Polytechnic Institute & State University Blacksburg, Virginia 24061 (703) 231-6271.   James R. Graham (Newsletter Editor and Co-Manager of INTER-L), 4301 Terry Lake Road, Fort Collins, Colorado 80524 (303) 493-0207

NAFSA: Association of International Educators, 1875 Connecticut Avenue, N. W., Suite 1000, Washington, D. C. 20009-5738 (202) 462-4811. Computer Services-Daniel Sauter, Director of Computer Services, (and NAFSA/Central Liaison to MicroSIG) and Rakan Saraiji, Computer/FIPSE Project Assistant.   Publications-Steven Kennedy, Director of Publications Kate McDuffie, Coordinator, Publications Fulfillment.

E-MAIL DISTRIBUTION SERVICES

Independent Federation of Chinese Students and Scholars in the U. S. (IFCSS), 733 15th Street, N. W., Suite 440, Washington, D. C. 20005 (202) 347-0017.

INTER-L: Discussion List for NAFSAnet Members and International Educators, in General, James R. Graham, CoManager and Bernard E. LaBerge, Co-Manager (See MicroSIG above for contact information).

SECUSS-L: List Service of NAFSA's Section on U. S. Study Abroad), Arthur Neisberg, SECUSS-L Manager, Study Abroad Coordinator, Office of International Education, 409 Capen Hall, State University of New York at Buffalo (SUNY-Buffalo), Buffalo, New York 14260 (716) 636-3912 and James R. Graham, Co-Manager (See MicroSIG above for contact information).

SLART-L: List Service on Second Language Acquisition, Research and Teaching, Fred Davidson, Assistant Professor Division of English as an International Language (DEIL), 3070 Foreign Languages Building (FLB), University of Illinois at Urbana-Champaign (UIUC), 707 South Mathews Urbana, Illinois 61801 (217) 333-1506.

TESL-L: List Service for Teachers of English as a Second Language, Anthea Tillyer, International English Language Institute, Hunter College, New York, New York and Susan Simon, The City College of New York, New York.

TFTD-L: Thought For The Day, Dan Galvin, Texas A & M University, College Station, Texas.

250 Technology in Student Affairs

U. S. State Department Travel Advisories, Craig Rice UNIX Systems Specialist/Network Analyst, Academic Computing Center, St. Olaf College, 1520 St. Olaf Avenue, Northfield, Minnesota 55057-1098 (507) 646-3631.

LEARNING CENTER PROGRAMS

Study Skills Resources

Computer-Assisted Study Skills Improvement Program (CASSIP), WFB Enterprises, 1225 Nineteenth, Beaumont, TX 77706.

College Success, Twin Tower Enterprises, Inc., 12345 Ventura Boulevard, Studio City, CA 91604 (Video Tape).

How to Survive in College, The Center for Humanities, Box 1000, Mount Kisco, NY 10549 (Video Tape).

The Time of Your Life, Cally Curtis, 1111 North Los Palmas Avenue, Hollywood, CA 90038 (Video Tape).

Time Management System, Time-Life Video, Box 644, Paramus, NY 07653 (Video Tape).

Entrance Examinations Resources

DAT Preparation Course, GMAT Preparation Course, GRE Preparation Course, LSAT Preparation Course, MCAT Preparation Course, Graduate Admissions Preparation Services, 500 Third Avenue West, Seattle, WA 98119 (Audio Tape).

Interactive Learning Systems LSAT Program, Interactive Learning Systems MCAT Program, Interactive Learning Systems, Inc., 6153 Fairmount Avenue, Suite 213, San Diego, CA 92120.Sandra Smith's Computer Review for the NCLEX-RN, National Nursing Review, 342 State Street 116, Los Altos, CA 94022.

The Official Software for the GMAT Review, The Official Software for the GRE Review, Educational Test Service, CN6106, Princeton, NJ 08541-6106.

The Perfect Score (SAT), Mindscape, Inc., 3444 Dundee Road, Northbrook, IL 60062.

Video Review for the GMAT, Video Review for the GRE, Video Review for the LSAT, Video Review for the MAT, Video Review for the SAT, Video Aided Instruction, Inc., Box 332, Moslyn Heights, NY 11577 (Video Tape).

Word Attack, Word Attack Roots and Prefixes, Davidson and Associates, Inc. 3135 Kashiwa Street, Box 13204, Torrance, CA 90505.

Science Resources

Body Language, EXP, 12 Bella Vista, Iowa City, IA 52240.

Body Works, Harper and Collins, 10 East Fifty-third Street, New York, NY 10022.

Chemical Nomenclature, Merlan Scientific Ltd., 247 Armstrong Avenue, Georgetown, Ontario, Canada L7G 4X6.

General Physics, Cross Education Software, Box 1536, Ruston, LA 71270.

Introduction to General Chemistry, Introduction to Organic Chemistry, Chemrain, Organic Stereochemistry, Compress, Box 102, Wentworth, NH 03282.

Introductory Genetics II, DSR, Inc., 34880 Buncker Hill, Farmington, MI 48018.

Physics: Elementary Mechanics, Control Data Publishing Company,Inc., Box 261127, San Diego, CA 92126.

Protein Synthesis, Genetic Engineering, Helix Educational Software, Inc., 47-09 Thirtieth Street, Long Island City, NY 11101.

The Body Transparent, Britannica Software, 345 Fourth Street, San Francisco, FL 94107.

The Cell and Cell Chemistry Series, Queue, Inc., 338 Commerce Drive, Fairfield, CT 36430.

The Living Cell, The Nucleus, The Plasma Membrane, The Cytoplasm, Cell Differentiation, Decoding the Book of Life, Cancer: A Genetic Disease, Muscular Dystrophy: The Race for the Gene, Coronet/MTI Film and Video, 420 Academy Drive, Northbrook, IL 30062.

Video Lessons for Conceptual Physics, Addison-Wesley Publishing Company, Jacob Way, Reading, MA 01867-9984 (Video Tape).

Mathematics Resources

Alge-Blaster, Davidson and Associates, Inc., Box 13204, Torrance, CA 90505.

Math Lab, Avery and Barker, 10893 Leavesley Place, Cupertino, CA 90514.

The Algebra Problem Solver, H and N Software, Box 4067, Bricktown, NJ 08723.

The Calculus Toolkit, Exploring Calculus, Mathematical Modeling with Math CAD, Master Grapher, 3-D Grapher, Addison-Wesley Publishing Company, Education Software Division, Jacob Way, Reading, MA 01867-9984.

For All Practical Purposes: Introduction to Contemporary Mathematics, W. H. Freeman & Company, 41 Madison Avenue East, Twenty-Sixth Floor, New York, NY 10010.

Introductory Algebra, Addison-Wesley Publishing Company, Jacob Way, Reading, MA 01867-9984.

Understanding Elementary Algebra, Introductory Algebra, Intermediate Algebra, Scott Foresman and Company, 1900 East Lake Avenue, Glenview, IL 60025.

Teaching Evaluation Resources

Teacher-Course Evaluation Project, Office of Instructional Development and Evaluation, 417 Dodge, Northeastern University, 360 Huntington Avenue, Boston, MA 02115.

RECREATIONAL SPORTS AND WELLNESS PROGRAMS

Tournament Scheduling

20,000 Leagues, Sports Stats, Inc., 320 Brookes Drive, Suite 231, Hazelwood, MO 63042.

Auto Scheduler, Amalgamated Softworks, Ltd., 1600 - 18th Avenue N.E., Box 18084, Minneapolis, MD 55418.

Game Time Scheduler, All American Sportware, 90 High Street, Newtown, PA 18940.

League Scheduler Plus, MicroSport Software, 427 Sheidley, P.O.Box 254, Bonner Springs, KS 66012.

League Scheduling, Programmed for Success, Inc., 503 Vista Bella, Suite 7, Oceanside, CA 92056-2513.

League Scheduling System, INFO 2000, Ind., 620 19th Street, Suite 117, Niagara Falls, NY 14301.

Sports Data Systems, P.O.Box 12268, St. Paul, MN 55112.

The Robin Tamer, Ruthven & Associates, Suite 904-1231, Richmond Street, London, Ontario Canada N6A 3L9.

Tournament Director, (tennis), Triangle Software P.O.Box 58182, Raleigh, NC 27658.

Fitness/Wellness Programs

Alternate Computer Services, 609 W. Lunt Avenue, Schaumburg, IL 60193.

ATA Information Services, Inc., 1677 Elk Boulevard., Del Plaines, IL 60016.

Body Logic, P.O.Box 162101, Austin, TX 78716.

Computer Outfitters, 4633 East Broadway, Tucson, AZ 85711.

Fitness Software Vendors, ATA Information Services, 1677 Elk Boulevard, Des Plains, IL 60016.

HealthCheck Software, 16801 Addison Road., Suite 137, Dallas, TX 75248.

HMC Software, 3001 LBJ Freeway, Suite 244, Dallas, Tx 75234.

Institute for Aerobics Research, 123000 Preston Road, Dallas, TX 75230.

JennWare Corporation, 200 N. James #3, Plainfield, IL 60544.

MacClub, 42 Areo Camino, Suite 214, Goleta, CA 93117.

MicroCache Systems, 123 Stadley Rough Road, Danbury, CT 06811.

MTD Computer Services, 8050 Seminole Office Center, Suite 300, Seminole, FL 34642.

Statistical Applications

MicroStat, Ecosoft Inc., P.O.Box 68602, Indianapolis, IN 46268.

SPSS, SPPS Inc., 444 N. Michigan Avenue, Chicago, IL 60611.

Systat, Systat Inc., 1127 Asbury Avenue, Evanston, IL 60202.

Miscellaneous

Bowling League Secretary, Mighty Byte Computer Inc., 12629 E. Tatum Boulevard., Phoenix, AZ 85032.

Calendar Creator (calendar producing program), Power-up Software, P.O.Box 7600, San Mateo, CA 94403-7600.

Golf Handicapper, Carnegie Computer Corp., P.O.Box 16343, Pittsburgh, PA 15232.

PageMaker (desktop publishing), Aldus Corporation, 411 First Avenue, South, Seattle, WA 98104-2871.

Paradox (database Management), Borland International, 1800 Green Hills Road, P.O.Box 660001, Scotts Valley, CA 95066-9933.

Quattro Pro (spreadsheets), Borland International, 1800 Green Hills Road, P.O.Box 60001, Scotts Valley, CA 95066-9933.

Sports Desk (desktop management), Soft-Run Software, 68 Pine Hill Estates, Kenova, WV 25530-9737.

Sybervision-Golf, Tennis, Racquetball (videotape instruction), Sybervision, 2450 Washington, San Leadro, CA 94577.

Time Line (project management), Symantec Corp., 505 B San Marin Drive, Novato, CA 94945.

Top Priority (personal management system), Power-Up Software, P.O.Box 7600, San Mateo, CA 94403-7600.

Toss (The Official's Scheduling System), Micro Computer Resources, LTD, P.O.Box 174, 8962 East Hampton, Denver, CO 80231-4996.

WordPerfect 5.1 (word processing), WordPerfect Corp., 1555 N. Technology Way, Orem, UT 84057.

STUDENT HEALTH PROGRAMS

Medical Practice Management System: (Medical Clinic Package), Business & Professional Services, P.O.Box 16512, Mobile, AL 36616.

RX-80: (Pharmacy Package), Condor Corporation, 2060 Oak Mountain Drive, P.O.Box 189, Pelham, AL 35124.

RX-90: (Pharmacy Package update), Condor Corporation, 2060 Oak Mountain Drive, P.O.Box 189, Pelham, AL 35124.

STUDENT LIFE PROGRAMS

4th Dimension, ACIUS, 10351 Bubb Road, Cupertino, CA 95014.

Compute-A-Rush, D&D Digital, 111 Lynn Avenue, Ames, Iowa 50010.

CricketGraph, Computer Associates International, Inc., 1240 McKay Drive, San Jose, CA.

dBase, Ashton Tate, P.O.Box 2833, Torrence, CA 90509.

FileMaker Pro, Claris Corp., 5201 Patrick Henry Drive, Santa Clara, CA 95052.

PageMaker, Aldus Corp., 411 First Avenue S., Seattle, WA 98104.

Questa, Questa Corp., P.O.Box 400, Pleasanton, CA 94566.

Ress, Integrated Management System, Ltd., 2301 Harley Drive, Madison, WI 53711.

TicketMaker Professional, TicketStop, 235 Northup Road, Bellevue, WA.

Welber System, Elihu R. Welber, 634 30th St., San Francisco, CA 94131.

Word/Word for Windows/Microsoft Excel, Microsoft Corp., One Microsoft Way, Redmond, WA 98052.

WordPerfect, WordPerfect Corp., 1555 Technology Way, Orem, UT 84057.

Appendix B:

Glossary

adapter A device used to compatibly connect one piece of equipment to another.

analog computer The first generation of computers developed in the 1950s. It measured changing physical variables such as temperature, pressure, and electrical impulses and converted them into numerical quantities which could then be manipulated or "computed" electronically. It required temperature, dust, and vibration controlled environments to work effectively. Contrast with digital computer.

analog data A physical representation of continuous information that assimilates an exact representation of original data. The electrical impulses carried by a telephone channel, for example, are an analog data representation of the original voice data. Contrast with digital data.

analog-to-digital converter A device that converts continuous analog signals (i.e. telephone signals) to discrete digital data used in present day digital computers. See modem.

application programs The programs (see software) that enable a computer to produce useful work such as ledger sheets, written documents, student records, and inventory lists. Contrast with system programs.

artificial intelligence The capability of a computer to perform functions normally associated with human intelligence, such as reasoning and learning.

batch processing The processing of computer data as a group that has been accumulated over a period of time or only needs to be done periodically.

baud A unit for measuring data transmission speed. One baud is one bit of computer data per second. It takes 8 bits to represent one character. Therefore, 2400 baud equals 300 characters per second.

binary digit Either of the characters 0 or 1. This is the standard coding system utilized in all digital computers.

bridge A dedicated microcomputer that is equipped with a special hardware board and used to connect two similar computer networks. Bridge board adapted computers are required at each network site and are usually connected together by a telephone line and modems at both sites.

bridgeware Computer programs that are used to translate software written for one type of computer into a format required by another type of computer.

byte A group of adjacent binary digits read by a computer as a group to encode a single piece or character of data. The most common byte contains 8 binary digits.

CAD Acronym for **Computer-Aided Design**. The process of using a computer's graphic display and design capabilities to assist the designer in creating and/or altering the designs and drawings for physical items and structures, such as buildings, furniture, autos, airplanes and clothing.

CD-ROM Acronym for Compact Disc, Read-Only Memory which is a laser technology data storage and retrieval system for use with computer and video systems. It looks and works much like a compact disc used in audio stereo systems only it is usually larger in diameter and made to be read by a special video or computer system. Data is stored as three-dimensional pits on a plastic disc, sealed with a protective coating, and designed to be read by a laser.

CD-ROM disc The hard disc used to input information into a CD-ROM. They are designed to be read by a laser beam rather than a magnetic head to retrieve stored data. This eliminates wear of the disk surface and prolongs the useful life of the CD-ROM almost indefinitely. A single CD-ROM disc can store almost the equivalent of 720 floppy disks (360K bytes on a standard floppy disk).

CD-ROM drive The piece of equipment that is connected to the computer or video player via a cable that reads data from a CD-ROM disc into the video machine's or computer's internal memory.

central processor/central processing unit (CPU) The component of a computer system that contains the arithmetic logic unit and controls the interpretation and execution of the computer's instructions.

COBOL The acronym for Common Business Oriented Language which is a high-level language developed primarily for data processing applications.

communication server A dedicated microcomputer (PC) with appropriate software that is connected to a pooled set of modems for the purpose of sending and receiving data over telephone lines to and from other computer systems both on and off campus.

compatible The quality possessed by a computer system that enables it to process data and programs originally developed for another type of computer system.

compatible software Programs that can be run on different computer systems without having to be modified.

converter A device that converts data in one form into data in another form. See analog-to-digital converter and modem.

CP/M The abbreviation for the disk operating system developed by Apple Computer, Inc. in the late 1970s for its original line of Apple computers.

CPU The abbreviation for **Central Processing Unit** (see above)

database management program Software that allows the user to logically collect, store, relate, update, and retrieve all or part of a data file.

data link The equipment that permits the transmission of information in data format.

database programs Software programs designed to manage a series of information items for a group of individual entities. Each piece of data is a field, each group of fields about a single entity is called a record, and each set of records is called a file. The logic behind database software programs is similar to the manner in which office filing systems have been historically maintained, but it is all done electronically instead of using file folders and filing cabinets.

debug The process of detecting, locating, and removing mistakes in a computer program or system.

decision table A listing of all the contingencies and proceed/stop decisions that need to be considered in the design of any computer program.

dedicated terminal A computer terminal that is reserved for a particular special use or task.

dedicated computer system A computer system or work station that is programmed and configured to do one primary function, such as word processing.

default A general instruction written into a computer program to tell the computer what to do if no contradicting specific instruction is given by the user or included in the application program.

desktop computer Another term for a personal or microcomputer system containing a microprocessor, input (i.e. keyboard) and output (i.e. printer) devices, and data storage device (i.e. hard disk and/or floppy disk drive).

desktop publishing program An application program that allows a microcomputer to be used to produce reports, newsletters, brochures, and other publications if the computer is connected to a high-quality printer. Desktop publishing software displays on the computer screen exactly what the printed page will look like and also allows the user to incorporate graphs, drawings, pictures, and other graphics into a typeset looking document of professional quality.

digital computer The present generation of computers. They utilize and manipulate digital data to perform arithmetic and logic operations on such data. Contrast with analog computer and analog data.

digital data Data represented in a discrete and discontinuous form (i.e. 1s and 0s). Contrast with analog data which is represented in continuous wave form.

digital-to-analog converter A mechanical or electronic device that converts discrete digital data to continuous analog signals. See modem and contrast with analog-to-digital converter.

disk A magnetic device used to store information and programs that has been encoded into digital data and is readable by a computer. The disk can be made of either a sheet of flexible plastic (referred to as a floppy disk) or a rigid plastic platter (referred to as a hard disk).

disk drive A device that reads data from a magnetic disk and copies it into the computer's memory and writes data from the computer's memory onto a disk for storage.

diskette Another name for a floppy disk (see below).

disk operating system (DOS) The internal operating system utilized by the computer to store and retrieve data from magnetic disks, allocate disk storage space, and manage other functions associated with disk storage.

dot-matrix printer A type of printer that creates text characters with a series of closely spaced dots.

double density disk A disk that can store twice the amount data in the same space as a normal or single density disk.

double-sided disk A disk capable of storing information on both of its surfaces or sides.

download The process of transferring data from a large computer data file, usually maintained by a central computer system, to a smaller remote computer system such as a desktop computer. Contrast with upload.

downtime The length of time a computer system is inoperative due to a malfunction.

dumb terminal A computer terminal with no processing capability and minimal input and output capabilities. It is only for the visual display of data and files contained in another computer system.

duplexing The use of duplicate computers and/or peripheral equipment so that the system will continue to function in the event of a malfunction of one component of the system.

electronic mail Also called **E-mail**. The communications technology that permits the sending, receiving, storing, and forwarding of digital messages from one personal computer to another over telephone data lines.

encoder A device that transfers output from manual keyboard entry to already recorded data from another source to machine-readable format, such as a floppy disk.

Ethernet A computer network transmission system that allows audio, video, and computer data to be transmitted across campus. Compare to optical fiber below.

facsimile Also referred to as **FAX**. A precise (exact) reproduction of an original document.

FAX machine The communications device that is capable of scanning a paper image, encoding it into electronic data which can be transmitted over telephone lines, receiving and decoding a data transmission sent from a similar machine, and duplicating the original image on some form of paper.

fiber optics A data transmission medium made of tiny threads of glass or plastic capable of transmitting very large amounts of data at the speed of light (see optical fiber below).

fiche Also referred to as **microfiche**. A sheet of photographic film containing multiple microimages. See microfiche below.

file When used in computer jargon, the term refers to a collection of related records that is treated as a basic unit within a computer data storage system.

file backup Copies of data files that can be utilized to replace or restore a data file that has been damaged or destroyed.

file maintenance The process of updating data files to reflect any changes made to the original data files. File maintenance is usually done on a very regular cycle to ensure the currency of file data.

filename For IBM and IBM compatible computer files, it is the 12 character alphanumeric label used to identify a particular file. For Macintosh computers the filename may be up to 32 characters in length.

fileserver A microcomputer that is dedicated to storing systems data and all of the software necessary to operate a local area network (LAN).

finder A portion of the computer's internal operating system program that organizes and displays files stored on disks in such a way that it can retrieve them in random fashion when called for by the user by their assigned filename.

flexible disk Same as floppy disk (see below).

floppy disk A flexible magnetic oxide-coated mylar disk protected by a plastic or paper envelope that is used to store computer data at a relatively low cost.

fuzzy logic The methodology being tried by computer scientists to enable computers to recognize and process imprecise data and/or instructions.

font A collection of printing characters of a particular size and style. Each computer and non-impact type printer (i.e. ink-jet or laser) must be equipped with font software in order to print in different sizes and styles.

gate An electrical device that uses a logic circuit to control the processing of two or more inputs into one output.

gateway A dedicated computer that is used to connect two distinctly different communications networks together.

grandfather file The name given to the third of three master files used in a commonly used data security system. The other two files are called the son file and the father file. Three duplicate master files are maintained so that if a malfunction occurs during processing or file updating, the most recent error-free copy can be used to reprocess or recover the data.

hacker The term used to describe a person who tries to learn how to use a computer or computer program through trial and error rather than in a more meaningful way.

hard copy The printed copy of the image displayed on the computer monitor or contained in the computer's memory.

hard disk A computer's main data storage device that is either mounted in its own case and connected to the computer's microprocessor with a cable and/or is permanently mounted inside the computer's housing cabinet. A single hard disk has the storage capacity of several million characters by bytes of information. Newer desktop computers usually contain at least 80-250 megabytes of hard disk storage.

hardware The physical equipment that makes up a computer system, such as the microprocessor unit, keyboard, auxiliary disc drive, monitor, printer, converter, adaptor, and modem.

hardware configuration The arrangement of the various pieces of equipment that comprise a computer system and the cables and devices that connect them and allow them to communicate electronically with each other.

Hertz Abbreviated **Hz**. The unit of electricity that describes cycles per second.

host computer The central controlling computer in a network of computers or the central processing unit (see CPU) that provides the computing power for dedicated terminals and other peripherals that are connected to it.

hybrid computer system A system that uses both analog and digital equipment.

icon A tiny on-screen symbol that is used to identify a program, command, or data file in the graphic computing environments utilized in Macintosh computers and in Windows software developed by Microsoft Corporation for use with MS-DOS operating system computers.

impact printer A device that imprints by applying pressure to raised type against an inked or carbon ribbon onto a piece of paper. Examples are daisy-wheel and thimble printers. Contrast with nonimpact printer.

import To read a file created by one program into the data base of another program.

ink-jet printer A device that prints by spraying a thin stream of ink onto a piece of paper in the form of alphanumeric characters or graphical images. Contrast with impact printer such as a daisy-wheel printer.

input The information a computer takes into the main data storage unit so that it can be processed. Contrast with output.

input device A device used to enter data into a computer, such as a keyboard, modem, or converter.

inputting The process of entering data into a computer system.

interactive multimedia The term used to describe the fusion or interactivity of video technology with the power of computer, CD-ROM, and THOR-CD technology. Interactive multimedia combines speech, enhanced music, video images, animation, and computer capabilities into a unified system.

interactive program Permits two-way communications between a computer system and the operator. The operator is able to modify or terminate a program as well as receive feedback from the computer program for verification or guidance.

internal memory or storage The data that is stored in and controlled by the computer's central processing unit (CPU).

keyboard The main input device used to key programs and data into a microcomputers storage system.

keyword A set of words or letters and symbols that have specific meaning to a MS-DOS type computer program and are thus used to give commands to the computer's operating system. An example is DIR which is a MS-DOS computer command to produce a directory of the files stored on a floppy disk.

kilobyte Commonly abbreviated K and used as a suffix to describe memory size. One kilobyte or K represents 1024 bytes of data.

LAN Acronym for **Local Area Network** A network of computer hardware and software systems within a limited distance, such as a building, portion of a building, office suite, or room, than is connected by dedicated communications channels.

lap-top computer A notebook or briefcase size portable computer capable of running on battery power and usually weighing less than ten pounds.

laser The term laser is actually an acronym for **Light Amplification by Simulated Emission of Radiation** but has come to be used as a term to describe a "device" that uses the principle of electromagnetic wave application by simulated emission of radiation rather than the process itself. Lasers operate in either the visible, infrared, or ultraviolet regions of light depending on their specific applications.

laser printer A nonimpact type printing device that places character images on a rotating drum using a laser beam of light. As the drum rotates, the laser exposed areas pick up toner power which is then fused onto the paper. Laser printers are fast and quiet and their print-quality is very high.

Liquid Crystal Display (LCD) A method of displaying alphanumeric characters and other graphics to appear by reflecting light on a flat crystalline substance. LCD technology is widely used in calculators, watches and other portable devices, such as notebook computers, that require a thin profile display screen.

logging-in The process of establishing communication with and verifying the authority to use the computer system and/or network.
logging-off The process of terminating communication between the user and the computer system and/or network.

Macintosh Systems 5-7 The operating system software developed in the 1980s by Apple Computer Inc. to run its Macintosh line of computers. System 7.1 is the operating system used by all newer Macintosh computers.

macro A single keyboard command used to instruct the computer to complete a series of tasks. Macros are stored in the computers internal memory and recalled through the use of functon and control keys.

MS-DOS The operating system software developed by Microsoft Corp in the early 1980s that was adopted by the IBM Corporation to run its line of personal computers (PCs). This operating system has also been adopted by most other computer manufacturers in order to make their computers compatible with IBM hardware and software programs. It is currently the dominant microcomputer operating system used in the industry, but it is being strongly challenged by IBM's recently released OS/2 operating system software (see below).

mail-merging The process of automatically printing form letters with individualized names and addresses from a mailing list file. A mail-merge program merges address information from one file with textual information from another file.

megabyte Approximately one million bytes or one thousand kilobytes of data.

megahertz Abbreviated **MHz**. A measure of electrical frequency equal to one million cycles per second. Used to define the speed with which a computer is capable of processing data. Early models of personal computers usually operated at 12 MHz or less. Present day PCs operate at speeds in excess of 33 MHz.

memory The term used to describe the amount of data that a device, such as a hard disk or floppy disk, is capable of storing.

microchip The principal electrical part used in the manufacture of computers. It is a tiny silicon chip with thousands of electronic components and circuit patterns etched onto its surface.

microcomputer A small and relatively inexpensive class of computers often referred to as PCs, personal computers, desk-top computers, and home computers. They are fully operational computers that use microprocessors as their central processing unit (CPU).

microfiche Also see fiche. A small sheet of microfilm upon which up to 270 pages of computer output can be stored.

microprocessor An integrated circuit chip that contains the basic arithmetic, logic, and control elements required to process electronic digital data.

minicomputer A computer that is generally more powerful than a microcomputer and less powerful than a mainframe computer.

mips Acronym for **Million Instructions Per Second**. Measure used to describe the average number of machine language instructions a computer can perform in one second.

modem Acronym for **Modulator/Demodulator**. A device that translates digital pulses from a computer into the analog signals required for telephone transmission and visa versa. The modem enables communication capabilities between computer equipment over common telephone transmission equipment.

monitor A visual display terminal used with microcomputer systems. They come in two types: monochrome (usually white, amber or green) and color (usually designated as VGA or RGB, depending on whether the monitor is for a Macintosh system or IBM/IBM compatible system). The monochrome monitor is the least expensive and produces a sharp easy to read display.

motherboard Also called **system board**. The main circuit board within the housing of a microcomputer into which printed circuit cards, boards, and modules are connected.

mouse A device that is connected to the keyboard of a computer system and used to move an electronic cursor or arrow around on the display screen.

multi-user system A system where two or more people, using different terminals, can access one computer simultaneously.

network A system of computer systems and terminals that are connected by a communications channel.

network interface card (NIC) A device that is attached to a computer's motherboard that allows it to be connected to a computer network.

node Any computer terminal, device or other communications station connected to a computer network.

nonimpact printer A printer that uses heat, laser technology, electricity, ink-jet technology, or photographic techniques to print output. Contrast with impact printer.

notebook computer A portable computer that uses a flat panel liquid crystal display instead of a cathode ray video tube type monitor.

off-the-shelf Refers to a software program that has been standardized and mass produced and is readily available to a consumer from a software vendor or supplier.

on-line Term used to describe when a piece of computer equipment or device is connected to the central processing unit of a computer and communication is possible between the two.

270 Technology in Student Affairs

operating system Abbreviated **OS**. The internal software that controls the execution of computer programs and commands. It regulates such things as input/output control, data storage, data manipulation, sequencing of internal operations, debugging, and related functions.

optical character reader Also called **optical scanner**. A computer input device that converts human readable data into reflected light images which are recognized by their shapes as digital characters readable by a computer.

optical fiber A thread of highly transparent glass that is pulsed very rapidly to carry a stream of binary signals which can be read by a computer. The use of optical fibers for networking computer systems is rapidly replacing Ethernet and other cable systems because they can carry a much higher volume of data and are immune to the electrical interference that often cause disruption and data loss in those other communications mediums.

OS/2 The operating system developed by IBM in the late 1980s to run its current line of PS 2 computers.

output Term used to describe the final result of data that has been processed by a computer and transferred from the computer's internal storage unit through some type of output device.

outputting The process of producing useful information from a computer system.

packaged software Software that is sold by a vendor in the form of a package containing both the software program and its operating instructions.

parallel input/output The transmission of computer data in such a way that each data bit has its own wire. This allows for the simultaneous transmission of data along different wires. Contrast with serial input/output.

password Special word(s), symbol(s), and/or alphanumeric code(s) assigned to a computer user for identification, accounting, and security purposes. The user must correctly enter the password into

Appendix B 271

the computer before the user will be permitted to gain access to the computer network's central processing unit.

PC The abbreviation for **personal computer**. A moderately priced microcomputer.

peripheral equipment The input/output units of a computer system which are connected by cables or telephone lines to the central processing unit of a computer system.

portable computer A microcomputer system that is small, light weight, can be operated on battery power, and may be easily moved from one location to another. To achieve this portability they also use a thin profile liquid crystal display (LCD) screen rather that a conventional video display monitor.

PostScript A page description language developed by Adobe Systems for designing page layouts on microcomputer systems.

program Another name for **software**. The series of computer instructions that determine the manner in which a computer will read, store, manipulate and output data. There are two general types of programs: those which are used to control and regulate the internal operations of the central processing unit of a computer called operating systems; and those that are used to manipulate and process input data into useful output data called application programs. Examples of operating systems are MS-DOS, OS/2, and Macintosh System 7. Examples of application programs are spreadsheet, word processing, data base management, and desktop publishing programs.

programming language A scheme of formal alphanumeric and symbolic notation that is used by a computer programmer to instruct the computer's central processing unit to perform specific functions. There are literally hundreds of programming languages in existence, but the one most commonly used in microcomputers today is called BASIC.

proprietary software A program that is owned or copyrighted by an individual or business. It is illegal to copy or use this software without permission or purchasing the right to use or copy it.

public domain software Software that is not protected by copyright laws and is, therefore, free for all to use or copy without fear of legal prosecution.

RAM Acronym for **random access memory**. The working memory of the computer into which the user can randomly enter information or instructions and randomly read stored data in order to execute applications programs. Most newer microcomputers used in colleges and universities come equipped with 2-4 megabytes of RAM but can be upgraded to 4-8 megabytes for a relatively small additional cost. The greater the RAM, the greater the computer's capability to efficiently operate complex programs with large databases.

ROM Acronym for **read-only memory**. A memory file that cannot be changed by the user but does not lose its program when the computer's power is switched off. In most microcomputers the BASIC language interpreter and operating systems are contained in the computer's central processing unit in read-only memory.

remote terminal A device for communicating with a computer that is physically separated by enough distance so that a communication facility like a telephone line must be used rather than a cable or wire.

retrieval The extraction of data from a data file.

RGB monitor A color monitor that uses red, green, and blue color "gun" (like a television picture tube) to produce a high quality electronic color display of computer data.

scanner An optical device that can recognize a specific set of visual symbols based on the light reflected by the symbols' unique shapes (see optical scanner).

serial input/output The transmission of computer data in which the bytes of data are sent one by one over a single wire. Contrast with parallel input/output.

software The program or instruction that tells a computer what to do (see program).

software license A contract signed by the purchaser of a software product in which the purchaser agrees not to make unauthorized copies or use of the software.

spelling checker A specific computer program, usually part of a word processing program package, that compares entered words against a list of properly spelled words and informs the user of possible spelling mistakes and correct spelling alternatives.

spreadsheet program Software that creates an electronic numerical table, or spreadsheet, which allows large columns and rows of numbers to be quickly changed according to parameters established by the user. Columns may contain either original data or a formula to calculate new data from data entered in one or more of the other columns. Each time any cell in one column is altered, all the dependant formula cells in other columns are automatically recalculated. Sections of the spreadsheet may also be moved or copied at will without inhibiting the recalculation of the dependant data. This type of software is very useful for asking "what if" type questions and for performing numerical forecasts without tedious manual calculations.

storage capacity The number of items of data that a storage device is capable of holding. Capacity is usually stated in terms of computer bytes (byte, kilobyte, and megabyte).

storage device A device used to store data for a computer system (see hard disk and floppy disk).

supercomputer The largest, fastest, and most expensive mainframe type computer currently available. Most universities use supercomputers for academic computing in the areas of theoretical physics and mathematics which involve the complex processing and storage of massive amounts of data.

surge protector A device that is plugged into a standard 110-volt electrical outlet, into which computer equipment is plugged, that filters out short surges of high voltage to protect the equipment from being damaged by those surges. Because high voltage surges can damage both computer hardware and software it is vital that surge protectors be used with all computer equipment.

system board The main circuit board of a microcomputer (also called motherboard).

system programmer The person who plans, creates, controls, revises and maintains the use of a computer's operating system.

system programs Also called operating system. Programs that control the internal operations of a computer system. For microcomputers, system software is built into or added to the central processing unit of the computer by the manufacturer and sold to the user as part of the computer system. Contrast with application programs which are generally sold separately or included in the sale of a microcomputer "package" by a vendor or manufacturer as part of a marketing strategy.

teleprocessing The use of telephone lines to transmit data between remote locations or between two computer systems. Also requires the use of modems and/or analog-to-digital and digital-to-analog converters.

terminal A device used to input programs and data to a computer and to receive output from a computer.

terminal access unit (TAU) A high speed modem that is used to connect terminals in local and wide area networks.

thermal printer A nonimpact type printer that produces output on heat-sensitive paper.

THOR-CD The name given by the Tandy Corporation to a compact disc technology it invented in 1990 that is capable of being erased and re-recorded. It can repeatedly record, play back, store and erase music, data or video on a disk that can be used with all existing CD audio and CR-ROM players.

touch-sensitive screen A display screen on which the user can enter commands by pressing designated areas of the screen with a finger or object.

track ball A device used to move a cursor around on a computer display screen. Compare to mouse.

type font A set of characters in a consistent and unique typeface that is used for printing of computer output (see font).

UNIX An operating system developed by AT&T and Bell Laboratories. Because it is a very powerful operating system with several high-level utility programs and capable of running a number of jobs at one time, it is frequently used in minicomputers that control office automation systems, accounting and billing systems, and for controlling local and wide area networks.

user-friendly A term used to describe computer hardware and software that requires little instruction to use in a meaningful way.

utility programs Application programs that are generally included by the computer vendor or manufacturer with the original equipment purchase which are used to facilitate commonly needed services such as transferring data from one medium to another, editing text, and handling data files. These programs facilitate the efficient operation of the computer for a number of different applications and uses.

VAX The designation given by the Digital Equipment Corporation to its large minicomputer systems which are commonly found on many college campuses.

virtual reality A term meaning "appearing to be", rather than "actually being". It is also used to describe the use of computer technology to generate video images that do not actually exist but appear to exist. An example of such technology is the special effect that was used in the motion picture Terminator 2 in which the lead character "appeared" to melt as he walked through objects and then become whole again.

voice mail Messages spoken into a telephone that are converted into digital form, stored in the computer's memory, and then reconverted into voice form when recalled.

WAN Acronym for **Wide Area Network** Linkage of computer hardware and software between buildings and/or between campuses through the use of a dedicated communications medium such as Ethernet or fiber optics.

word processing program Software that allows the computer to be utilized for routine typing tasks as well as for such things as making variations in formats and type styles within a single document, moving blocks of copy within a document and between documents, conducting spelling checks, inserting graphs and tables produced by other programs, storing, and saving documents and files, and personalizing routine correspondence by using the mail merge function.

workstation A configuration of computer equipment designed for use by one person at a time.

WYS/WYG An abbreviation for What You See Is What You Get. It is used to describe word processing programs that generate screen images that are identical in position and type appearance to the final output printed document.